Wilma Mankiller

Recent Titles in
Women Making History

Wilma Mankiller

A LIFE IN AMERICAN HISTORY

Tamrala Swafford Bliss

Women Making History
Rosanne Welch and Peg A. Lamphier, Series Editors

 ABC-CLIO®

An Imprint of ABC-CLIO, LLC
Santa Barbara, California • Denver, Colorado

Library of Congress Cataloging-in-Publication Data

Names: Swafford Bliss, Tamrala, author.
Title: Wilma Mankiller : a life in American history / Tamrala
   Swafford Bliss.
Description: Santa Barbara, California : ABC-CLIO, [2023] | Series: Women
   making history | Includes bibliographical references and index. |
Identifiers: LCCN 2022046069 | ISBN 9781440873867 (hardcover) | ISBN
   9781440873874 (ebook)
Subjects: LCSH: Mankiller, Wilma, 1945-2010. | Cherokee Indians—Kings and
   rulers—Biography. | Cherokee Indians—Social conditions. | Indian
   leadership—North America. | Cherokee women—North America—Politics and
   government. | Cherokee women—Biography.
Classification: LCC E99.C5 M3384 2023 | DDC 973.04/975570092
   [B]—dc23/eng/20220927
LC record available at https://lccn.loc.gov/2022046069

ISBN: 978-1-4408-7386-7 (print)
      978-1-4408-7387-4 (ebook)

27 26 25 24 23   1 2 3 4 5

This book is also available as an eBook.

ABC-CLIO
An Imprint of ABC-CLIO, LLC

ABC-CLIO, LLC
147 Castilian Drive
Santa Barbara, California 93117
www.abc-clio.com

This book is printed on acid-free paper (∞)

Manufactured in the United States of America

Contents

Series Foreword

We created this series because women today stand on the shoulders of those who came before them. They need to know the true power their foremothers had in shaping the world today and the obstacles those women overcame to achieve all that they have achieved and continue to achieve.

It is true that Gerda Lerner offered the first regular college course in women's history in 1963 and that, since then, women's history has become an academic discipline taught in nearly every American college and university. It is also true that women's history books number in the millions and cover a wealth of topics, time periods, and issues. Nonetheless, open any standard high school or college history textbook and you will find very few mentions of women's achievements or importance, and the few that do exist will be of the "exceptional woman" model, ghettoized to sidebars and footnotes.

With women missing from textbooks, students and citizens are allowed to believe that no woman ever meaningfully contributed to American history and that nothing women have ever done has had more than private, familial importance. In such books we do not learn that it was womens' petitioning efforts that brought the Thirteenth Amendment abolishing slavery to Abraham Lincoln's attention or that Social Security and child labor laws were the brainchild of Frances Perkins, the progressive female secretary of labor who was also the first woman appointed to a presidential cabinet.

Without this knowledge both female and male students are encouraged to think only men—primarily rich, white men—have ever done anything meaningful. This vision impedes our democracy in a nation that has finally become more aware of our beautiful diversity.

The National Bureau of Economic Research said women comprise the majority of college graduates in undergraduate institutions, law schools, and medical schools (56 percent in 2017). Still, women's high college attendance and graduation rates do not translate to equal pay or equal economic, political, or cultural power. There can be little argument that American women have made significant inroads *toward* equality in the last few decades, in spite of the ongoing dearth of women in normative approaches to American history teaching and writing. Hence, this series.

We want readers to know that we took the task of choosing the women to present seriously, adding new names to the list while looking to highlight new information about women we think we know. Many of these women have been written about in the past, but their lives were filtered through male or societal expectations. Here we hope the inclusion of the women's own words in the collection of primary documents we curated will finally allow them to speak for themselves about the issues that most mattered. The timeline will visually place them in history against events that hampered their efforts and alongside the events they created. Sidebars will give more detail on such events as the Triangle Shirtwaist Factory Fire. Finally, the chapter on Why She Matters will cement the reason such a woman deserves a new volume dedicated to her life.

Have we yet achieved parity? We'll let one of our subjects—the Honorable Ruth Bader Ginsburg—remind us that "when I'm sometimes asked when will there be enough [women on the supreme court]? And I say when there are nine, people are shocked. But there'd been nine men [for over 200 years], and nobody's ever raised a question about that."

Introduction: Why Wilma Mankiller Matters

The life story of Wilma Mankiller illustrates the power of perseverance despite continuing challenges. Wilma wanted to be remembered as the person who restored faith in the Cherokee people (Mankiller 1993). She certainly accomplished that—and much more—as a trailblazer, treaty rights activist, feminist activist, community developer, and Cherokee leader.

Her inspirational life story coincides with major federal Indian policy that had both devastating and welcoming effects on American Indian communities from the 1950s through the 1990s. During the Termination and Relocation years of the Eisenhower administration, Wilma and her family moved to San Francisco for better opportunities, as promised by the Bureau of Indian Affairs. Urban poverty and few opportunities met them in California. Wilma experienced culture shock on a variety of levels and found solace at the San Francisco Indian Center. Here she interacted with other young Indian people from all around the country and slowly became interested in national Indian affairs and in her own Cherokee heritage. Wilma learned many lessons about grassroots activism and negotiating with the federal government on behalf of Indian people during this period (Blansett 2018, 85).

The Red Power Movement of the late 1960s and early 1970s emerged out of frustration, hope, and bringing diverse Indian people together from around the country. Tribal sovereignty and protection of Indigenous human rights, including political reform through intertribalism, became the new focus for urban Indians. As the Red Power Movement coincided with the Civil Rights Movement, Wilma and her friends learned many valuable lessons about nonviolent direct action to exact change. It was in

San Francisco and Oakland, and particularly at the Indian Center, that Wilma became involved in Indian Rights, the American Indian Movement, and the second wave of the women's rights movement, but with a Native focus (Lobo 2002). During these years, Wilma discovered her calling as she worked toward the improvement of the lives of women and all Indian people, especially her fellow Cherokees. The movement provided her with confidence and a sense of purpose.

Returning to eastern Oklahoma in 1977 and needing work, Wilma sought an entry-level job at the Cherokee Nation. The Ford administration passed the highly significant Indian Self-Determination and Educational Assistance Act of 1975 and it was a key factor in Wilma's effective community development work. A major facet of this legislation is the ability of tribes to contract for work that was previously maintained by the Bureau of Indian Affairs. This was a huge step forward in self-determination efforts for tribes. Wilma became very adept at grant writing and sought to improve rural community services in the areas of housing, health care, and education. She was the founding director of the Cherokee Nation Community Development Department, and one of her earliest accomplishments was receiving a federal grant for improvements in the Bell Community in 1982.

Under the supervision of Wilma, the Bell community came together and completed a waterline of 26 miles within their local community so that they could have running water in their homes. It was during this project that Wilma became interested in the Kenwood community as the next project to undertake, and her work there inspired her to enter tribal politics. She also met her husband, Charlie Soap, during this time, and he encouraged her to enter tribal politics. She had an epiphany that the most effective way to exact change was to work within the existing system and be in control of that change.

Wilma's community development challenges became even greater by her entrance into the male-dominated tribal council environment of the Cherokee Nation. Despite tremendous sexism, the Cherokee people elected Wilma as the first woman deputy chief, in 1983; and in 1985, they appointed her principal chief of the Cherokee Nation. She once remarked she experienced far more discrimination because of her gender than because of her being an Indian, and gender discrimination was the most painful time in her life (Mankiller 1993). Choosing to ignore the gender bias and overt sexism, Wilma focused her energy on community development, health, and educational services for rural Cherokee communities. Through her leadership efforts, Wilma took the Cherokee Nation to a position of strength by imparting the lessons of self-help she had learned in San Francisco and Oakland. Yet, she also reminded her communities that the Cherokee people always helped one another for the common good, an institution known as *gadugi*. She continued to lead the Cherokee people as chief as she was reelected in 1987 and 1991.

While Wilma was learning about the governance of the Cherokee Nation and contributing to community development projects, she experienced a series of health challenges. Her strength and determination in overcoming each illness and continuing with her work with the Cherokee people is admirable. Because of her health issues, she did not seek reelection in 1995 and instead continued her activism throughout the country until her passing in 2010.

Wilma Mankiller led her people through difficult times. Her story reflects the struggle of an Indigenous woman in America—a very distinct woman in a very distinct America—and illustrates how the American mosaic is a work in progress. Yet, it works positively when we work together for the good of all, as Wilma reminded us. She was a Cherokee woman and a person who believed in a cause greater than herself. As the author of two books and many speeches, her writings are an account of her beliefs and the factors that contributed to her strength and leadership. While she had no interest in school until she returned to Oklahoma in 1977, she received a highly valuable education of another type while in California and while fighting sexism in her community. As a single mother to two teenage daughters, her interest in school turned to social work and, coupled with her activist training, gave her a tremendous skill set through which she governed the Cherokee tribe under extraordinary circumstances.

When Wilma thought of the Cherokee Nation, she thought of the people in the Cherokee communities. Her biography is a study of life and human nature, driven by tenacity against enormous personal and professional challenges. She grew up in extreme poverty with a father of Cherokee lineage and a mother of Dutch and Irish lineage; Cherokee culture was dominant in their home. This knowledge of Cherokee culture sustained her tenacity and strength and she often remarked that having a cause greater than herself made all the difference in her life.

The Cherokees, through their mutual aid institution of *gadugi*, exemplify the cooperative activities associated with their social capital. They also adhere to the Harmony Ethic, which is a traditional tribal concept among the Cherokees embodying the fundamental characteristics of non-aggressiveness, non-competitiveness, the use of third-party negotiators to avoid interpersonal confrontations, and generosity. Cherokee author Marilou Awiakta described how, under the modern name of Community Development, the traditional pattern of the town council still functions as effectively as it used to. People convene, discuss, and decide what they need and what skills they can pool to "get the job done" (Awiakta 1993). The leadership style of Wilma embodied these actions.

Wilma Mankiller matters because her life coincided with the evolution of Cherokee traditional belief. She combined the concepts associated with *gadugi* with contracting services directly with the Bureau of Indian Affairs to exact the changes most desired by the members of the communities. Lakota activist scholar Vine Deloria Jr. astutely argued that tribal traditions were an ongoing process. Both he and Joseph Mathews, an Osage author, argued that "the success or failure of American Indian communal societies have always been predicated not upon a set of uniform unchanging beliefs, but rather upon a commitment to the groups and the groups' futures" (Warrior 1995). The non-Indian societal norms, which Indians were told to imitate, existed in a constant state of chaos and change. Wilma reminded Indian people of their own societal norms and encouraged people to have confidence in those tribal traditions.

Deloria stated, "The awakening of the tribes is just the beginning. Traditionalists see the movement as a fulfillment of ancient Hopi and Iroquois religious predictions of the end of white domination of the continent" (Deloria 1969, 246). Traditions that kept tribes together and maintained tribes in the ways of their ancestors have regained primary importance. As Deloria suggests, "The problems of Indians have been ideological rather than social, political, or economic" (Deloria 1969, 256). Under Wilma's leadership, Cherokee communities illustrated this point by continuing to adhere to their traditional beliefs and institutions despite tremendous policy changes and constant efforts at assimilation by BIA officials. English professor Robert Allen Warrior (Osage) stated, "The Indian situation at the turn of the century was a battle of community values versus individualistic chaos rather than a battle of one set of cohesive, livable values against another" (Warrior 1995). While the eastern Oklahoma–Cherokee communities suffered from social, political, and economic maladies, the one constant that drove them to persevere was the Cherokee identity associated with *gadugi*. Assisting community members who were in need was one aspect of what it meant to be Cherokee.

Tribal nations have a history of establishing institutions consistent with their culture, traditions, and environment, and this tradition often relied on individual and family property rights. By necessity, Cherokee society was dynamic, not static. Anthropologist Eleanor Leacock noted that "Indian ways of today are nonetheless Indian." Indian cultural traditions continued to develop with constant integration of innovations into characteristically Indian ways and Indian views (Neely 1991). Under Wilma's leadership, Cherokee communities and their tradition of *gadugi* showed this cultural evolution as the tribal leaders and members continuously integrated elements of non-Indian society into their traditions. A modern Cherokee identity emerged from this integration as the tribal communities kept their traditional views throughout their growth and development in the late 20th century.

At the end of the tragic "Trail of Tears" in 1839, Cherokee settlements along the Grand River reflected the tribal divisions caused by the fraudulent signing of the Treaty of New Echota. The Ross Party, predominately full-bloods, settled east of the river and the Treaty or Ridge Party settled west of the Grand River. The Treaty Party, led by those who signed the Treaty of New Echota, was a majority mixed-blood community and its members became ranchers and business leaders and often intermarried with whites. They were socially and culturally assimilated, yet proud of Cherokee ancestry. By 1930, only one-tenth of the 4.5 million acres allotted from the Dawes Act of 1887 remained in Cherokee hands. Also known as the General Allotment Act, the Dawes Act authorized the federal government to subdivide communally held lands in Indian Territory into allotments for Native heads of households. Those not enrolled in the tribe did not receive land. The Oklahoma Cherokees have 17,718 acres in trust land allotted. The tribal government comprises a principal chief and an 11-member executive committee governing body. It is important to understand the land masses involved, as Cherokee people associate the *gadugi* with land held and maintained by kinship groups and clans within each Cherokee community. The *gadugi* is a traditional tribal institution comprising work crews who come together and perform work for the good of the community. After decades of control by the federal government through the Bureau of Indian Affairs, the Cherokee Nation emerged as a model of the significance of cultural institutions to community development.

The late 20th century represented a period of trial and error as the tribal communities attempted several enterprises to reach local autonomy. Many Cherokee people rediscovered what made them a successful society prior to European contact through the traditional tribal value system of *gadugi*. While both internal and external forces constantly sought solutions to economic and community development efforts, the traditional value system of *gadugi* remained within Cherokee communities and helped reinforce the notion that they could always reach their goals of local sovereignty. Despite all the federal government policy changes that affected the Cherokee communities, Wilma's leadership reawakened the *gadugi* spirit and helped reestablish a positive community identity.

Wilma identified the ways in which the Cherokee Nation communities shared resources and maintained relational obligations and commitments, or social capital, a set of informal norms and values shared by a group of individuals. Wilma and her husband, Charlie, reminded the community residents of the role of *gadugi* in accomplishing community development plans. The meaning of the term *gadugi* has developed over the centuries, from signifying a work crew to being included as a facet in the Cherokee traditional knowledge system. Traditionally, *gadugi* was a mutual aid work group organized by kinship groups in each community. The most current usage of the term *gadugi* means working together for the good of the community.

The meaning of "community," *na v nu ha da lv*, within this biography, focuses on the Western Cherokee non-reservation lands. The people living on those lands define "community" as kinship based. This stems from the traditional clan system, which included seven distinct clans found within each town. "Traditional" beliefs, as used throughout this book, refer to the tribal cultural beliefs among the Cherokee people, passed down through oral teachings from one generation to the next. Wilma began her political career working with traditional Cherokees in their isolated communities and this work influenced the rest of her work, writing, and activism.

Wilma Mankiller matters because her leadership and the evolution of the Cherokee institution of *gadugi* allowed community members to seek a better life for themselves and future generations, exhibiting tribal self-determination. Through community development efforts, Wilma and community leaders used both internal and external entities to assist in their community building efforts on their own terms.

During her tenure as chief, Wilma opened three rural health centers, expanded the Head Start program, and opened a center to prevent drug abuse. She also helped found the organization Women Empowering Women for Indian Nations. As a working single mother of two daughters, Wilma's story reminds readers that dedication to family and community is for the betterment of all. She inspires Indigenous and non-Indigenous people all over the world.

Wilma received many awards and honors for her effective leadership and activism, including the Presidential Medal of Freedom in 1998. The sheer volume of testaments to her character and integrity since her passing reflects the reason why Wilma Mankiller matters. There have been two movies produced on her life—a film released in 2013 entitled *The Cherokee Word for Water* and a documentary in 2017 entitled *Mankiller*. The United States Mint also honored Wilma in 2015 as one of the four female finalists to be placed on the 20-dollar bill, replacing Andrew Jackson.

Most recently, in 2022, Wilma became one of five women in American History to be honored on the new quarter. The American Women Quarters Program of the United States Mint celebrates women who made significant contributions to the development and history of America. Wilma's life matters because she is the rare person highly revered among Natives and non-Natives, Democrats and Republicans.

Wilma always educated Indians and non-Indians, seeking to improve knowledge about Indian people and correct the persistent negative stereotypes. The Cherokee Nation has rebuilt itself again and again. Wilma's life story reflects one remarkable Cherokee woman's journey during the time she helped rebuild communities with the Cherokee Nation and rebuilt her own life in the late 20th century. The story of the Cherokee people is one of hope, survival, and tenacity; they are tenacious people who have had to revitalize their communities repeatedly. They have held on to their traditional tribal customs. Wilma's life story reminds us of the importance of working together for the common good and what we can learn from traditional tribal knowledge.

1

Mankiller Flats

In 1984, Deputy Chief Wilma Mankiller participated in the reunion between the tribal council of the Cherokee Nation of Oklahoma and the tribal council of the Eastern Band of Cherokee Indians on the historic Cherokee lands in eastern Tennessee. This meeting, the first full tribal council since the beginning of the Trail of Tears in 1838, occurred at Red Clay, Tennessee, on the Georgia state line. Red Clay served as the last capital of the original Cherokee Nation prior to removal. The state of Tennessee declared Red Clay a 275-acre state historical area in 1979. A highlight of the joint tribal council was the dedication of an eternal flame monument at the state park (Maltby 1984). The eternal flame, carried by two runners from the Eastern Band Cherokee reservation, became a symbol of building one fire—to put away differences, come together as a people, and work for the common good. The fire still burns at Red Clay and this event had a great historical and emotional impact on the Cherokee people.

At the reunion, Deputy Chief Wilma explained: "We're one tribe in a historical sense, we expect to, one, sort of renew an old kinship and, two, explore a lot of issues that might be common to both tribes" (Maltby 1984). The Eastern Band comprised the descendants of those who had escaped into the caves and hills during the Removal roundup. Those in attendance at the reunion also included Tennessee governor Lamar Alexander and Iron Eyes Cody, who was depicted as a Native American crying when he saw pollution in the Keep America Beautiful—Ad Council television spots in the 1970s. About 20,000 people attended, including at least 3,000

1

Cherokees from North Carolina and several hundred Cherokees from Oklahoma. Wilma's ancestors had survived an America in transition from rural to urban and from assimilation to self-determination. Their journey to present-day Oklahoma was a story of resilience and community.

Being descendants of survivors of the Trail of Tears is integral to the identity of Oklahoma Cherokees. Wilma's great-great-grandfather, *Kaskun-nee* Mankiller, survived the Cherokee Trail of Tears in 1839 and her grandfather, John, *Yo-na*, established a home in a place that became known as Mankiller Flats, one of Wilma's greatest passions. A kitchen utensil belonging to Wilma's aunt also survived the trail and became a beloved item of the family.

When colonial American leaders created a new government at the end of the 18th century, Indigenous governments already existed. Approximately 60 Cherokee communities endured in four regions across the southeastern United States: the Lower Towns in South Carolina; the Middle Towns in western North Carolina; the Valley Towns in southwest North Carolina and northeast Georgia; and the Upper and Overhill Towns in eastern Tennessee and northeast Alabama. Commonly known as the Cherokee Old Towns, ties of kinship connected the residents of these communities rather than ideology or allegiance to a political leader (Stremlau 2011, 23). These matrilineal and matrilocal clan-based communities consisted of Cherokee women remaining with their birth families after marriage and throughout their lives and the husband relocating to the wife's home community.

A gendered division of labor existed in the Old Towns with women as gatherers, growers, and processors of food. They also grew and spun cotton. Both women and men cultivated food in multiple locations with the majority of their corn in large, communal fields. Mankiller remarked, "In historical times, Cherokee people cared a great deal about balance. An important part of that balance was a measure of equity between men and

---

THE SEVEN CLANS

The seven Cherokee Nation clans are the *a ni ka wi*, or Deer Clan; *a ni way ha*, or Wolf Clan; *a ni wo di*, or Paint Clan; *a ni gi lo hi*, or Long Hair Clan; *a ni ga to ge ioi*, or Wild Potato Clan; *a ni so ho ni*, or Blue Clan; and the *a ni tsi squa*, or Bird Clan. The Cherokee traditional clan system was matrilineal. When a young man married and left his mother's house, he typically went to live among the clan of his wife, who often remained in the community of her mother's clan. More than the father of a Cherokee child, the matriarchal uncle was responsible for teaching traditional values to the young children of his sister.

women. Women often served as consultants in matters of importance to the community, the clan, the family and the nation, in the capacity of female tribal dignitaries, called War Women or Pretty Women, and a women's council." Women even occasionally accompanied men to the battlefield as warriors. The profoundly religious Cherokees of this time believed that the world existed in a precarious balance and that only right or correct actions kept it from tumbling. "Wrong actions could disturb the balance" (Mankiller 1993, 20). This is the approach Wilma took as the first female leader of the Cherokee Nation in Oklahoma in the mid-1980s.

In the 19th century, a Cherokee woman known as Nancy Ward held the position of "Beloved Woman," receiving this honor for her skill in mediating between Cherokees and whites and for her skill at peacemaking. British officials and non-Indian settlers often mocked tribal leaders of the Cherokee Nation for having women in leadership roles, and some whites called them a "Petticoat Government." Such mocking became one of several reasons that led Cherokee men to slowly push Cherokee women to the background and take charge of all tribal decision-making that involved whites.

The gender roles of Cherokee men and women complimented one another, yet Cherokee women did enjoy a greater degree of autonomy than their European counterparts. Feminism and Indianness shaped Wilma's sense of self and her political leadership. The Cherokee people descended from the Iroquois and in the Great Law of Peace, the chain of culture is the chain of women linking the past with the future. In Cherokee historical times, Cherokee people lived in semiautonomous villages and towns, each with unique characteristics (Rector 2002). The relationships in Cherokee settlements existed between people who lived together for many years in the same location in small communities and shared Cherokee culture and traditions. These extended relatives from a primary kin group lived scattered throughout their southeastern domain in autonomous villages, with each village having a war chief and a peace chief, sometimes called a Red Chief and a White Chief, charged respectively with the external and internal affairs of government. In times of war, the Red Chief made decisions and in times of peace, the White Chief became the main influencer in advising the people. Each chief had a council of advisers. It is certain that Cherokee women played an important and influential role in traditional town governments (Mankiller 1993, 19).

Reciprocity and living according to traditional values became important attributes of Cherokee culture. In dozens of tradition-oriented Cherokee communities in eastern Oklahoma, traditional values existed in a widespread self-help water-and-housing movement, which is often considered as a return to a time when Cherokee people lived responsibly for one another and helped one another. A good Cherokee is respectful to others, always keeps his or her word, and helps other people. When Cherokee people lived in the southeast, little ambiguity existed about what it meant to be a good person. "The good man dealt cautiously with his fellows, turned away to avoid threatened face-to-face conflict, and when overt conflict did occur, withdrew from the offenders" (Gearing 1962, 36). Prudent in relationships with others, a good person conducted his or her affairs with honor, respect, and dignity. "Being a Cherokee is a way of thinking and a way of knowing" (Anderson 1992). Everyone had clearly defined roles and understood the rules of conduct governing rights and correct actions. Wilma came to personify this "good person" identity. Among conservative traditional Cherokees, the Cherokee ethos, or the basic principle of their values, is harmony. This principle of harmony directs Cherokees to avoid discord and embrace the importance of being circumspect, quiet, and distant. The harmony ethic teaches Cherokees to mind one's own business and exhibit no counteraggression. These values are a standard of decency and by this measure, a person gains or fails to gain a good repute (Gearing 1962, 32).

Each Cherokee settlement would conduct an annual Green Corn ceremony for the purpose of rekindling relationships, requesting forgiveness for inappropriate conduct during the previous year, and cleansing the mind of negative thoughts toward others. Those who participated in the ceremony were forgiven for past offenses and their fellow participants never spoke of the offense again. No one was supposed to leave the ceremony with grudges or animosity toward others. A symbolic but very important feature of this ceremony was that each house in the village extinguished its home fire and relit it from a central ceremonial fire, as accomplished at Red Clay at the 1984 tribal reunion. Placing a very high premium on restoring harmony and balance in the community, the fire ceremony encouraged Cherokee people to keep a good, clean mind. *Du yuk tu*, meaning "the right way," represented the idea of balance. An underlying belief upheld that thousands of negative, hateful, vengeful, or jealous thoughts left unchecked would permeate the being, ultimately resulting in violent action or severe illness. These ceremonies continued as settler colonialism emerged throughout the traditional Cherokee lands.

As the new United States formed, national leaders decided that an Indian policy had to be created to deal with the remaining Indian communities. In 1802, Thomas Jefferson decided that the federal Indian policy for southeastern tribes was assimilation and Natives would all be better off if they relocated to the newly acquired territories west of the Mississippi River explored by the Lewis and Clark Expedition. He signed the Georgia Compact that year, promising to aid in the eventual removal of the Cherokee from Georgia. A group of Cherokees—around 2,000 to 4,000 people— voluntarily moved as a result of the Jackson-McMinn Treaty in 1817 and settled in the Arkansas Ozarks. Some Cherokees, who did not desire to assimilate to the ways of white farmers, voluntarily moved west at the end of the 18th century and the beginning of the 19th century. These early settlers lived between the White and Arkansas Rivers in present-day Arkansas and became known as the Old Settlers of the Cherokee Nation West. Wilma stated,

> Some of the Cherokees who moved west before the Trail of Tears were promised by the United States that in exchange for land in the eastern part of the country, they would be left alone forever. Believing this promise, they settled the area, built farms and communities, and began their lives over again, far from the political, social, and economic systems they had always known. They left behind not only their kinspeople, but essentially everything they were familiar with to come to the new land in the West. Not long after, they realized the United States would break its promise to the Cherokees again and intrude on their new homeland as well. Betrayal by the United States government was by then a familiar story to the Cherokees. (Mankiller 1993, 58)

This plan of assimilation was the first among many to attempt to "solve the Indian problem" for the United States.

Demand for the Cherokee to move increased once gold was discovered in Dahlonega, Georgia in 1828. In 1830, President Andrew Jackson authorized the Indian Removal Act, which proposed to move all Indians west of the Mississippi River, and this period became known as the Removal period. It took eight more years to institute the new federal Indian policy as the Cherokee chief, John Ross, led a series of attempts to have the policy overturned. In *Cherokee Nation v. Georgia* (1831) and *Worcester v. Georgia* (1832), the U.S. Supreme Court ruled in favor of Georgia in the 1831 case, but in the Worcester case, the following year, the court affirmed Cherokee sovereignty. None of this mattered to Andrew Jackson, who ignored the ruling of Supreme Court justice John Marshall and allowed white settlers the illegal move onto Cherokee lands. A small group of mixed-bloods, who did not represent the Cherokee Nation or any of the Cherokee people, signed the Treaty of New Echota on December 29, 1835, successfully giving away most of the Cherokee southeastern land to white settlers for lands in Indian Territory west of the Mississippi River. Former Cherokee chief Major Ridge, his son John, and his cousin, Elias Boudinot, signed the treaty without the consent of most of the Cherokee people and that is what made it illegal and fraudulent.

Because of the signing of this illegal treaty, in the summer of 1838 President Martin Van Buren decided that the Cherokee Nation had to leave the southeast to make way for white settler colonialization. Van Buren ordered the U.S. Army, under the command of General Winfield Scott, to round up all Cherokee people and place them in stockades to await removal to

Indian Territory. Those who could escape into the many caves throughout the traditional southeastern Cherokee lands. The U.S. federal soldiers placed those who could not escape in 31 camps, eventually bringing this down to 23 stockades near Cherokee towns. One was in Fort Payne, Alabama, with the rest located in Tennessee. In these stockades, the Cherokee men, women, and children awaited the long journey west. While they were kept there, in an act best described as inhumane, many of them died of exposure or hunger. The Cherokee removal involved 645 wagons and 5,000 riding horses at a cost of over $1 million, deducted from the amount paid for the southeastern homelands. This illegal and reprehensible action against the Cherokee people became known as Trail of Tears. Of the 17,000 Cherokees who began the trek, over 4,000 perished along the trail (Conley 2005, 157).

Beginning in the fall of 1838 and lasting into winter 1839, some Cherokees traveled by boat along the Tennessee, Ohio, Mississippi, and Arkansas rivers into Indian Territory and thousands more walked the roughly 1,500-mile journey (depending on the starting point). Although Chief John Ross was of Cherokee blood to only one-eighth degree (since he also had some Scots-Irish ancestry), the Cherokees considered him one of the best leaders among them, and he always had the best interests of the most traditional among the tribal members. Chief Ross led one of the 13 groups who walked. As mentioned earlier, about 4,000 Cherokee people died on the way to Indian Territory and the cultural memory became the "trail where they cried" for the Cherokees and other removed tribes (Cherokee Nation Cultural Resource Center website, n.d.).

Arriving in present-day Oklahoma, then known as Indian Territory, Cherokee communities ended the Trail of Tears in 1839. The earliest Cherokee settlements in Oklahoma developed along the Arkansas River in the valley lands and divided into districts bound by the Grand and Arkansas rivers on the west and south, respectively. These districts became organized for administrative purposes and were named Cooweescoowee, Delaware, Saline, Flint, Goingsnake, Sequoyah, Illinois, Canadian, and Tahlequah. Geographically, the Springfield Plain encompassed the communities in the Delaware, Goingsnake, and Flint districts, with many springs for fresh water. The Sequoyah district, in the valley lowlands, had a smaller population.

Setting out to reestablish their communities and rebuild the Cherokee Nation, the Trail of Tears survivors established Tahlequah as the first town, in 1839, with Fort Gibson created next, by 1857. Building on its commitment to public education, the tribe established public schools in 1841 and had as many as 21 schools throughout the communities in the Cherokee Nation by 1858. Through the hard work of Chief John Ross, two exceptional seminaries, or preparatory schools, for young Cherokee scholars began to operate within the nation by May 1851—the Cherokee National Male Seminary near Tahlequah and the Cherokee National Female Seminary at Park Hill. "The establishment of a school exclusively for Cherokee women was thought of as quite radical because most white Americans at that time regarded females as intellectually subordinate to men" (Mankiller 1993, 122). This was also when the role of women started to be diminished within the Cherokee Nation as the traditional matrilineal system gave way to the patriarchal system. Slowly, the power Cherokee women once held in their communities was increasingly diminished, with the men increasingly asserting community control.

A period of rapid growth continued throughout the 1850s and became known as the "Cherokee Golden Age" because of the many advances made in building homes, schools, churches, and stores. By 1867, 32 public schools existed, and by 1870 there were 2 additional high schools and 100 primary schools. The Black members of the Cherokee communities attended one high school. Twelve mission schools and an orphan asylum also served the Cherokee youth. The mixed-bloods insisted on an all-English curriculum, so by 1874, the full-blood settlement schools permitted the Cherokee language and texts to be available to the students (Mails 1996, 279). Scattered across the Cherokee communities dense enough in population to sustain a school, 65 public schools were in existence by 1875.

Besides the infrastructure and social institutions, the Keetoowah Society resurfaced in the Cherokee Nation after Removal as a powerful secret society. Derived from the name Kituwah, an ancient town in the old nation forming the nucleus of the most conservative element of the tribe, one purpose of the society became the cultivation of nationalism among the full-bloods opposing the more progressive mixed-bloods. Extended to The Creek Nation of Indians, members served the Union during the war known as "Pin Indians" and opposed every effort to destroy the Cherokee national self-government. The Pin organization was formed among members of the Baptist congregation at Peavine, Goingsnake District and numbered at least 3,000. The secret signs of the Pins included a way of touching the hat as a salutation and a particular way of holding the lapel of a coat, first drawing it away from the body then giving it a motion as if wrapping it around the heart (Mooney [1899] 1972, 225–226).

The Keetoowah Society, formed in 1855, held a political purpose and was not a strictly traditionalist movement, as most of the leaders were Christians. Group members resolved to "define a true Cherokee patriot as a full-blood, true to traditional values, national unity, and Cherokee self-determination" (McLoughlin 1993, 156). Not only was Keetoowah the name of an ancient Cherokee town on the Little Tennessee River, but it also referred to the *ani-kutani*, the spiritual and political elders of the nation, charged with preserving the tribe's sacred rituals and myths.

Mostly leaders among the full-blood Northern Baptists, the missionary Jones brothers formed a society to oppose the members of the pro-slavery, Southern rights, mixed-blood group known as "Blue Lodge" from an off-shoot of the Treaty Party and their descendants. The Keetoowahs supported the Union while the Blue Lodge supported the Confederacy. The Keetoowah Society also revived the old Cherokee religion with greater emphasis on medicine and dance grounds.

The Keetoowahs created a constitution and began wearing an insignia on their jackets consisting of crossed pins, earning the moniker of "the pins" (McLoughlin 1993, 158). By 1861, they had 2,000 members, with only full-bloods allowed. These two groups, the Keetoowahs and the Blue Lodge, came to represent the polarization within the Cherokee Nation. For many Cherokees during this period, embracing Christianity became a revitalization movement, as many local preachers delivered the weekly sermon in the Cherokee language. "The movement successfully integrated cultural identity, class identity, ethnic identity, and political idealism in a pietistic form of political action largely resembling the Free Soil movement in northern states" (McLoughlin 1993, 160). Yet, it was not to last, as the Civil War soon came to Indian Territory.

At the onset of the Civil War, the Treaty Party, comprising those who had signed the fraudulent Treaty of New Echota, chose to side with the Confederacy and be in full support of slavery. The Ross Party and the Keetoowahs favored the Union, but Chief Ross wished to remain out of the conflict because the Treaty Party had the support of most mixed-bloods and the Knights of the Golden Circle, a secret society established in the mid-19th century to oppose the Union. Chief Ross looked to the Keetoowah Society for support and reluctantly joined the Confederacy in 1861. "Old feuds and past troubles returned to haunt our people. Many innocent victims were caught in the cross fire. In only a few terrible years, nearly two decades of prosperity for the Cherokees were swept away by vicious guerilla fighting" (Mankiller 1993, 127). The Civil War destroyed much of the newly created Cherokee Nation West.

In September 1865, delegates from the Five Tribes (the Cherokees, Creeks, Chickasaws, Choctaws, and Seminoles) and other tribes gathered in Fort Smith, Arkansas, with representatives from President Andrew Johnson's administration. The federal officials informed the Five Tribes that they had violated their treaties by siding with the Confederacy and declared that the Cherokee citizens had given up all treaty rights. Their real motivation was to gain Indian lands for railroads and white settlement. The 1866 Cherokee Treaty abolished slavery and granted tribal citizenship to all former slaves in the Cherokee Nation. The terms also stipulated that it had brought the Cherokee Nation back under the protection of the United States.

Chief John Ross died in 1866 and his nephew, William Potter Ross, fulfilled through appointment the rest of his term. William Ross also became the first editor of the tribal newspaper the *Cherokee Advocate*, which continued publication in 1870 after a hiatus that had begun in the late 1850s. In 1867, Assistant Principal Chief Lewis Downing, a former lieutenant colonel in the Union army, became principal chief. Throughout his tenure, he focused on the increasing demands for the opening of Indian Territory to white settlers, as the railroads came to Cherokee lands by 1870. The fullbloods organized within the Downing Party. Lewis Downing was chairman of the Keetoowah Society during the Civil War and assistant principal chief. He served as chief from 1867 until his death in 1872, when William Potter Ross became principal chief for a second time. The Keetoowah Society divided into small groups with local chiefs. In 1874, Budd Gritts reorganized the society and reunited the organization. Keetoowah member Dennis Wolf Busheyhead served as principal chief from 1879 to 1887. "The Downing Party was reorganized in the late 1880s, and from that time until the United States greatly diminished the Cherokee government in 1907, almost all the principal chiefs of the Cherokee Nation came from the Downing Party" (Mankiller 1993, 130). The Cherokee Nation began to prosper again with the replenishment of livestock, cultivation of thousands of acres of crops, and appearance of new homes and stores. When the Cherokee people controlled their own affairs, they prospered. When outsiders, including the federal government, attempted control, chaos ensued.

The next federal Indian policy to attempt to "solve the Indian problem" was the Allotment Period. Until the development of the railroad in the 1880s, no other formal towns besides Tahlequah and Fort Gibson had existed among Cherokee communities in Oklahoma. The completion of the railroad in 1889 had a significant impact on the development of the region. The Dawes Act of 1887, also referred to as the Allotment Act, developed a federal commission that created a final tribal member roll for the Five Tribes (also known as the Five Civilized Tribes). The Dawes Commission then allotted a share of previously communally held lands to the approved individual members of these five tribes. Wilma exclaimed, "As a student of Native American history, I realize that the question of United States citizenship for native people was addressed in the Dawes Act, or the General Allotment Act of 1887." This was the law that prepared Native people for the eventual termination of tribal ownership of land by granting 160-acre allotments to each Indian family, or 80 acres to an individual. All of the allottees were to become U.S. citizens. Even though Theodore Roosevelt called the Dawes Act "a mighty pulverizing engine to break up the tribal mass," the Act failed because Native Americans considered land not as a possession but as a physical and spiritual domain shared by all living things. "Many of our people were reluctant to turn away from the traditional view of common ownership of land" (Mankiller 1993, 6). The application process began in 1896 but ended two years later when the Curtis Act required applicants to reapply. During this second round of applications, the Dawes Commission came up with the Final Rolls of the Citizens and Freedmen of the Five Civilized Tribes in Indian Territory (National Archives website, n.d.). John *Yona* Mankiller, Wilma's paternal grandfather, whose father survived the Trail of Tears, was one of those allottees.

The intent of allotment became the "liberation" of Indians from their connection to community. In other words, the intent was to break up extended families and undermine those who worked for the common good. In effect from 1887 to 1934, the Dawes Allotment Act resulted in the confiscation of millions of acres of land from Indians. The Five Tribes were initially excluded from the Act, yet in 1890, Congress appointed the Jerome Commission to deal with Indian Territory tribes in Oklahoma territory between 1889 and 1893. Then, in 1898, the Curtis Act was passed, ending Indian tribal governments, and in 1907 Oklahoma became a state. The Curtis Act abolished all tribal law and tribal courts and prohibited tribal councils from creating any new laws without the express approval of the president of the United States (McLoughlin 1993, 376).

In the 1890s, many traditional Cherokees, including those in the Keetoowah Society, opposed allotment. As leader of the Nighthawk Keetoowahs, Redbird Smith openly opposed allotment and refused to register, as required by the new law. "The more traditional Keetoowahs retreated into the hills of eastern Oklahoma to pursue their spiritual beliefs" (Mankiller 1993, 169). Then, in the 1890s, the mixed-bloods regained authority in tribal leadership. The Redbird Smith Movement, centered on the dance aspects of the ancient religion, was formed. From 1880 to 1890, approximately 25,000 whites settled in towns near the rivers. The full-bloods further isolated themselves. When allotment became the new federal Indian policy, the full-bloods ignored it for being contrary to their belief in shared and cooperatively-tended lands (Mails 1996, 275). The typical full-blood community in 1880 had a log church building with two or three extended families in log homes spread along a stream. There was also a smokehouse and gardens of corn, cotton, and beans, as well as a smaller home garden next to the house. Families shared duties of plowing, planting, harvesting, and homebuilding. "Leadership was provided by 'Little Captains,' who were the local officers of the Keetoowah Society" (Mails 1996, 276). The shared duties included the work of the men and women from the community. The men often did the more physically demanding work of cutting wood or clearing a garden spot, while the women cooked a large meal to share.

Most were Baptists and they used the church building for social dinners, quilting bees, and other activities, besides the church services in the
Cherokee language. There was also a Cherokee-language bible and hymns
translated into Cherokee. Political and religious life intertwined with
political meetings also held in the church. Missionaries vehemently
opposed the stomp dances held on medicine grounds (a medicine ground,
also known as a stomp ground, is a ceremonial gathering place and there
are many throughout northeastern Oklahoma), so they gradually declined
until the conservative full-bloods, who were not Baptists, formed the Redbird Smith Movement around 1896 (Mails 1996, 277). Conjuring for healing continued and many of the religious concepts of the movement came
from prayers of medicine men who collected them in books in the Cherokee syllabary. Most full-bloods kept knowledge of the ancient myths. Smith
held the opinion that the ancient teachings of the wampum belts had been
lost and his movement attempted to restore the more traditional ways back
to the tribe.

In 1896, the Keetoowah Society appointed Redbird Smith and a committee to retrieve and retain land and religion previously lost or in danger
of being lost. The messengers carried their secret messages at night and the
followers became known as the Nighthawk Keetoowahs. Redbird recovered the seven sacred Cherokee wampum belts and entrusted them to the
elders of the Cherokee, Creek, and Shawnee (Mails 1996, 279). During the
Creek visit, the Four Mother's Society was created and became a resistance
organization of full-bloods from the Five Tribes. It resembled the old intertribal councils with the retention of attorneys and sent delegates to Washington. This led to the reinstatement of the all-night dances at the medicine
grounds.

At Keetoowah meetings, Cherokees joined in all-night stomp dances
and feasts, after these dances were first revived on Blackgum Mountain in
1896. The Curtis Act of 1898 dissolved tribal governments and the Four
Mother's Society refused to accept this action. In 1902, federal officials
arrested and jailed Redbird and other leaders for not enrolling in the allotment program. After the approval of the Dawes Commission in August
1902, most members of the Cherokee Nation finally enrolled, but the full-
bloods again withdrew from social activities. Former members of the
Keetoowah Society formed the Night Hawks, a secret society not representing the Keetoowahs. The Keetoowahs pulled out of the Four Mother's
Society and then refused to take part in the tribal business or in new agreements between the United States and the Cherokee Nation (Mails 1996,
283). After authorities released Redbird from jail in 1902, he created a ceremonial dance ground, or medicine ground, in his home community. It
was called the Deep Branch Fire and later came to be known as Redbird's

Ground (Mails 1996, 284). Within the next year, there were 23 dance grounds. By 1916, a generalized Cherokee ceremony was in use, as was the old White Town form of government organization.

In a letter to Federal Judge Joseph A. Gill in Muskogee dated May 16, 1903, the Keetoowahs stated their purpose as loyalty to the U.S. government and the preservation of the Cherokee property as agreed to by previous treaties. Composed of those who were Cherokees by blood and who did not speak or understand English, they supported the Union Army and respectfully objected allotment (Mails 1996, 283). Wilma remarked, "The Keetoowah Society is still very well respected among our people, especially those who understand its historic role in the Cherokee Nation and the importance of continuing our tribal traditions such as ceremonial dances" (Mankiller 1993, 169). In the period of assimilation and allotment, the conservative Cherokees withdrew from active community development activities, while both conservative and progressive Cherokees became dependent on the Bureau of Indian Affairs (BIA) for major decisions on their education and health (Gulick 1958, 250).

In the late 19th century, Indian reformers often referred to as the "Friends of the Indians" failed to understand the extended kinship systems. Comprising missionaries and various wealthy white people, these Indian reformers thought they knew what was best for the Indian communities and therefore did not attempt to learn anything about Native culture. The reformers believed the lack of motivation among Indian men accounted for the lack of achievement of self-sufficiency. The main goal of the reformers continued to be eradicating tribal culture and language and transforming Native beliefs into those held among white people. Wilma stated, "In a time when the pressure to assimilate was tremendous, quite a number of Cherokees, including (Redbird) Smith's followers, managed to preserve the old Cherokee spirituality, ceremonial dances, and the idea that land should be held in common for the general use of everyone. They also perpetuated belief in personal responsibility and community interdependence" (Mankiller 1993, 171). By the end of the 19th century, adult children established households near the community of either the wife's family or the husband's family. Cherokee grandmothers passed on their knowledge of the Cherokee worldview to their children and grandchildren and, as matriarchs of their families, they had much influence (Hewes 1942b, 276).

Maintaining their Native culture and traditional tribal knowledge did not come easy. The Cherokee people spent a great deal of time moving large numbers of the population to appease others. The relocation of the Cherokees did not stop with the punitive terms imposed by Andrew Jackson or with the tragic Trail of Tears, and that initial relocation became the beginning of more to come. While the purpose of the Allotment Act of 1887 was to divide and distribute tribal lands among Indians, attempting to make them white farmers, the consequence was the breakup of tribes, fragmented lands, and surplus lands made available for white occupancy.

Because of the economic development associated with the railroad, by 1902 ten towns existed with over 200 people each; the residents were largely mixed-bloods or more-assimilated Cherokees. Between 1903 and 1910, land in the Cherokee Nation was subject to allotment. Full-bloods received 720,000 acres and Cherokees of less than one-half Indian blood, including intermarried whites, received 810,000 acres. Cherokee freedmen, former slaves associated largely with the mixed-bloods, received 148,000 acres. In 1907, the Cherokee Nation lost its political autonomy and was incorporated into the state of Oklahoma with 17,718 acres in trust land allotted. By 1930, only one-tenth of the allotted remained in Cherokee hands, and those not enrolled did not receive land. Most traditional Cherokees hesitated in enrolling and signing anything that had to do with the federal government due to their personal experiences with Removal during the Trail of Tears. By 1934, two-thirds of the land held by Indians at the time of allotment had passed into the hands of non-Indians (Cahn and Hearns 1969, 94).

Besides the disastrous allotment program, missionaries and federal boarding school leaders decided that education seemed the best route to assimilation efforts. The missionaries sought to eradicate all vestiges of Native culture through a Christianization policy and because most of the adults resisted, they worked with the children, often against their will. Government and boarding school officials forcibly took the children away from their families, their elders, their tribes, their language, and their heritage, isolating them so they would forget their culture. The boarding school concept seemed the most effective means for the federal government to deal with what its officials always called "the Indian problem." Wilma recalled, "After first trying to wipe all of us off the face of the earth with violence, they attempted to isolate us on reservations or, in the case of many people such as the Cherokees, place us in an area that the government called Indian Territory. All the while, they systematically conjured up policies to kill our culture. So, the federal government rounded up Indian youngsters and forced them to attend boarding schools whether they wanted to or not. This was true for most tribes, not just the Cherokees" (Mankiller 1993, 7). The assimilation efforts continued through much of the 20th century.

By the time of Oklahoma statehood in 1907, whites outnumbered Indians throughout the former Indian Territory (Hewes 1942b, 276). John W. Hoffman, entrepreneur, began buying timber rights in the traditional community of Kenwood area in 1913 and by 1920, over 1,000 people lived there and worked in the timber industry. Hoffman's company employed 300 men in creating railroad ties and finished lumber. Once Hoffman's company had depleted the timber supply they abandoned the company town, reflecting the boom-and-bust dynamic centered around the creation of the railroad (Howell 2017, 195). This occurred throughout eastern Oklahoma, resulting in no permanent wage-earning opportunities for anyone.

Reporting on the status of the various efforts to solve "the Indian problem," a commission of specialists from various fields, including education and health care, published the Meriam Report in 1928. This first report on the administration of American Indian programs concluded that the federal government assimilation and allotment policies had failed. Because of the destructive policy of the Dawes Severalty Act, or the allotment policy, Indian-owned lands declined in total acreage from 155 million acres to 48 million acres by 1934. Seeking another governmental solution, Commissioner of Indian Affairs John Collier sought the passage of the Indian Reorganization Act (IRA) in 1934 within the Franklin Roosevelt administration, ending the allotment process. This legislation further provided funds for tribes to purchase more lands, offered government recognition of tribal constitutions, and repealed the prohibition on American Indian languages and customs.

John Collier often overlooked the Indian perspective in his efforts at legislative reform, resulting in a major failing of this progressive law. Most tribes agreed the IRA government could be an improvement, so many tribes and bands throughout Indian Country approved reorganization. However, 78 tribes voted against the IRA, including the eastern Iroquois, the Navajo (Dine'), and the Yakima. Acknowledging the "one-size-fits-all" approach to Indian legislation failed in 1935, the Oklahoma Indian Welfare Act extended provisions of the IRA to Oklahoma tribes. Collier recognized the threat to tribal sovereignty, cultural preservation, treaty rights, and territorial integrity posed by those seeking assimilation (Shreve 2011, 32). After World War II, new ideas to help Indians join mainstream American culture emerged that decidedly embraced more conservative and conformist actions, once again transitioning into the emerging Termination and Relocation policies.

From the 1920s up to the 1940s, many of the more traditional Cherokees avoided places and events near the emerging towns. People became afraid and avoided social situations, and the traditional tribal knowledge of *gadugi* disappeared in its original form (Wahrhaftig 1978, 451). By 1942, the lands allotted to the full-bloods was only around one-third the acreage originally allotted to them (Hewes 1942a, 401). These Ozark residents comprised only one-twelfth of the total population but possessed over one-sixth of all the Cherokee lands. The poor land quality and scattered distribution of family lands became overwhelming factors in the vast poverty in the Indian districts of the Oklahoma Ozarks. The practice of leasing land to white farmers became more prevalent in the mid-20th century, and a lack of capital and the inability to obtain credit also contributed to the poverty (Hewes 1942a, 411). The *gadugi* existed as a work group in 1942 and later became "an occasion" rather than an organization among the Oklahoma Cherokees. A *gadugi* crew then became a form of disaster relief or a work party of traditionalists coming together to accomplish a specific task. Most often these work groups formed through the ceremonial sites, or stomp grounds.

Another Cherokee removal occurred three years before Wilma was born. The relocation of 1942 was not nearly as devastating or on the same scale as the tragedy of the Trail of Tears, but for the Native people displaced, it was just as upsetting and catastrophic. This removal occurred in the early days of World War II when the U.S. Army enlarged Camp Gruber, a military installation with an extensive reservation near Muskogee, Oklahoma. To accomplish its plan, the government condemned eight tracts, or 32,000 acres, of restricted Cherokee property. The land grab included the homes on allotments of 45 Cherokee families. Sixteen of those families raised livestock as self-sufficient farmers. Given only 45 days to pack up their belongings and abandon their homes, none of the families received compensation for improvements on their properties and none of them received relocation assistance. Most of the families had cattle, hogs, and poultry, and gardens. Not only was the compensation for the land inadequate, it often took years for it to be paid to the Cherokee families.

In the Greenleaf Hills near the rural, traditional community of Braggs, Camp Gruber served as one of the eight Prisoner of War camps built across Oklahoma. The new military installation also created a 35,000-troop facility. Today, the site is a training center for Homeland Security and Weapons of Mass Destruction and a specialty tactical training center for the Department of Defense military, law enforcement, and federal agencies.

Just after World War II, community development clubs emerged to create a new type of organization for rural people to clarify and solve their own problems. Similar clubs existed in each of the seven districts of the Eastern Band of Cherokee Indians (EBCI) in western North Carolina. In the mid-1950s, two of these clubs among the EBCI successfully extended electric power poles into their communities and one built its own clubhouse. For a while, participation in these clubs decreased, yet the community clubs in districts within the Cherokee Nation in eastern Oklahoma came to have more of an important role in the 1970s and 1980s.

In the 1940s and 1950s, many conservative Cherokees continued to live together in loosely grouped clusters, similar to the Cherokee Old Towns. The eastern wooded and Ozark portion of the Cherokee Nation served as both a cultural hearth and home to most Cherokees in eastern Oklahoma. There was a continuity of purpose despite the changes in families; they remained largely egalitarian, flexible, inclusive, and decentralized, with extended families, and this provided order and stability (Stremlau 2011, 47). A fear of whites existed because of the negative experiences of removal, allotment, and boarding schools. In the 1950s, anthropologist Robert K. Thomas (Cherokee) correctly identified maintaining harmonious relations and sharing resources and labor as being central to the Cherokee value system, and he observed that the culture of *gadugi* remained central to the Cherokees in Indian Territory (Stremlau 2011, 93). Communal resource ownership was a form of social welfare and also minimized competition. Some Cherokees sought protection of common interests rather than individual wealth, and many sought self-sufficiency. The formal institutions for organizing collective work and political decision-making and interpersonal relationships persisted, just not as evidently as it used to be (Wahrhaftig 1978, 455). The Free Labor Companies, volunteer labor based on the traditional *gadugi*, were still active in 1958, with limited participation and only for the benefit of needy individuals (Gulick 1958, 250). Pride in Cherokee schools and teaching values fostered social harmony and self-sufficiency, yet Cherokee settlements surveyed in the 1950s existed in extreme poverty and an extreme drought in 1955 made conditions much worse. Within this sense of place, Wilma spent her formative childhood years.

The Mankiller family surname is associated with an old military title; it used to be given to a person who safeguarded a Cherokee village. *Asgaya-dihi* means "Mankiller" in English. The Mankiller name survived in her family as a surname for four generations; it was originally not a name at all, but a rank or title used only after one had earned the right to it. Calling someone Mankiller was similar to calling a person Major or Captain (Mankiller 1993, 3). Since the name "Mankiller" referred to a military position for the village lookout, each Cherokee community had one, though Wilma said the name may have had other meanings as well, such as those stemming from the past. Wilma explained, "We know that in the Cherokee medicinal and conjuring style, Mankillers were known to attack other people to avenge wrongs that had been perpetrated against themselves or others they served. This Mankiller could change things, often for the worse. This Mankiller could change minds to a different condition, could make an illness more serious, and even shoot an invisible arrow into the body of an enemy. In the eighteenth century for example, there was the Mankiller of Tellico, the Mankiller of Estatoe, and the Mankiller of Keowee" (Mankiller 1993, 12). Later in her travels, teaching, and lecturing, when someone made a derogatory inference regarding her name, she would often tell them she had earned it and that usually shut them up. "The name Mankiller carries with it a lot of history. It is a strong name.

I am proud of my name—very proud. And I am proud of the long line of men and women who have also been called Mankiller" (Mankiller 1993, 13).

After settling in the community of Rocky Mountain on allotted lands that came to be called Mankiller Flats, Wilma's paternal grandfather, John Mankiller, joined the U.S. Army and fought in World War I. Her paternal grandmother, Bettie Bolin Bendabout Canoe Mankiller, died in 1916 from influenza. Her aunt (her father's half sister) Jensie Hummingbird helped raise her father, Charley, from the time he was two years old. Jensie also helped raise Charley's sister, Sally. Charley Mankiller was born in his father's house on November 15, 1914. "At the time of his birth, much of the land that had been allotted to the Cherokees was being taken away by unscrupulous businessmen with the cooperation of Oklahoma's judicial system. Unspeakably greedy people would arrange to be appointed guardians of Cherokee children, and then take control of their individually allotted Cherokee land" (Mankiller 1993, 5). This happened often in the early 1900s after the discovery of oil in Oklahoma. Charley had only one full sibling, his older sister Sally. She married a full-blood Cherokee named Nelson Leach, and they lived on a portion of Mankiller Flats.

Boarding school officials forced both Charley and Sally Mankiller to attend the Sequoyah Training School near Tahlequah. The school began as an orphan asylum. Wilma remembered, "The Cherokee National Council passed an act establishing the asylum in 1871 to provide housing for children orphaned by the Civil War. The war was fought partly in the Cherokee Nation, and Cherokees served in both the Union and Confederate armies. Later, the orphan facility became an asylum for Indian people who experienced mental or physical problems of such severity that they could not cope without assistance. Finally, it was turned into a boarding school for Indian children" (Mankiller 1993, 6). Federal boarding school education had the primary purpose of indoctrinating the Native children into accepting the dissolution of their cultures and the superiority of the Euro-American value system. In the government boarding school, Charley encountered such beliefs and practices.

Much mental and physical abuse occurred at the boarding schools, including widespread sexual abuse of the young men at the schools. Wilma remembered her father being conflicted about his educational experiences at school, as he often received punishment yet developed a good relationship with the superintendent, Jack Brown. Charley also developed a love of books in school, which he passed on to Wilma and her siblings. Charley's traditional family life helped counteract much of the anti-Cherokee boarding school experience. Wilma recalled, "I am thankful that even though my father was raised in such a boarding school environment, he did not buy into everything that was being taught. Fortunately, he came from a

---

THE POCAHONTAS CLUB

The mixed-bloods developed their own cultural pattern as represented in the Indian Women's Pocahontas Club, created in June 1899 in the Cooweescoowee District in Claremore, Oklahoma. It began as a social club and then began accepting male members and transitioned into more of a literary club with other activities. Dr. Emmet Starr, Cherokee historian, became its president in 1906 and Will Rogers became one of the more popular members due to his quick wit and noted oratory skills. The Pocahontas Club disbanded in 1929 due to a lack of participation but was reestablished in 1937 in the wake of renewed interest in Cherokee heritage and culture. In 1947, the club became a member of the National Congress of American Indians and remains active even today.

---

strong family, and because of his traditional upbringing, the school was not successful in alienating him from his culture. He was a confident man, and to my knowledge, he never felt intimidated in the non-Indian world" (Mankiller 1993, 9).

Wilma's maternal grandmother, Pearl Halady, was born in 1884 in Washington County, Arkansas. In 1903, when she was 19 years old, she visited the community of Wauhillau, a new settlement of Cherokees and white pioneers in Indian Territory. There Pearl met Robert Bailey Sitton. They married within the year and established a home near the community of Wauhillau, where Robert's parents, William and Sara Sitton, lived. After two years, Robert and Pearl moved to a small farm near the community of Titanic. Robert worked for the railroad, and his work caused the young family to move frequently. They finally settled on a small farm near Rocky Mountain. Wilma remembered, "I have heard it said that there was not a job on the farm my grandmother would not tackle, including plowing the fields. Folks described her as being spunky. Some years after my grandfather died and her children were raised, she sold her farm and moved into the town of Stilwell to run a boardinghouse" (Mankiller 1993, 11). Robert and Pearl Sitton had seven children. Wilma's mother, Clara Irene, was the youngest.

Clara Irene Sitton was born in Adair County, Oklahoma on September 21, 1921. Her parents Robert and Pearl were from the Sitton and Gillespie families of Dutch and Irish stock. Wilma stated, "My mother's ancestry goes back to North Carolina, where her kinfolk from the Sitton side were some of the first iron-makers, while the Gillespies were craftsmen who turned out fine long rifles" (Mankiller 1993, 9). Wilma's mother and father had a whirlwind courtship and married in 1937, when they were 15 and

21 years old, respectively. Wilma recalled how against the relationship her grandmother was. "Although her oldest daughter, Sadie, had married a mixed-blood Cherokee, Grandma Sitton did not approve of my father because he was a full-blood Cherokee" (Mankiller 1993, 11). The couple married in the Baptist Church in the Mulberry community on March 6, 1937, after which Charley took a job cutting railroad ties—it was the main source of income in the area during the Great Depression in the 1930s. During this period, many Cherokees made money cutting railroad ties to supplement their subsistence farming, but the work was dangerous (Wahrhaftig 1978, 449). Charley did not serve in World War II. Wilma remarked, "I suppose if my father had not fallen off a log while cutting trees for railroad ties, I would not have been born. But his leg injuries prevented him from enlisting in the military service and going off to war" (Mankiller 1993, 32).

Wilma had three older brothers (Louis Donald, born in 1937, Robert Charles, born in 1940, and John David, born in 1943) and two older sisters (Frieda Marie, born in 1938, and Frances Kay, born in 1942). She had two younger sisters (Linda Jean, born in 1949, and Vanessa Lou, born in 1953) and three younger brothers (Richard Colson, born in 1951, James Ray, born in 1956 in Oklahoma, and William Edward, born in 1961 in San Francisco) (Mankiller 1993, 38).

Wilhelmina "Wilma" Pearl Mankiller was born in the W.W. Hastings Indian Hospital in Tahlequah, Adair County, Oklahoma on Sunday, November 18, 1945. Her parents established their home in Mankiller Flats in Adair County on the Cherokee County line in eastern Oklahoma. Bounded by the Cherokee Hills on the north and the Cookson Hills on the south, Adair County had the highest percentage of American Indians compared to any other county in the United States in the mid-20th century (Mankiller 1993, xvi). The community closest to Mankiller Flats was Rocky Mountain, which had a small grocery store, a gas station, and a school. The one hundred acres of family land called Mankiller Flats became part of Wilma's heritage and pride.

The house her father built had a wood stove for heat, no electricity, no running water, and an outhouse. The family hauled water from a spring a quarter of a mile away. Yet, Wilma was a happy little girl. She loved the springtime, and her family's home had a lot of dogwoods and redbud trees and a variety of wild flowers. Wilma recalled how her entire family loved the outdoors and her mother could name every tree, bush, flower, and edible plant in the woods. Wilma's father must have known somehow that she would also develop a love of flowers because he gave her the Cherokee name *A-ji-luhsgi Asgaya-dihi*, which means "little flower and protector of the village" (Mankiller 1993, 42). Wilma remembered the smell of burning wood in the house and the sound of rain on the tin roof. She also had a rather negative memory of opinionated, white Oklahoma ladies offering her a ride as she walked daily to or from her school in Rocky Mountain (a six-mile roundtrip). They also offered clothing, saying, "Bless your heart." Wilma viewed this as condescending pity, which she felt was unnecessary.

The Mankiller family attended neither church nor medicine grounds regularly, but they occasionally attended the Echota Baptist Church as well as the traditional all-night ceremonial stomp dances, and Wilma had fond memories of both. She remembered the importance of the ceremonial dances, community clubs, and Cherokee stories. "My father's stories were important to all of us. Our main forms of entertainment were storytelling and visiting. Either we went to see other families, or folks visited us. Mostly we saw other Cherokee people" (Mankiller 1993, 37). Charley enjoyed telling stories, as did other members of the community. One story was about the Cherokee Little People.

The Little People are a group of little people who are said to inhabit the wilds and caves of North Carolina, Tennessee, and Georgia; the Natives called them *Nunne'hi*, meaning "people who live anywhere," and *Yunwi Tsunsdi*, or "Little People." They are said to be just like human beings in appearance, only smaller in stature, in some traditions no higher than a man's knee; they are also said to be imbued with various powers, such as the ability to vanish at will, teleport from place to place, and live forever. Inclined to sing and dance, the *Nunne'hi* also protected the forest and helped lost travelers. Often, hunters would tell of hearing the drums of *Nunne'hi* in the distance, although it was said that to try to track the sound to its source was futile, with the sound always seeming farther away.

The Mankiller household, where people visited often and stayed for long periods, constantly buzzed with activity. Some people Wilma remembered visiting during her childhood were her aunt Jensie Hummingbird, and Jim and Maudie Wolf (Jim was a traditional Cherokee healer and Maudie was a ceremonial dance leader). She also remembered her aunt Sally Leach and Sally's husband, Nelson, as well as her great-aunt Maggie Gourd, her dad's cousin, who was also a Cherokee storyteller (Mankiller 1993, 40).

Most people young Wilma knew spoke Cherokee as their first language, and her home was bilingual. During her youth in the early 1950s, the family worked a large garden and always had good food—fresh or canned—on the table for the large family. Wilma remembered bartering with neighbors for eggs or milk and eating what they grew in their garden. Being raised in that environment with the sense of community extending beyond her immediate family helped Wilma discover the power of community relationships. Seasonal employment also helped the Mankiller family, as did cutting timber and being part of harvest crews. Her father and oldest brother Don often harvested broomcorn in Campo, Colorado, to supplement the family income. This money helped purchase new winter coats and shoes for school.

According to Wilma, the first time she ever felt different or ashamed of being poor was when she started attending school in the Rocky Mountain community. One day, a girl at school saw her flour-sack underwear and told other girls, who laughed at her. While there may have often been a lack of money in the Mankiller home, there was absolutely no lack of love and affection. A great love of books also existed, as Wilma recalled they were always around the house as far back as she could remember, and the love of reading became the best gift her father ever gave her (Mankiller 1993, 44).

The community around Mankiller Flats in the 1950s existed in isolation with only dirt roads, no television or telephones, and mostly Cherokee speakers. Wilma learned three valuable lessons from those early childhood days by watching other people around her. She first noticed the sense of interdependence among the traditional Cherokees, who often had to depend on one another to survive. She also learned to have a good mind and be positive. Last, she learned that the Cherokee people often viewed problems as challenges rather than as a reason to give up. Before she was 30 years old, Wilma had begun to live her life based on these three observations.

Not giving up on assimilation, in yet another attempt to "solve the Indian problem," the federal government developed the Termination Act of 1953, intended to assimilate individual American Indians into mainstream American culture by dissolving Indian trust status. This particular federal Indian policy intended to grant all privileges and rights of citizenship to American Indians. In actuality, the Act ended tribal sovereignty and freedom, trusteeship of the reservations, and exclusion of Indians from state laws. Wilma recalled, "The government's primary objectives in the policy of termination were to break up the system of Indian reservations across the country and to lure native people from their homeland through the program of relocation" (Mankiller 1993, 63). Before termination, the Indian Health Service gave health care to many tribes, but with the termination policy, many of the Natives no longer had access to hospitals, clinics, or health care. Between 1953 and 1966, Congress ended 109 tribes, terminating the trust relationship, and withdrew federal services such as education and health care funding, with disastrous results. The Klamath tribe in Oregon became especially affected by the new termination policy.

In response to the Termination Act, the Bureau of Indian Affairs (BIA) instituted a voluntary relocation program to urban areas. Reservation-based and rural American Indians could choose to move to metropolitan areas such as Denver, Chicago, Los Angeles, Seattle, Cleveland, and San Francisco. The BIA promised relocation assistance, that is, assistance in locating housing and employment. The Mankiller family heard and read about the wonderful opportunities for Indians to get good jobs, obtain good education for their kids, and leave poverty behind once and for all. In reality, the program gave the federal government another opportunity to remove Indian people from their culture and lands. Wilma stated, "Instead of guns and bayonets, the BIA used promotional brochures showing staged photographs of smiling Indians in 'happy homes' in the big cities of America" (Mankiller 1993, 69).

After much debate among her mother, father, and oldest brother, the Mankiller family moved, yet Frieda, the eldest daughter and a senior at Sequoyah High School, remained behind. Her father, Charley, believed leaving the poverty and the severe drought of 1955 behind in Adair County, Oklahoma, was best for his family. Wilma's entire world until this point had been a 40-mile radius from her family home at Mankiller Flats, and she had only briefly traveled to Muskogee, Stilwell, and Tahlequah. Before boarding the train heading west, the Mankiller family ate bowls of chili at the Stilwell Café and barely spoke, as young Wilma tried to remember every detail about her homeland.

2

The Streets of San Francisco

The Mankillers selected San Francisco as their land of opportunity because Irene's mother, Pearl Sitton, had moved from Oklahoma to Riverbank, California, in 1943 after Robert died and she remarried. The farming community of Riverbank, about 90 miles east of San Francisco, allowed young Wilma to identify this move with the movement of her ancestors to a strange, new place after the Trail of Tears. "The government wanted to break up tribal communities and 'mainstream' Indians, so it relocated rural families to urban areas. One day I was living in a rural Cherokee community, and a few days later I was living in California and trying to deal with the mysteries of television, neon lights, and elevators. It was a total culture shock" (Mankiller 1993, xx). For Wilma, the culture shock manifested itself in days of crying.

Wilma recalled that the U.S. government, through the BIA, was again trying to settle the "Indian problem" by removal. "I learned through this ordeal about the fear and anguish that occur when you give up your home, your community, and everything you have ever known to move far away to a strange place." "I wept tears that came from deep within the Cherokee part of me. They were tears from my history, from my tribe's past. They were Cherokee tears" (Mankiller 1993, 62). The Mankiller family relocated one month before Wilma's 11th birthday in October 1956, and she often referred to it as her family's own personal Trail of Tears. Although their relocation was voluntary, Wilma still associated the move with a great loss. For the first time in her life, Wilma began thinking about what it must

23

have been like for her Cherokee ancestors when the government troops made them give up their land, houses, and everything they owned at gunpoint and move to a faraway land. "It was a time for me to be sad" (Mankiller 1993, 68). During the first decade she lived in San Francisco, Wilma experienced different cultures, new technologies, high school graduation, marriage, motherhood, radical politics, and the nascent feminist movement. Each experience shaped her naïve beliefs and influenced her opinions on poverty, politics, and her identity as a young Cherokee woman.

By the time World War II happened, the Bay Area population had doubled over the previous decade, increasing competition for affordable housing and jobs. San Francisco attracted a variety of workers during and after World War II. In 1946, Stanford University created the Stanford Research Institute to promote the economic development of the west coast, and in the mid-1950s, Hewlett Packard, then Xerox, Lockheed, ITT, IBM, Sylvania, Admiral, and others followed by setting up offices. Many migrants from Oklahoma and Mexican Americans and African Americans from the lower Mississippi River Valley moved to the region and by the end of the war, the African American population in the San Francisco Bay Area had increased from 20,000 to 65,000 (Abbott 1993, 19). Most of these new residents of the Bay Area had to live in overcrowded public housing facilities because less than 1 percent of housing existed for them. As with many other large American cities, a decline in the city occurred as white residents moved out into the suburbs. The city center increasingly deteriorated into several "skid row" areas, or districts as they are known in San Francisco, including the Tenderloin District, south of Market Street, and parts of Bayview-Hunters Point. The influx of thousands of American Indians made the housing shortage even more severe.

After traveling from Stilwell, Oklahoma to San Francisco, the Mankiller family found a temporary home in the dilapidated Keys Hotel, located in the red-light area within the downtown Tenderloin District. Suddenly surrounded by concrete, hard-faced men, asphalt, prostitutes, steel, broken glass, and neon lights, Wilma and her siblings felt they had landed on another planet. The noises of the sirens from police and ambulances became the most curious and frightening sounds and Wilma thought they sounded like wolves. "Wolves surrounded me. But they were not four-legged or fanged or covered with fur. They were a species all their own" (Mankiller 1993, 76). After a few weeks at this location, the BIA found an apartment for the family in the Potrero Hill District. It was a tiny place yet close to the rope factory where Charley and Don found a job earning $48.00 a week.

Wilma soon encountered people of other ethnicities in San Francisco, such as the Mankiller family's Mexican American neighbors, the Roybals and their children, who became good friends. Jerry and Carmen Roybal taught the Mankillers how to maneuver in the big city; they taught Wilma and her siblings how to ride a bicycle, roller skate, and use an elevator and a telephone. Yet, this was also when Wilma discovered that the other kids appeared to be far more advanced than her and her siblings in social skills and academic abilities; it led to her increasing sense of isolation. Wilma began her new school in the fifth grade and experienced ridicule by other students for her last name and accent; they bullied her because of the "country" way she talked and dressed. She and her younger sister Linda sat up late into the night reading to each other as practice to lose their Oklahoma accents. Because of these experiences, she despised school and never felt comfortable there.

Wilma's growing sense of detachment came during the first instance of racism she encountered in San Francisco. Wilma and her family quickly learned of ethnic intolerance and that poverty and prejudice persisted (Mankiller 1993, 102). Soon after they had arrived in the city, a woman approached her mother and told her she had "n----r children." Then the strange woman called Wilma's mother an "n----r lover." Most people were not so blatant in their racial intolerance and just made comments under their breath or behind one's back. While the Deep South experienced racial strife and direct action emerged under the direction of Dr. Martin Luther King and the Southern Christian Leadership Conference, some Southerners remained intolerant of others Wilma felt an association to her new neighbors of color, as they were all treated as less than those with Caucasian features in San Francisco.

Feeling sad and homesick for Mankiller Flats most of the time, during the early months in San Francisco and especially when she became older, Wilma thought back to the past and to her ancestors who had walked the Trail of Tears to become the Cherokee Nation West. "The experiences of those who made that journey to Indian Territory remain an unrivaled lesson in courage and hope" (Mankiller 1993, 77). Wilma often reflected on her ancestors who had survived the removal from the southeast and how they had rebuilt their lives time and again.

The mid-20th-century American Indian diaspora from rural areas and reservation communities into western cities became one of the largest internal migrations of Americans. As an unplanned consequence, urban American Indians organized their own institutions and business networks in the San Francisco region as well as in other cities. The idea of a collective Indian identity also emerged to keep their tribal identities in the city. This unexpected Native response to the termination and relocation policies created national, regional, and local groups. Government policies and mission school policies were designed to eradicate Indian language and culture. The 1953 Termination policy intended to close the BIA and the reservations and abrogate all treaties.

Indian efforts to oppose assimilation efforts began in May 1944 in Denver, as the National Congress of American Indians (NCAI) lobbied for self-determination, tribal sovereignty, treaty rights, and territorial integrity. The NCAI mission became the protection of Indian land rights and improved educational opportunities. The Termination policy of 1953 allowed states to assert legal jurisdiction over Indian reservations without tribal consent, to transfer federal Indian responsibilities to states, and to relocate Indians to urban areas. The NCAI slogan was "Self-determination rather than Termination." The NCAI lobbied intensively against the termination policy. Other national Indian organizations emerged after the termination policy seeking to negotiate the newest plan by the federal government and find ways to improve the lives of American Indians, reservation-based Indians, and urban Indians. The NCAI began six-week summer workshops in Colorado created by D'Arcy McNickle (Cree/Irish) to teach tribal sovereignty, treaty rights, cultural preservation, and self-determination with the focus on federal Indian policy, social theory, and Native history.

After the Great Depression and World War II, Indigenous people throughout the world began to decolonize, revolting against their European colonizers. Anthropologists Robert "Bob" Thomas (Cherokee), Murray and Rosalie Wax, Fred Gearing, Robert Rietz, and Albert Wahrhaftig taught the workshops on American Indian affairs. A Cherokee traditionalist, Bob Thomas encouraged a nationalist framework within the philosophies rooted in tribalism, sovereignty, self-determination, treaty rights, and cultural preservation. After the workshops ended, both Thomas and Alfred Wahrhaftig continued work with the Cherokees in eastern Oklahoma in the 1960s and 1970s. Participants in these NCAI workshops read Ruth Benedict's *Patterns of Culture*, Robert Redfield's *The Folk Society*, John Collier's *Indians of America*, and Edward Spicer's *Cycles of Conquest*, stressing cultural relativity and considering all cultures viewed on an equal level. The 1950s Denver workshops functioned similarly to those workshops taking place at Fisk University in Nashville among young African American students, but with a different purpose of seeking treaty rights more than civil rights.

Although termination and relocation of American Indians to urban centers officially became federal Indian policy in the 1950s, Indians had been moving to cities throughout the 20th century. By the mid-1950s, approximately 3,000 reservation Indians, mostly from the southwest region of the United States, were moved to housing developments in Chicago and then moved to other cities. The YWCA and the BIA operated an Indian Employment Office at the Oakland Post office in the 1920s. The YWCA also sponsored an Oakland social club called the Four Winds Club, the only Indian organization in the Bay Area until the American Friends

Service Committee, a Quaker group, transformed it into the Intertribal Friendship House (IFH) in 1956. The Quakers supported the retention of Indian identities and advocated for the support of treaty rights (Smith 2012, 35).

The IFH played a key role in the Bay Area, becoming one of the first Indian-focused, multiservice, urban organizations in the nation. The directors and volunteer staff offered programs and services such as summer youth programs, educational activities, elder programs, holiday meals, social services counseling, and crisis intervention. During these programs, Indian people became connected for mutual support and socialization (Lobo 1990, 11). One of the first people Wilma met upon arriving in San Francisco was Justine Buckskin (Klamath), who volunteered at the IFH, and the two became life-long friends.

The Oakland BIA Relocation office opened a year before the Mankiller family arrived in San Francisco and offered adult vocational training intended to complement the relocation program. Also, in 1955, St. Vincent De Paul Society opened the American Indian Center in the San Francisco Mission District. This was one of the community centers in which Wilma and her family became actively involved. An American Indian Baptist Church also opened in 1958 in Oakland, primarily for the tribal people from Oklahoma, and the church officials also sponsored a monthly pow-wow (Fortunate Eagle 2002, 30).

After 1958, Indians in San Francisco found one another during Sunday afternoon Golden Gate Park picnics that grew into singing and drumming occasions. The IFH began working with the United Council of the Bay Area Indian Community. As Cy Williams (Chippewa) stated, "There are a lot of Indian clubs forming right now, and maybe by working together we could do better for our people" (Fortunate Eagle 1992, 25). A great need existed for Indian leadership in those Indian clubs. The Council of Area Leaders became the Bay Area American Indian Council.

Wilma met more Indian people from other reservation communities and discovered that the BIA promise of a better future produced an even tougher life. She learned that many urban Native people endured poverty, emotional suffering, substance abuse, and poor health because they had left their homelands and communities—they had left their social capital, or social safety net. Reflecting on those early years, Wilma recalled, "Urban Indian families banded together, built Indian center, held picnics and pow-wows, and tried to form communities in the midst of large urban populations. Yet there was always and forever a persistent longing to go home" (Mankiller 1993, 73). Sad and lonesome most of the time, Wilma had to endure the worries and pressures of urban life and contend with the ordeals of adolescence becoming extremely unpleasant experiences for her. "I was nagged by anxiety, doubt, and fear that silently crept from the city's shadows with the thick bay fog to sit on windowsills and hover at doors. The hushed voices were more terrible than any beast's howls" (Mankiller 1993, 76). Knowing only the country and country ways, Wilma suffered from incurable homesickness aggravated by what felt like a permanent case of the blues. Her whole world seemed like a hopeless exercise that would never end.

After being in the city for over a year, the Mankiller family moved into a three-bedroom house in Daly City, approximately eight miles southwest of the Potrero Hill District. This is when her father became more involved in the San Francisco Indian Center. The move was an improvement for the family, but Wilma was still miserable in California and particularly in school there. Feeling alienated from other students, always uncomfortable, feeling stigmatized and insecure, and entering the seventh grade, Wilma felt mortified having to meet another group of new students. The students at Potrero Hill and in Daly City teased her mercilessly about her country accent and last name. Wilma and her sister Linda still read aloud to each other every night because, as with other kids, they also wanted to belong. Wilma simultaneously experienced puberty and reached her full adult height by age 12 and this caused people to think she was much older. She hated what was happening to her body. She hated school and the teachers and the other students, and she hated San Francisco (Mankiller 1993, 103).

Wilma's teen years became troubled, and she felt afraid and very alone as her self-esteem plummeted to its lowest point. She ran away from home at least five times over the next year and always went to her Grandma Sitton's house in Riverbank. Eventually, Charley and Irene allowed Wilma to remain in Riverbank with her grandma for the 1959 school year. Wilma attended eighth grade at Lone Tree School in Escalon, California. She liked Riverbank because other Oklahoma families who had moved to California during the Dust Bowl had settled there, and she felt more comfortable in the farming communities than in the big city. Wilma often returned there during the summer breaks from school, and as she grew older, she began to cruise around the valley town of Modesto, the model for the town in the 1973 film *American Graffiti* and the place where the director of the film, George Lucas, spent his youth in the early 1960s.

Grandma Sitton outlived another husband, sold her house, and gave the money to her son and daughter-in-law, Floyd and Frauline. That money purchased a dairy ranch north of Riverbank near Escalon. Grandma Sitton then moved in with them and their four children. After a rocky start, because of Wilma's competitiveness with her cousins and her sensitive nature, Wilma developed a bit of self-confidence. When she first started living on the dairy farm, Wilma would become provoked at the slightest irritant and described her cousins and herself as "pure country" (Mankiller 1993, 105). She and Grandma Sitton milked the cows every morning.

Wilma's primary job was to keep the barn clean and she also worked in the large vegetable garden. Her grandmother was opinionated, outspoken, very independent, and deeply religious; she often sang gospel songs, loved to garden, and valued hard work. Wilma inherited her work ethic from her father and Grandma Sitton. Her grandmother had a tremendous influence on Wilma and taught her the value of hard work and being an independent lady.

Besides Wilma's personal changes that were brought on by adolescence, there was a major change in the Mankiller family when her eldest brother, Don, met and married a Choctaw woman named LaVena. Their marriage meant some loss of income for the Mankiller family, as Don and LaVena moved to their own place. With the decrease in income in the household, Wilma and her family had to leave the three-bedroom house in Daly City and move to a cheaper place called Hunters Point, a rough housing project approximately 16 miles away on the other side of San Francisco but closer to the Indian Center on Mission Street. Hunters Point was often referred to as Harlem West.

In a peninsula extending into the San Francisco Bay, the Hunters Point-Bayview District housing project sat in a 21 square mile area of southwestern San Francisco, with approximately 50,000 people living there in 10,224 housing units as of 1960 (Hippler 1974, 13). The San Francisco Housing Authority listed 95 percent of the residents as African American and 5 percent as white and Samoan (Hippler 1974, 15). Forty percent of the residents belonged to/lived in single-mother households. The buildings in Hunters Point were constructed of concrete with six-unit apartments in groups of three or four placed side-by-side about 30 yards apart. Each group of homes shared a common courtyard area and a small playground. There was a panoramic view of the rest of the city from the top of the hill in Hunters Point, yet the area was poor, isolated, and dependent, with minimal white contact and new outdoor activities Wilma had not seen before, such as juvenile delinquency and gangs. One other relocated Cherokee family lived there, but most residents were African Americans. Wilma's perceptions of the world took shape here as she realized that all authority figures in her life were white people. The black culture at Hunters Point also had a profound influence on Wilma's life, with part of her continuing education in the world of urban poverty and violence being the gang activity between African Americans and Samoans (Mankiller 1993, 109).

Women from the Third Street and Bayview community centers near Hunters Point held the power in the community, as mothers as well as in other roles; they usually acted as the heads of their households when it came to making economic decisions. Because Wilma's paternal grandmother had died before Wilma's birth, she felt a special affinity toward the older women in her community at Hunters Point. She came to know the women there as being especially strong and that they were considered the mothers of the entire community. Here, Wilma's sociopolitical view of the world materialized. Her views of white culture emerged—she saw them as people who held all the power and authority. She became immersed in African American culture, whose people had no power. Unlike most teens her age who listened to Pat Boone, the Beach Boys, or Elvis, Wilma and her best friends, Johnnie Lee and LaVada, listened to Etta James, Dinah Washington, Sarah Vaughan, B.B. King, and other rhythm and blues musicians. Their favorite radio stations were KDIA in Oakland and KSOL in San Francisco, which played the latest hits in R&B music of the late 1950s.

Wilma shared an upstairs bedroom with her sister Linda and the two often either stared at the water in the bay or down at the streets below, where the African American and Samoan street gangs fought constantly for territory. Wilma learned about the constant struggle against racial prejudice and to keep kids away from drugs while interacting with a diverse population full of frustration and alienation. It became more important to appear a fighter than a good student. Youth learned about "telling it like it is." There was also much self-hatred among the youth there, as living in poverty and feeling powerless to control aspects of daily life created a sense of helplessness and despair quite similar to what was seen at the Indian reservations or allotment lands in eastern Oklahoma. Wilma became streetwise at Hunters Point.

All these social issues aside, Wilma had fond memories of the women in that community. She was quite moved by their perseverance: "Poverty is not just a word to describe a social condition, it is the hard reality of everyday life. It takes a certain tenacity, a toughness to continue on where there is an ever-present worry about whether the old car will work, and if it does, will there be enough gas money; digging through piles of old clothes at St. Vincent de Paul's to find clothing for the children to wear to school without being ridiculed; wondering if there will be enough to eat" (Mankiller 1993, 110). The African American women of Hunters Point possessed a quiet strength and grace in their struggle to survive and this made an impact on young Wilma's growing knowledge of womanhood.

Once they moved to Hunters Point, the Mankillers became more active in the Indian Center, located approximately 4.5 miles from their new home. Situated on 16th Street in the Mission District, the San Francisco Indian Center became a sanctuary for Wilma. After school, she often rode the city bus to the Indian Center and hung out with other Native teenagers. Her dad, Charley, moved from working in the rope factory to working as a longshoreman and a shop steward and union organizer for a San Francisco spice company. Charley also became more involved in urban Indian projects and even appeared on a local television program advocating for an Indian health clinic in the city. He always brought people home from the

Indian Center who needed a meal or help in other ways and often kept a $20 bill in the back of his wallet in case a family needed it. Wilma sometimes participated in the all-night poker games held at her home and she became a skilled poker player. The Indian Center in the Mission District became exceptionally important as more newly urban Natives discovered what a sham the relocation program actually was, and it removed the deeply important sense of place highly valued among most Indian people. Wilma inherited her father's tenacity and his willingness to help others in need.

From the time she was a young child, Wilma had debated with her father on daily topics, including political subjects. Like many descendants of Trail of Tears survivors, Charley became a Republican who wanted nothing to do with the Democrats, the party of Andrew Jackson. In spite of their political differences, Wilma loved spending time with her dad, at home and at the Indian Center.

Tragedy struck the Mankiller family in 1960. Wilma's older brother Robert (Bob) worked with a friend named Louie Cole (Choctaw) picking apples in Washington State. To save money, the boys lived in a sharecropper's cabin on the orchard property. Early one morning, when it was cold and dark, Bob reached for what he assumed was the kerosene they used to help light the woodstove and instead grabbed gasoline. After he threw it in the stove, the cabin exploded in flames and the boys struggled to get the deadbolt open to escape. Louis Cole suffered substantial burns but Bob's injuries were greater. After seven days in the hospital, Bob died. His parents buried him in the Oakdale Citizen's Cemetery in Oakdale, CA, near Riverbank and Escalon, and Grandma Sitton. Fifteen-year-old Wilma admired her older, carefree brother Bob for his good looks, athleticism, and happy attitude and his death devastated her. The family went to the Indian Center for comfort and solace during this time of much grief. That same year, Wilma's mom, Irene, became pregnant with her eleventh and last child. Baby William brought joy to the Mankiller family nine months later.

Wilma had met Louie Cole the previous year, which she had spent with her Grandma Sitton in Riverbank. He became her first boyfriend. Her next boyfriend, whom she met at the Indian Center, was Ray Billy (Pomo), who maintained an active involvement in the IFH activities. The Wednesday Night Dinner at the IFH served as a platform for supporting and exchanging information on Indian affairs. The Mankiller family too shared holiday dinners there with other Oklahoma Indians.

During her teen years, Wilma devoted much of her time to the Indian Center, and this contrasted with her nondescript participation in high school activities. She held fond memories of the Indian Center. Native people always talked about the coming change, and that made the Indian

Center an exciting place to be. The emerging national Civil Rights Movement provided many ideas to urban Indians about ways to seek more attention from the federal government so they would honor the treaty rights. Wilma remarked, "Even before the 1960s, the entire Bay Area had become a magnet for artists and rebels who were ready and willing to act as the merchants of change. Now a generation was getting its voice, testing its wings, I was part of that generation. San Francisco was the place to be. We were ready to proceed with the decade and with our lives" (Mankiller 1993, 116).

Reflecting on the move to California, Wilma noted, "What kept us together, I think, as a family during that period of time was the Indian Center, which was a place where many other families like ours, sort of refugees, I guess you could say in the city, gathered at the San Francisco Indian Center and shared our experiences and kind of tried to build a community there. . . . But what I learned from my experience in living in a community of almost all African-American people, and what I learned from my experience in living in my own community in Oklahoma before the relocation is that poor people have a much, much greater capacity for solving their own problems than most people give them credit for. Throughout the sixties, my entire family considered the Indian Center to be a stronghold" (Mankiller 1993, 112). Wilma did not have many fond memories of high school and was not at all interested in school, except for literature. Her favorite teen memories were of the San Francisco Indian Center.

Single mothers at the Indian Center also made quite an impression on Wilma. They gathered at Justine Buckskin's house on Saturday nights, preparing for a big night out by applying makeup and spraying massive amounts of Aqua Net hairspray to hold their tall beehive hairdos, a common style among whites at the time. Wilma and Linda babysat their kids and thought their lives were so exciting. Justine became a major influence in young Wilma's life and always encouraged her to continue her education. School became a bit more tolerable when Wilma joined the Junior Achievement Club and enjoyed it. She did not, however, enjoy the home perm her mom gave her while in high school, which was a disaster (in lieu of going to the beauty shop for a professional permanent curling treatment, many American mothers gave their unsuspecting daughters home perms in the 1950s and 1960s).

Wilma loved reading and music. She learned about leadership from watching the volunteers at the Indian Center.

A societal shift transpired in San Francisco in the early 1960s, and young Wilma witnessed it all. There was unease and ambivalence among teenagers of the late 1950s, immersed in angst and pop culture influences. Due to the "Duck and Cover" atomic bombing drills in schools, what had been underground flowed to the surface (Gitlin 1993, 82). "Where it's at" became a popular catch phrase, similar to "telling it like it is," and rhythm and blues music morphed into rock 'n' roll. The Beat writers told of disaffected materialism; writer Herb Caen had coined the term "beatnik" a few years earlier (Gitlin 1993, 52). The 1960s began with images of four Black youths at a segregated lunch counter in North Carolina. By April, young African American activists were organizing sit-ins in 54 cities in nine states across America. In May 1961, the Freedom Rides into Birmingham, Alabama, and Jackson, Mississippi, covered by the media, influenced a growing movement.

The migration of thousands of Indians from reservations and rural communities to western cities during the 1950s and 1960s led to the creation of community organizations to help one another. The sovereignty struggle that emerged against the termination policy became increasingly successful. One example is the National Indian Youth Council (NIYC), which was founded in 1961 after the American Indian Chicago Conference illuminated a schism between the young-and-educated Indians and the elder tribal leaders. Indians from various tribes gathered to begin a movement because they believed the older leadership was not aggressive enough in seeking fair and equitable treatment. The NIYC activists believed the practice of direct action and Indian control over education was the best way to keep the ideals of the tribal elders (Shreve 2011, 14). As an evolution of the intertribalism begun by earlier generations, the 10 youths who formed the NIYC believed Indian affairs had become so bad "it was time to raise some hell" (Steiner 1968, 40). Led by Mel Thom as council president, the NIYC became influential throughout Indian Country and well known in the San Francisco Indian Center through their publication, *The American Indian*.

Contrary to popular belief about members of the Red Power movement, the Native activists who advocated for Red Power ideology came mostly from reservations and rural areas. Women also played pivotal roles, and this may be because of the matrilineal traditions of many Native people (Shreve 2011, 5). The NIYC held that direct-action methods were the way forward in the continuing struggle for sovereignty, self-determination, treaty rights, and cultural preservation. Clyde Warrior (Ponca) emerged as a junior leader in 1961 in Norman, Oklahoma, and he had a gift for oration in terms of pointedly articulating a growing frustration and sense of urgency. He attended the Chicago Conference in 1961, with a focus on self-determination. Self-determination means a people determine their future through the development of policies that meet their needs as they have defined them. The NIYC stressed intertribal fellowship and matters such as how to be self-sufficient and how to run their own organizations.

Social science researchers have always had much interest in relocated Indians, and earlier work focused on acculturation while more recent studies have focused on cultural persistence. Bay Area Indians created institutions to meet their needs and they also transformed Indian identity by reinforcing traditional tribal knowledge (Lobo 1990, 15). The Social Survey of American Indian Urban Integration (1961–1964) investigated the success of the jobs training programs. The two largest groups were 14–23 year olds at 25.8 percent and 24–35 year olds at 45.2 percent, with 64.7 percent males and 35.3 percent females for southeast tribes (Willard 1997, 43). BIA employees encouraged relocatees to seek independent housing rather than live near other Indian people.

Throughout the mid-to-late 1960s, the Bay Area Indians became more vocal against federal Indian policy. Activism among Indian youth occurred all around and especially on college and university campuses. A group of demonstrators from the Bay Area Indian Council picketed three employment assistance offices dressed in powwow regalia and directed media attention toward Indian problems in that area in June 1963 (Willard 1997, 41). The abusive tactics of Theophilus Eugene "Bull" Connor—Jefferson County's public safety commissioner and a racist—in Birmingham, Alabama, showed the world the struggle involved. He authorized the use of firehoses and police dogs to attack and drive away young African American demonstrators. These actions, which appeared on the national nightly news in May 1963 also had a big impact on the San Francisco state campus. Connor was vehemently opposed to any actions in favor of advancing the civil rights of people of color, and he had many supporters. In reaction, in the summer of 1963, the United Freedom Movement of the Congress of Racial Equality (CORE), the National Association for the Advancement of Colored People (NAACP), and the Baptist Minister's Union were begun in order to mobilize on a national scale and educate on the civil rights of others in America (Barlow and Shapiro 1971, 43).

Wilma also experienced significant change as she finally graduated high school in June 1963 and moved in with her older sister Frances. Wilma found a pink-collar office job in a finance company performing clerical work and loved her new independence. More excitement came after her old neighbor Carmen Roybal introduced her to a handsome young man at a Latin dance. Hector Hugo Olaya de Bardi was a 21-year-old college student and soccer player from Guayaquil, Ecuador. Wilma called him Hugo. His father was an Ecuadoran physician and his mother was from an Italian family of old money. Hugo had moved to America with his father as a child and was studying accounting and business at San Francisco State College when he met Wilma. He was dark, macho, and sophisticated, with not a drop of Indian blood, according to Wilma. That summer in 1963 was a series of days working at the finance company and nights out with Hugo having dinner. The young couple frequented nightclubs and Hugo introduced Wilma to areas of San Francisco she had not visited before. Wilma described it as a partying relationship as he introduced her to many exotic foods, forms of music, and cultures.

After dating all summer, the couple became engaged in October 1963, and on November 13 of the same year they flew to Reno, Nevada, and were married in a wedding chapel by a Justice of the Peace. After they returned to San Francisco, Hugo's father gave them $1,000 as a wedding gift and the newlyweds went to Chicago for their honeymoon. They boarded a bus and took off. It was on the long bus ride that Wilma thought seriously about her impulsive decision to marry Hugo and decided to just make the best of it. They were still in Chicago when the news came that President John F. Kennedy had been assassinated. The honeymoon quickly ended, as did the era of Kennedy-led politics and optimism.

Another cultural watershed occurred in 1963 with the publication of Betty Friedan's *Feminine Mystique.* This book certainly had an influence on the young and headstrong Wilma. Friedan argued that women caught within "the mystique" were in danger of losing their personal identity to that of being a good wife and mother. This widely read book created a cultural split among American women, between those completely fulfilled in domesticity and those who sought a higher purpose for their individual life. Women's roles changed after World War II as more women entered the workforce and sought to become engaged citizens outside of the home, and Wilma became influenced by this new perspective on personal identity as a young, modern woman in urban America. Other social changes occurred as women had begun enrolling in colleges in large numbers by the mid-1960s. Added to that, the liberal social climate and the desire for self-fulfillment played a role in the mixed feelings many women had about whether or not they wanted to have a traditional role in a marriage. The 1960s became a decade with many single adults who were products of the postwar Baby Boom. In 1962, Helen Gurley Brown published *Sex and the Single Girl*, and in later years, she published the new and provocative magazine, *Cosmopolitan*. Consciousness-raising groups also emerged throughout San Francisco as women began to critique sexism.

Returning from their honeymoon, Hugo and Wilma Olaya moved in with his cousin Tito Bastidas who lived with his wife Rose in the Mission District. While completing his degree in accounting at San Francisco State College, Hugo began working the night shift at Pan American airlines. Two months later, Wilma became pregnant with their first child. She struggled with high blood pressure and edema through most of the pregnancy and had to leave her job at the finance company. Eventually, after 27 hours of labor, Wilma's first child, Felicia Marie Olaya, entered the world on August 11, 1964. During this time, Wilma also experienced ongoing kidney problems. Needing more room for the growing family, the young couple moved into a new place in San Francisco. Wilma settled into her new role as wife and mother and shopped, cooked, and cleaned. Yet, she always had a nagging sensation of discomfort, physically and emotionally. Wilma's experiences as a housewife echoed the feelings Betty Friedan had described in *The Feminine Mystique*. Less than two years later, and after a much easier pregnancy and delivery, Wilma gave birth to her second child, Gina Irene Olaya, on June 15, 1966. Yet, her uneasiness continued.

Between 1964 and 1970, over 20 million young Americans turned 18 years of age and had to register for the Vietnam War draft (Gitlin 1993, 192). From 1964 to 1966, radical politics continued to grow on the University of Berkeley and San Francisco State College campuses. Students wanted to break out of the traditional classroom and become relevant to real-world problems and urgent social issues. The students discovered that the more their interest in social conditions increased, the more the authorities remained unresponsive and uncooperative. Rather than trying to influence those resisting change, they decided to help create political alternatives. Berkeley students opposed the trivial activities of sororities and fraternities and sports and wanted to become more involved in politics. The liberal student political party, SLATE, active from 1958 to 1966, opposed nuclear testing, segregation, capital punishment, and compulsory Reserve Officers' Training Corps (ROTC) on campus (Barlow and Shapiro 1971, 36). San Francisco State College was a commuter college and began to become affected by political stirrings in the Spring of 1960 as the Southern sit-ins became more publicized. Students, faculty, and counselors created a "Philosophy Statement on Student Activities," saying that "students are respected as adults and citizens in the community and, as such, have all the rights and responsibilities of adults and citizens to participate in college and community affairs." This became the impetus for the Berkeley Free Speech Movement in 1964 (Barlow and Shapiro 1971, 41). The New Left emerged in the fall of 1964 in Berkeley and the Free Speech Movement arose after campus administration banned student political activity on campus property. By 1965, the New Left was synonymous with community organizing and community involvement programs emerged.

Among the American Indian communities of the Bay Area, the Mission District in San Francisco had the effect opposite to the one intended with assimilation, as it gave way to Native intertribal nationalism and intertribal community building. Coalition politics emerged out of the different ethnic groups living in the Mission District. Community activists started community action programs. Vine Deloria Jr. (Santee Sioux) served as the executive director of the NCAI from 1964 until 1967. During that time, he urged Indian leaders to ground their leadership in the traditional values of their tribes and communities. That is just what Wilma did as she began learning more about her Cherokee heritage.

THE NEW LEFT

The New Left was a political and social movement that began in the 1960s to gain civil rights and protest against the escalating war in Vietnam. The Students for a Democratic Society (SDS) and the women's movement emerged from this broad organization and influenced an entire generation of young people to stand up for their rights and challenge the establishment in order to ensure a more just society. The social movements of the 1960s and 1970s triggered transformations that have resonated for more than half a century. Black freedom movements and uprisings as well as the women's liberation and gay liberation movements and the Native American, Chicano, and Asian American struggles yielded profound legal and cultural changes, effectively rewriting the rules of race, gender, and sexuality. Antiwar and countercultural activism by millions of young people of every background turned campuses and cities into both battle grounds and zones of social and cultural innovation, while helping to bring down two presidents and rearranging both the Democratic and Republican parties.

Reservation communities provided safety and a buffer against non-Indian culture. Indians in the Bay Area interacted with other Indians from their own or different tribes, for the same reason. Many Indian values were and still are incompatible with mainstream American values as cultural identity and traditions remain. During the early years of relocation, almost three-fourths of the Indians who moved to urban areas returned to their reservation communities (Ablon 1964, 297). With the increased pressures of urban life and the lack of a support network such as the one that existed on the reservation with an extended family, Indian communities formed at the several Indian Centers in the Bay Area as a means of survival. A core group of planners at each of these centers became increasingly vocal and defiant against whites and about having an intense Indian identity. This positive sense of personal identity was one of the major reasons for self-segregation among Indian populations. Urban Indians preferred to associate with other Indians due to shared experiences and similar cultural beliefs and traditions (Ablon 1964, 303). In 1964, Rupert Costo (Cahuilla) and his wife Jeanette Henry-Costo (Eastern Cherokee) created the American Indian Historical Society in the Mission District of San Francisco as a center for this growing sense of Indian pride.

Melvin "Mel" Thom (Walker River Paiute), a cofounder of the NIYC, illustrated a growing militancy within the organization in his essay "Indian War 1964" (Shreve 2011, 140). Thom argued that Indian people desired to be in charge of their own futures. The passage of the Economic Opportunity

Act (EOA) of 1965 and the creation of the Office of Economic Opportunity (OEO) were the beginning of economic self-determination. Thom advocated ways in which urban Natives could use OEO programs to contribute to solving their own problems (Shreve 2011, 152). The EOA and Community Action Programs (CAP) expanded social programs and provided a voice to the recipients. Indian militancy slowly increased, all the while maintaining a focus on sovereignty, self-determination, cultural preservation, and protection of treaty rights. The escalation of violence in Vietnam caused many young people to question traditional non-Indian American values, which further inspired urban Indians to band together, separate from the mainstream.

The NIYC had the goal of creating culturally sensitive classrooms with Native-centered curriculums. As more Indians came to the Bay Area, the United Council of the Bay Area Indian Community slowly became more militant, especially as Indians became excluded from the Lyndon B. Johnson administration's War on Poverty programs in 1964. Even the 1964 Civil Rights Act excluded Indians. The Bay Area Sioux Indians conceptualized the occupation of Alcatraz Island in 1964, with Belva Cottier as one of the primary leaders prompted by growing tensions because of the relocated Indians (Johnson 1996, 17). Indian people felt increasing anger toward the treatment by the BIA and resentment toward the treatment from their tribal councils. Wilma said the relocation policy was "nothing more than another direct assault on Native American rights and tribal identities" (Mankiller 1993, 63). Dillon Myer, the secretary of the interior, focused on destroying tribal governments.

BIA officials planned for the eradication of Indian culture as former tribal members assimilated into mainstream American society, but that plan backfired as traditional tribal knowledge continued to be taught in Indian communities. Developing yet another set of survival strategies, Indian people sought each other out as fellow tribal members or alumni of Indian boarding schools. Traditional tribal customs strengthened through an intertribal unit (Johnson 1996, 13). Not only did these units provide urban Indians with gathering places where they could be proud of their tribal heritage, they also provided Indian leadership. As more urban Indians became educated and politically active, they called for Indian self-determination.

Coming back to Wilma, three years into her marriage and after the birth of her two daughters, she felt increasingly restricted by housewifery and motherhood. She also felt her relationship with Hugo change. She grew restless and Hugo, too, longed for the days when they had fewer responsibilities. Another issue in their marriage was that their tastes, backgrounds, and value systems were different. Wilma often just wanted to visit her parents and play cards with them, and Hugo preferred to go to a nightclub and drink and dance. At the time, Wilma already knew the two of them were moving in different directions. One of the few commonalties the couple shared was being urbanites. In the mid-1960s, San Francisco and its surrounding area was an exciting and creative place to be. Plus, there were always people at her parents' house from the Indian Center and Indian culture was always being discussed. Remembering the debates she used to have with her father, Wilma explained, "We always argued about politics as long as I can remember. Once we got to California and had television, we would watch the evening news and argue about what was on the news, or whether rock 'n' roll was good or bad. I remember one six-hour argument about whether there should be a tax on auto imports" (Jones 1999).

Wilma became interested in the Chicano movement because of the people she knew in her neighborhood and her good friends the Roybals. The Chicano movement emerged from the Mexican American political movements, with support for Cesar Chavez and Dolores Huerta. There was also a rise in power politics in the Mission District with a local chapter of the Brown Berets opening an office on 16th Street, beside the Indian Center. The Brown Berets formed in 1967 in East Los Angeles as a pro-Chicano group and an offshoot of the Third Movement for Liberation. The Brown Berets emerged in defense of Hispanic rights in the region. In August 1965, the Delano grape fields strike led by Chavez, Huerta, and the National Farm Workers Association (NFWA) inspired student activists, including Wilma (Barlow and Shapiro 1971, 68). With the Brown Berets office being located beside the Indian Center, Wilma became interested in the plight of the national farm workers and the work of Chavez and Huerta in the San Joaquin Valley. Because of her previous days of working on farms, Wilma could identify with the workers and became active in their cause. Another group that caught her attention was the Black Panther Party in Oakland.

In the early 1960s, the Nation of Islam advocated black nationalism as it rejected Christianity and promoted self-improvement and black pride. Malcolm X was the most famous Black Muslim and fought to strengthen black communities. After his assassination in 1965, "Black Power" activists championed black communities and focused on poverty and social injustice. Some created day care centers and community job training programs and worked to improve health care and housing in urban areas. Others worked to end police harassment. In October 1966, Huey Newton and Bobby Seale founded the Black Panther Party in neighboring Oakland. Early in their activism, the panthers established alternative schools and free breakfast programs and stood up to the police and other white authority figures. Their message of self-help and racial pride resonated with Wilma. The radical Black Panther Party was also a militant self-defense group to protect blacks from police violence. They opposed the war and supported Third World revolutionary movements. Their Ten-Point program included "What

---

BLACK PANTHER PARTY

The Black Panther Party came into being in October 1966 in Oakland, California. Cocreators Huey P. Newton and Bobby Seale formed the group as a revolutionary organization with an ideology of black nationalism, socialism, and armed self-defense, particularly against police brutality. It was part of the Black Power movement, which broke from the integrationist goals and nonviolent protest tactics of the Southern Christian Leadership Conference led by Dr. Martin Luther King Jr. The name and symbol of a black panther came from a Black political party in Alabama called the Lowndes County Freedom Organization.

---

we want, what we believe," which inspired blacks to work within the political system. Riots began in San Francisco in July 1964 and continued for the next four years. The violence and fight over civil rights divided the nation and led to a new conservatism.

From her prior work, Wilma believed in the importance of education, good housing, and employment as the foundations of communities. She was slowly becoming an activist and she was raising her daughters that way too. Felicia and Gina received free McDonald's Happy Meals after they completed handing out all of their community flyers advocating the free breakfast programs of the black panthers. Wilma's first volunteering experience and association with the panthers led her back to her heritage at the Indian Center.

While volunteering with the Black Panther Party, Wilma continued her close association with the Indian Center in the Mission District. Her family had always kept ties with the center and she renewed her relationships with old friends there. Wilma stated, "The center was a hotbed of sedition, fortunately" (Mankiller 1993, 162). Although many Native people left the Bay Area and Los Angeles to return to their homes or reservations, California's Indian population remained substantial. Wilma and other Natives who remained in the urban environments found a new sense of self-esteem. The Indian Center became an important place for them to discuss issues and formulate plans, providing some sense of direction and pride. Wilma recalled the way the focus on Indian education emerged, "Soon, delegations of native people were appearing before the state board of education to demand fairer treatment of Native Americans in textbooks and curricula" (Mankiller 1993, 162).

For those seeking community friendships and places to meet, the San Francisco Indian Center and nearby Warren's Bar played a key role in creating an intertribal community. St. Vincent De Paul sponsored the San Francisco Indian Center until the mid-1960s, when the American Indian Council of the Bay Area began to manage it. The upstairs portion of the Center had a dance floor as well as meeting and sewing rooms, and the main level held a small snack bar and offices. The Center workers were involved in job counseling, social work, health outreach, and youth activities. During the winter of 1966–1967, the Indian Center had four women and one man on its board of directors (Steiner 1968, 224).

During a typical week, the activities included Indian dancing on Tuesdays, with a ladies' sewing club, Indian arts and crafts, girls' ping pong, and boys' pool tournament on Wednesdays. On Thursday evenings, members held a council meeting on job, housing, and welfare programs. Modern ballet class and a powwow took place on Fridays. On Saturdays, the members held a children's health clinic and a rock 'n' roll dance, which was followed by a movie screening on Sundays (Steiner 1968, 187).

Wilma's liberal political values gradually formed during the Civil Rights years of 1965 and 1966. A series of protests erupted on the campus of San Francisco State College in 1966, including rallies, sit-ins, teach-ins, and marches. Urban middle-class liberals shared the ideology of the anti-poverty programs of the Johnson administration. Community Action Programs of the OEO provided training grounds for young urban leaders, and the Indian communities took advantage of these programs (Abbott 1993, 104). Young non-Indians also became disaffected activists over issues such as the Civil Rights struggle, opposition to the Vietnam War, the Berkeley "Free Speech" movement, the New Left, and the emergence of hippie culture. Wilma witnessed these actions firsthand. The hippies took up residence in the Haight-Ashbury streets, where she often took Felicia and Gina in their frilly little-girl dresses to the street fairs and concerts. There was electricity in the air and revolution in the streets, not to mention an explosion of new music from Janis Joplin, the Grateful Dead, Jimi Hendrix, Jefferson Airplane, and The Doors. Wilma recalled, "Whenever I do pause to reflect, I find that many of my hopes and aspirations were formed during those wonderfully sad and crazy years of the 1960s in San Francisco" (Mankiller 1993, 157).

The Glide Memorial Methodist Church, a counterculture sanctuary presided over by Rev. Cecil Williams, also attracted Wilma (Mankiller 1993, 157). The church was located on the corner of Ellis and Taylor streets in San Francisco and funded by the Glide Foundation; it became one of the most liberal churches in the United States in the 1960s and 1970s. Church officials held consciousness-raising groups and sex education and health workshops. The foundation hired Rev. Lewis Durkham in 1962 and he hired Ted McIlvenna, Cecil Williams, and Don Kuhn for the Glide Urban Center, a new ministry connecting with marginalized people in the city.

Rupert and Jeannette Henry-Costo moved their organization, American Indian Historical Society, to the Haight-Ashbury district and reopened in 1967 as the Chautauqua House (Soza War Soldier 2013). Wilma was not only immersed in Indian culture but also the emerging counterculture. Then came the new women's movement.

The National Organization of Women (NOW) was formed in 1966 and quickly spread across the country, championing the cause of civil rights for women in America. It was started by a group of 16 women, with Betty Friedan as the first president. The organization aimed to ensure the full participation of women in mainstream American society. A new feminism emerged, known as "women's liberation." Initially focused on gaining equality for women within the protest movements of the 1960s, women's liberation with NOW made second-wave feminism a mass movement (the first wave occurred with the feminism associated with the women's suffrage movement of the Progressive era). At the same time, women of color challenged sexism within their own organizations and promoted personal and political alliances with male allies in racial nationalist groups.

Many of Wilma's hopes and aspirations for the future developed during these years, with lasting impact. She became positively influenced by the different cultures of the urban people and their ideas on politics, music, art, literature, theology, and world events. She was influenced especially by the emerging direct-action movements that involved standing up for what one believed was the right thing to do. These years proved seminal in Wilma's move from citizen housewife to Indian activist leader.

3

Cultural Awakening

The years from 1967 to 1976, which Wilma spent in San Francisco, resulted in tremendous growth in her education, activism, and personal identity. As she became increasingly involved in social justice and Indian issues at the Indian Center, her marriage grew ever more strained. In 1967, Wilma began taking courses at the nearby Skyline Junior College in San Bruno. Once she took a few classes and discovered she enjoyed it, she enrolled at the larger San Francisco State College. Justine Buckskin, who served as a volunteer at the Intertribal Friendship House of Oakland, always encouraged Wilma to attend college and took her to campus to ensure she registered properly.

Wilma continued working in law offices, typing briefs and wills, but became increasingly drawn to the activism and liberation events all around her. She also enjoyed going to school for the first time. At first, Hugo vehemently opposed Wilma's return to school because he wanted her at home taking care of him and the girls. He changed his mind once he saw how much Wilma enjoyed her courses, and he bought her books and a typewriter. He did not, however, support Wilma's continued association with her Indian friends and family. Hugo discouraged Wilma from visiting the San Francisco Indian Center, the urban bars, and the Intertribal Friendship House (IFH). These gathering places became informal institutions that served as networking centers and sources of information for the Indian community (Hurtado 2008). Community members shared information and discussed the latest books.

Between 1952 and 1962, thousands of Indians moved to cities, yet by the late 1960s the Johnson and Nixon administrations renounced the federal policies of Termination and Relocation. President Lyndon B. Johnson established an Indian desk in the Office of Economic Opportunity, which allowed funding for tribes and included Indian people in the decision-making processes that affected them. The key responsibilities of the Indian desk included coordinating government services for Indian people, promoting interagency cooperation, efficiently providing government services, and encouraging Indian people to take advantage of the opportunities.

Cultural integrity rather than cultural integration became one of the major issues for the urban Indian communities, as they embraced self-determination as the new goal and rejected integration. Indian activists sought the enforcement of treaty rights rather than individual civil rights. As the population of Indians continued to increase in the region in the 1960s and 1970s, the community organizations also increased and became more specialized, catering to specific needs in health, education, employment, and child welfare. A pan-Indian community emerged as well and in the late 1960s, Vine Deloria Jr. (Sioux) coined the term "Red Power."

By October 1967, the Resistance against the Vietnam War also emerged as young men began turning in draft cards and protests took place at Armed Forces Induction Centers. From 1964 to 1973, the U.S. military drafted 2.2 million American men over the age of 17 to serve in the Vietnam War. Opposition to the draft became a central issue in the antiwar movement. This was also a time of high school rebellions and protests in vocational schools, increasing demands for an end to police harassment, and calls for the development of a nonwhite curriculum. Many young students resented being excluded from the opportunity to obtain a college degree (Barlow and Shapiro 1971, 150). The deadliest part of the war began in the spring of 1968, with 20,000 American troops deployed and at least 500 U.S. soldiers killed each week in Vietnam.

The draft increased despite the draft resistance movement. A National Day of Draft Resistance was held on April 3, 1968. There was a decidedly "us against them, us against the United States government" mentality among urban American youth. The Students for a Democratic Society organized campuses around the nation to oppose permanent leaders and work toward participatory democracy. Columbia University's expansion into lands in Harlem and the conducting of secret war research led to huge demonstrations and a strike among students which occupied five buildings. On April 30, 1968, the police broke up the strike in violent fashion. The police attacked young protesters all over the country. Robert Kennedy traveled to San Francisco and the San Joaquin Valley on June 4, 1968, and young people loved him. Sirhan Sirhan killed Kennedy in Los Angeles two days later. The violence and unrest in the country signaled a great imbalance, and the mood of the country was of fear and anger as a war raged abroad and at home.

Wilma wrote of 1968 as a time when "the balance was off," and the events of the year support that opinion. She witnessed the assassinations of Martin Luther King Jr. and Bobby Kennedy, the Tet Offensive in Vietnam, turmoil on American college campuses, the creation of the American Indian Movement, the passage of the Indian Civil Rights Act, and the election of Richard Nixon as president. On the feminist front, the women's movement and the National Organization of Women (NOW) recruited more members. Within this atmosphere, many women of color did not trust the national mainstream women's organizations to be inclusive. The women's liberationists who gathered in San Francisco that year had a tremendous impact on Wilma's life at a pivotal time, as she grew increasingly distant from Hugo and her marriage. Bobby Kennedy influenced Wilma to become involved in mainstream politics after he visited the Cherokee Nation in 1968, while he was campaigning for the presidency. Indian people were experiencing a renewal of energy and purpose.

A student strike occurred on the campus of San Francisco State University in the fall of 1968. Led by the Third World Liberation Front, the students sought an ethnic studies department. Several liberation movements emerged during this time. The National Liberation Front believed the African American struggle in the United States had allies in the "third world" people of color and those struggling to free their lives of colonial imperialism. The political philosopher Frantz Fanon became the impetus for the "Black Liberation" struggle in America. The Black Panther Party adapted Fanon's writings as they viewed the black community as an oppressed black colony within the white mother country—an oppressed minority within a white society (Barlow and Shapiro 1971, 156). The student strike ended when police from multiple jurisdictions converged and arrested over 700 people and also with the creation of an Ethnic Studies Department. Indian activists differed in their ongoing resistance to land and resource conflicts.

Wilma's increasing community involvement and her continuing education made her realize she wanted to control her own destiny and not live a life based on someone else's dream (Mankiller 1993, 159). This was the beginning of the end of Wilma's marriage. As a husband, Hugo expected her to walk away from the Indian Center and her birth family, but by the time she was 23, Wilma knew she could no longer live a life defined by her husband. As she increasingly exerted her personal freedom, the tension between them became irreconcilable. She turned to the Indian Center and to her love of literature and music. She continued to grow in her musical tastes and learned to play the guitar. R&B artists released some of the best music of the 1960s and Wilma's favorite song by Aretha Franklin came out in 1967, "Respect."

The generation of Indians raised in urban environments became more vocal about Indian identity and empowerment. With this, leadership also changed, as Indian personnel replaced non-Indian leaders of the urban organizations. Native students LaNada War Jack Means (Shoshone-Bannock) and Lehman "Lee" Brightman (Lakota/Creek) formed the Bay Area–based United Native Americans and began publishing the newsletter *Warpath*, calling for war against the BIA (Langston 2003, 2). Much creativity and energy existed among those who had come of age in the multitribal urban Indian environment (Lobo 1990, 12). Wilma recalled, "Our experience with whites revealed that they could not be trusted. We would always remember the long line of treaties and promises. Most were as worthless as the politicians who drafted them. They were only pieces of paper filled with empty words as hypocritical as most of the white men's promises" (Mankiller 1993, 166). Previously, people and groups in charge of Indians and Indian programs were non-Indians, but that was slowly changing.

Ending a tumultuous decade, 1969 became a crucial year for Native people as the San Francisco Indian Center "became a hotbed of sedition, fortunately" (Mankiller 1993, 162). The American Indian Movement (AIM), which had emerged on the scene in 1968, became a national organization. Urban Indians in the Minneapolis-St. Paul area complained of police harassment and formed Indian patrols to monitor police activities in their neighborhoods, inspired by the actions of the Black Panther Party. Clyde Bellecourt, Dennis Banks, and George Mitchell, serving as patrol leaders, created AIM, which caused a revival of Indian nationalism and Indian pride throughout America, especially in cities with large Indian populations. The primary goal of AIM became turning the attention of Indian people toward a renewal of spirituality to impart the strength of resolve needed to reverse the ruinous policies of the United States, Canada, and other colonist governments. Urban Indian centers were hubs of social activity and some became active in political issues.

One of the fundamental problems faced by the Indians who relocated to the city was the risk of losing their identity and cultural heritage. It quickly became apparent to all relocatees that the BIA had oversold the opportunities for good jobs with good pay and a good place to live in the cities. Many urban Indians were faced with low-income housing, low pay, poor health care, crime, alcoholism, and high student dropout rates in schools (Lobo 2002, 3). Upon arriving in the city, families sought assistance from local churches and social services organizations in maneuvering city life. Many, however, blamed government officials for their current state and chose to form mutual aid societies instead. These societies not only aided newcomers but also helped preserve tribal identities. Slowly, Natives took control of mutual aid societies and social services organizations and added culturally oriented activities such as powwows, arts and crafts, and native language classes. These new urban Indian centers played a huge role in creating a space for people to meet, seek help or information, or take part in cultural events (Lobo 2002, 4). Wilma and many urban Indians became young revolutionaries-in-training.

Seeking the guidance of elders for leadership advice became part of the direct-action plans of Indian activism, marking a change from the NIYC and its emphasis on youth and new ideas. In the late 1960s, Tom Porter (Mohawk) and a group of elders traveled across the country from New York, educating others. The group traveled in a blue-green bus and a caravan of cars from community to community in Indian Country. In three-day meetings the group, calling themselves the White Roots of Peace, sought to revive traditional tribal knowledge and find ways to revitalize language and preserve ceremonies and traditions. Wilma's path of public service began after she heard Porter speak at one of the traditional unity caravan meetings at the IFH in Oakland. "It was as a result of Tom that I was drawn into public speaking and writing to share my experience with other people" (Adams 2001). Porter encouraged the participants to go back to their own communities and work for "the people" and also spoke of the importance of personal responsibility. He represented those ideals in his daily living.

Tremendous interest in American Indians emerged from the disaffected white youth culture in the late 1960s and early 1970s. Hippies viewed Indians as worthy of emulation, especially some of their traditional attire, and a nature-based value system. Many of these counterculture youths only knew the Hopi and Yaqui tribal traditions, through the writings of Carlos Castaneda and Hopi prophecies about revoking European American mainstream culture. The young counterculture devotees held a romantic notion of American Indians, with little real knowledge of their languages, customs, and value systems and the differences between the various tribes. The reality was very different.

High crime rates, gang activity, and high levels of unemployment plagued the neighborhoods in the Mission District and Hunters Point. The Mission Coalition Organization, created in 1968, took advantage of the federal government Community Action Programs in an effort to ameliorate these social issues. The organization worked mostly to keep low-income housing available in the district (Blansett 2018, 87). Samoans and Indians cohabited in the Mission District, with increasing tension. Richard Oakes (Mohawk) from Brooklyn, New York, arrived in the city and became one of the first volunteer neighborhood foot patrols to help keep the peace, and he later played a critical role in the occupation of Alcatraz (Fortunate Eagle 2002, 48).

On April 12, 1969, a committee formed by the National Council on Indian Opportunity (NCIO) and Peter McDonald (Dine') focused on learning about experiences of urban Indians in the San Francisco area. Oakes and other students created the Student Coalition of America Natives (SCAN). In a speech delivered by Oakes, he argued that the Indians have to stand up for their own rights (Blansett 2018, 155). Wilma learned about having the courage of one's convictions from Richard Oakes.

Under Gerald Wilkinson's leadership, following the death of Clyde Warrior in 1968, the NIYC joined with the AIM to protest federal Indian policy (Shreve 2011, 181). Adding to the explosion in American Indian activism was the influence of the publication in 1969 of N. Scott Momaday's Pulitzer prize–winning novel *House Made of Dawn*. This important novel is considered a classic in American Indian Literature for its exploration of the cultural identity of an urban Indian who returns to the reservation. Dee Brown's *Bury My Heart at Wounded Knee* highlights the federal government's wars against the Native communities in the American West. Native scholar and philosopher Vine Deloria Jr. published his groundbreaking *Custer Died for your Sins: An American Indian Manifesto*, and Edgar S. Cahn and David W. Hearne's collection of essays, *Our Brother's Keeper: The Indian in White America*, argued that the Indian's life is not his own to live as every aspect of it is controlled by the BIA (Lobo 2002, 5). Also, in 1969, Rupert Costo began publishing the scholarly journal *The Indian Historian* and Alvin M. Josephy published findings recommending a repudiation of the Termination policy, in calling for self-determination for Indian people to be a Nixon administration priority. These groundbreaking books and newsletters were probably discussed at the Indian Center and San Francisco State College and Wilma was influenced by their messages.

After a suspicious fire destroyed the Indian Center in October 1969, it began to function from a temporary location at 3189 16th Street (Blansett 2018, 91). The new site became the staging area for donors, volunteers, and the media to gather for information on Alcatraz. Lee Brightman then became the director and also president of United Native Americans (UNA), which he cofounded with LaNada War Jack. The same year, San Francisco State College created a new Native American Studies program and Richard Oakes became the student director. Additionally, UC Berkeley created a Native American Studies program, with LaNada War Jack as the student director (Blansett 2018, 99).

Then something happened that provided the focus Wilma had sought. "It all started in November of 1969, when a group of Native Americans representing more than twenty tribes seized a deserted island in the midst of San Francisco's glittering bay" (Shreve 2011, 192). The occupation of Alcatraz Island off the coast of San Francisco by the pan-Indian group, Indians of All Tribes, was born out of years of frustration over mistreatment of American Indians by the federal government. The occupation marked a new era in American Indian activism with an unintended consequence of relocation being the coming together of urban, rural, and reservation Indians. Under the Treaty of Fort Laramie in 1868, between the United States and Lakota, all retired, abandoned, or out-of-use federal land returns to the Native people from whom it was taken. "Citing a forgotten clause in treaty agreements that said any unused federal lands must revert to Indian use, they took over the twelve-acre island to attract attention to the government's gross mistreatment of generations of native people. They did it to remind the whites that the land was ours before it was theirs. The name of the island is Alcatraz. It changed me forever" (Mankiller 1993, 163). Alcatraz was a turning point in the movement for Wilma personally, as she visited her family there, gave them supplies, and kept the books on donations.

Indian activism was strong in the Bay Area because of the generation that had lived there for 10 years or more. This corresponded with a resurgence of nationalism on the reservations because of the mobility of the urbanites going back and forth. Students from area colleges and members of the San Francisco Indian Center led and supported the occupation of Alcatraz. Divisiveness plagued the occupation from the first day, as LaNada War Jack and Richard Oakes became unofficial leaders (Johnson 1996, 84). While men such as Oakes, Russell Means, and John Trudell received most of the attention, the women did much work behind the scenes and kept the basic services—such as the community kitchen, school, and health center—operating on the island. The women held everything together by providing sustenance and care for the children. The occupation of Alcatraz began Wilma's path toward revitalizing Native communities, and the Indian Center became a catalyst for her to focus on her own Cherokee heritage. She spent more time at the new Indian Center, which became a communication post.

The Indian Center instilled Native pride in history and heritage and encouraged young people to use that pride as a source of strength to navigate the urban environment. "In most ways I was a typical housewife at that time, but when Alcatraz occurred, I became aware of what needed to be done to let the rest of the world know that Indians had rights too. Alcatraz articulated my own feelings about being an Indian. It was a benchmark. After that, I became involved" (Mankiller 1993, xxi). Alcatraz sparked the notion of Indian sovereignty and political activism. Native nationalism emerged when assimilation efforts failed. Wilma also recalled, "It was idealistic, and the generosity of spirit of the people proved that we could change anything. Who I am and how I governed was influenced by Alcatraz. The way I viewed dissent was totally influenced by Alcatraz. People on the island were very strong about freedom of speech, freedom of dissent. I saw the importance of dissent in government" (Winton 2021). Wilma also became reacquainted with her good friend, Justine Buckskin Moppin (Klamath), who maintained an active presence at Alcatraz. Justine became a major inspiration to Wilma—she described her as the personification of the Cherokee concept of being of good mind, as she devoted her entire life to helping others and always had a positive attitude. Wilma became caught up in the idealism, the social movements, and the civil unrest throughout San Francisco. "I finally felt like a person who belonged to the time, yet I wanted to become more involved and was not quite sure how or what to do" (Shreve 2011, 192).

On November 10, 1969, NIYC, AIM, NCAI, and other intertribal organizations formed the American Indian Task Force, calling for greater Indian involvement in federal Indian policy (Shreve 2011, 192). The year 1969 was one of self-awareness, social upheaval, and finding solutions to inequality and discrimination. Wilma renewed relationships with people at the Indian Center and there was a new sense of self-esteem among the people there. Alcatraz changed federal Indian policy, as well as Wilma, forever.

Wilma met dozens of Natives from other tribes during Alcatraz, and meeting them changed her perception of herself as a woman and as a Cherokee. Wilma described her friend, Bill Wahpepah (Kickapoo/Sac & Fox), as one of the finest spokespersons for Indian rights in the country. She also became acquainted with AIM members Dennis Banks, Carter Camp, Vernon and Clyde Bellecourt, and Leonard Crow Dog. "The entire environment gave me courage," recalled Wilma. "Just as seeing women speak up had an impact on me, seeing Native people on the 6 o'clock news challenge the United States government—go and take over an island, and talk about treaty rights and the need for education and health care—had a profound impact. They could articulate things I felt" (Weinraub 1993).

The school on Alcatraz, which came into being on December 11, became the Big Rock School and operated from the prison's main cell block with 12 initial students from grades one through six and a preschool in the guard's quarters. The students learned basic California public school texts supplemented with Native studies, history, and culture (Johnson, Josephy, and Nagel 1999, 192). Stella Leach (Colville/Ogalala Lakota) assisted in the health clinic, Earl Livermore (Blackfoot), former director of the San Francisco Indian Center, taught arts and crafts, and Dr. Dorothy Lone Wolf Miller (Blackfoot) wrote grants and operated the health clinic (Fortunate Eagle 1992, 88). LaNada War Jack became knowledgeable in grant writing.

Community members Adam Fortunate Eagle, Grace Thorpe, and Wilma, among others, provided valuable support back at the Indian Center.

Wilma stated that who she is and how she governed were influenced by Alcatraz; she claimed her experience during the occupation was "an awakening that ultimately changed the course of her life" (Johnson 1996, 129). Working on the Alcatraz occupation from the new Indian Center, Wilma and other volunteers collected donations that were mailed in support of the Indians of All Tribes actions to 3981 16th Street, Alcatraz Relief Fund, Bank of California, San Francisco, CA. There were inadequate accounting records and the people lost control of the donations. One of the original occupants, Horace Spenser, estimated that over $20 million had been donated, although this could not be proven. Some people suggested Oakes misappropriated donations but this was not proven either (Johnson 1996, 159–161).

Wilma became immersed in the events surrounding Alcatraz, as she worked tirelessly at the Indian Center volunteering and fundraising. The occupation became a family affair as several of her siblings joined in. Her home became a hangout for other Natives to visit, plan, and dream of a brighter future. Her younger brother Richard was the first of the Mankillers to go to the island, followed by Vanessa and James; Richard also served on the Alcatraz Council. Wilma's younger sister Linda, recently separated from her husband, and her three small children stayed with Hugo and Wilma for a while. When Linda went to Alcatraz to visit, she ended up staying the longest, until June 1971, when the occupation ended. Wilma never stayed on the island, believing she could be of greater service at the command post of the new Indian Center. This was where most of the fundraising and all the communication to and from the island occurred. "Every day that passed seemed to give me more self-respect and sense of pride" (Mankiller 1993, 193).

Stella Leach (Colville/Oglala Lakota) created the health center on Alcatraz and later created the first American Indian Wellness Center in the San Francisco Bay Area. John Trudell operated "Radio Free Alcatraz" as a half-hour radio show five days per week, broadcast from KPFA in San Francisco and in New York and Los Angeles (Smith and Warrior 1996, 71). A leadership crisis emerged as power struggles and drugs increasingly became a part of the occupation scene.

A tragedy occurred on Saturday, January 3, 1970 when 12-year-old Yvonne Rose Oakes, the eldest daughter of Richard Oakes and Annie Marufo Oakes, fell three stories down a stairwell in one of the guard buildings. She suffered a fractured skull and brain injuries and died five days later at the U.S. Public Health Service Hospital in San Francisco. The Oakes family left the island and buried Yvonne on the Pomo Kashia reservation at Point Arena Mendocino County; they never returned to Alcatraz (*Desert Sun*, 1970).

While the Alcatraz occupation continued, Wilma discovered another occupation movement among a small group of Indians in the north of the state. The Pit River Indians comprised 11 bands in the northeast corner of California in the Shasta Mountains. Among them were the Achomawi, Ajumawi, and Kahi people. Wilma learned about the Pit River people and their fight against Pacific Gas and Electric Company (PG&E) over millions of acres of land. On June 5, 1970, the Pit River tribes issued a proclamation. Several hundred members of the Pit River tribes attempted to seize control of 3.5 million acres of land in Shasta County in northern California. While PG&E claimed clear title to the land, the tribal members argued that the land title was not valid. Parts of the lands were in the Shasta National Forest. In 1959, the federal government conceded that the Pit River tribes' claim to the lands was legitimate. The government maintained that the tribe had relinquished rights to the land as part of the Indian Claims Commission (ICC) settlement, a standpoint which the tribe rejected (Caldwell 1970). The ICC awarded California tribes $29 million as redress for land claims. Members of the Pit River tribes did not accept the 47 cents per acre settlement and instead desired to exchange their ICC monies for land occupied by PG&E, which was their land. The courts disagreed. The failure of the attempts of the Pit River people to regain traditional lands underscored the challenges associated with not having media coverage. The ICC involvement complicated the issue further (Smith 2012, 171).

After Wilma saw the news report about the Pit River tribes, she called their attorney, Aubrey Grossman, and volunteered to help. Wilma helped organize a legal defense fund at Grossman's San Francisco office, through which her association with Pit River lasted for five years. She often visited the Pit River people with Felicia and Gina. Grossman worked on both the Alcatraz and Pit River issues, and Wilma volunteered at his office in connection with both these issues. During her time as a volunteer she always worked in the background. She made the coffee and copies, wrote some speeches, but she still did not have the confidence to speak up. Not yet.

Eight months into the Alcatraz occupation on July 8, 1970, Nixon issued a "Special Message to the Congress on Indian Affairs," ending the Termination policy. Wilma stated, "The torch of protest and change was grasped by Native Americans. In 1969, the rage that helped to give a voice and spirit to other minority groups spread through Native people like a springtime prairie fire. And just as the tall grass thrives and new life bursts forth after the passage of those indispensable flames, we too were given a renewal of energy and purpose" (Mankiller 1993, 161). Because of Alcatraz, some Indian people began to find pride again.

The occupation of Alcatraz was a success in the ways it shaped public opinion and policy (Lobo 2002, 4). The creation of Native American studies departments in the late 1960s offered valuable information and promoted a positive Indian self-image. The media attention given to the Alcatraz occupation led to an increase in public support and a series of laws initiating a major shift in federal Indian policy (Smith 2012, 111). After Alcatraz, the following policies—intended to assist Indians—emerged. In December 1970, the Nixon administration returned 48,000 acres to the Taos Pueblos in New Mexico and two years later they returned 21,000 acres to the Yakima tribe in Washington State. The Boldt court case decision in 1974 reaffirmed the rights of Washington's Indian tribes to fish in accustomed places. Also, in 1974, the Indian Financing Act was passed, to help finance the economic development of Indians and Indian organizations. The Indian Self-Determination and Educational Assistance Act of 1975 was a game changer for tribes. This Act authorized the Secretary of the Interior, the Secretary of Health, Education, and Welfare, and other government agencies to enter into contracts directly with Indian tribes to provide services. Also, the Johnson O'Malley Act was revised in 1975, updating regulations and authorizing contracts for the education of Indian students. Finally, the Indian Health Care Improvement Act of 1976 provided for improved services and facilities at federal Indian health programs. Alcatraz provided a sense of hope, raised political consciousness, and succeeded in moving Indian affairs into the mainstream media; it turned Indian self-determination into reality.

Wilma credited the Alcatraz occupation with helping many Native people. She gained more self-respect and pride and the activism helped her and many others return to the concept of "having a good mind." She met many people during the Alcatraz occupation who had a profound impact on how she perceived herself as a woman and as a Cherokee (Mankiller 1993, 196). She developed more courage, and seeing other Indian women speak up had an impact on her.

Wilma had long believed something was wrong with her because she was so unhappy in the traditional role of a housewife. However, when she began listening to what other Native people and activists were saying, she started thinking that perhaps they could improve education and health care for their community. She also witnessed the women's movement growing and saw other women standing up for their rights, so she began to think maybe it was not just her.

The cultural and political radicalism of the 1960s in San Francisco saw the Civil Rights struggle, the Free Speech movement, the antiwar movement, the second-wave feminist movement, the counterculture movement, the Black Panther Party, the Brown Berets, the Red Power movement, and the American Indian Movement. There was a duality of fierce individualism and a pursuit of common interests. The social activist theories of Saul Alinsky influenced student activists, who demanded a measure of control over their own lives, and organized the disenfranchised and dispossessed to defend their own interests and effect social change. Alinsky was the author of the 1971 book *Rules for Radicals*, which was meant as a guide for community organizers among low-income communities. Alinsky's goal was to empower the organizers to help those without power gain social, political, and economic power within their communities and to be able to unite grassroots organizations to gain lasting change in government, labor, and communities. He offered guidance on community organizing, testing purpose, means and ends and communication and tactics and called for working within the system to exact change and offer hope.

Wilma discovered that mixing with and learning from other Indians from different tribes in an urban environment created increased political consciousness and a renewed interest in Indian heritage. She held a strong belief in the importance of maintaining traditional values and applying them to solve tribal problems from within the communities. AIM and Alcatraz rallied Indians from all backgrounds to demand public recognition of Indian traditions and their historical treaties with the U.S. government. The Indian activists rejected the choice between living in the modern world and being a traditional Indian, believing that one could do both.

By early 1971, the Alcatraz occupation had turned into a disaster. The early occupiers understood that the occupation was a statement of sovereignty and self-determination for all Indian people. The new leadership, however, became more interested in partying, power, and money and less in treaty rights (Weinraub 1993). Another issue with the occupation became the Ohlone people, the original inhabitants of the island, as they had not been consulted or contacted about the occupation. Yet, other Indian organizations and individuals continued in their efforts at gaining self-determination.

While the Alcatraz occupation was still going on, Wilma experienced a family tragedy when she learned her dad, Charley, had been diagnosed with end-stage polycystic kidney disease. Prior to this, Charley and Irene had finally reached a stable period in their lives, having moved to their own home in Monterey, California after the children were all grown up. Then Charley began experiencing high blood pressure and kidney problems. At the same time, Wilma also began having severe urinary tract infections and discovered she had the same kidney disease as her father. Charley's disease became increasingly difficult for Wilma as she was so close to him; they shared the same birthday week in November and she had always sought his approval and support. She spent Thanksgiving 1970 at her parents' new home in Monterey and could share a quiet meal with her dad in his bedroom, which was no small feat in a family of 10 children and their children. During that last Thanksgiving meal, Charley told Wilma he was so proud to have raised a daughter who had become a "revolutionary." He passed away just three months later on February 20, 1971, at age 56. All the Mankillers traveled back to Mankiller Flats in Rocky Mountain, Oklahoma, and buried Charley Mankiller in nearby Echota Cemetery.

After the death of her father, Wilma immersed herself in her community work and school. She transferred to San Francisco State University and also continued volunteering for the Pit River tribes until the mid-1970s, providing help in fundraising for the tribes' legal defense fund. She also learned how to do paralegal work and gained experience in treaty rights and international law. She had learned from her father that to be alive was to be engaged in the world around you and to try to be of some service.

As Wilma exerted her personal freedom, the tension between her and Hugo increased. He had forbidden her from buying a car, but she did anyway. She wanted a car to be more mobile, and he vehemently opposed the idea, so she went to the bank, withdrew enough money, and bought herself a little candy apple red Mazda. Breaking free from Hugo's control, Wilma and her daughters, Felicia and Gina, began traveling to Indian cultural events all over California and had a great time learning about different California Indians. Sitting at home with Hugo, Wilma often glanced over at him from across the room, wishing she could fulfill his expectations of her. He was a good man, but their differences were just too great. Her two previous boyfriends had been Indian and shared values and experiences similar to hers, while Hugo and his extended family held non-Indian mainstream values. He enjoyed the company of his soccer mates and partying at social gatherings.

While her marriage foundered, the San Francisco Indian Center activists nurtured Wilma's intellectual, emotional, and spiritual development and led her into the field of social work. Additionally, her volunteer work there galvanized her sense of identity and purpose, leading her into her future of leadership. She learned the value of bringing together diverse views, finding common ground, and adapting to different perspectives. Her time with the Pit River tribes became an internship program for leadership development (Dullien 2016, 18). Wilma also developed close friendships during the days and nights she spent with the Pit River people.

The home of Raymond and Marie Lego (Pomo) in Yurok Country became one of the gathering places for the work related to the Pit River citizens. The Legos maintained a garden, hunted, and lived a simple life, reminding Wilma of her Cherokee relatives back in eastern Oklahoma. This is where Wilma learned about treaty rights and international law

(Mankiller 1993, 204). Wilma and her daughters visited several Pomo people she had first met at Alcatraz, as she continued learning about Indian issues.

Wilma, Felicia, and Gina also spent much time at another Pomo rancheria near Santa Rosa—the Pomo Kashia rancheria in Sonoma County. Many AIM warriors from Wounded Knee were also at the Kashia rancheria in 1973, at the home of Rags and Ida Steele, the parents of Wilma's friend Maxine Steel. Wilma's brother Richard and Maxine's brother Charles were at Wounded Knee. Wilma and others often enjoyed a glass of red wine under the stars and Felicia and Gina enjoyed camping out. The girls loved Kashia, there was a whole alternative world far from their urban environment in those mountains. "Rags worked at a local winery, so we always had fine wine with our meals and plenty of it afterwards as well" (Mankiller, *Every Day Is a Good Day*, 2004, 49). Wilma also attended a spiritual gathering on the Colville reservation that year with Maxine and their kids.

Reflecting on her time working with the Alcatraz occupants, Wilma recalled that "in a way it reminds me of a flame that kind of died down and was just a very low, low flame and then the flame never went out, it never went away and Alcatraz sort of relit that and out of that fire came all those different people spread in all the different directions to do incredible work and the people from Alcatraz had a profound impact on the lives of people throughout this country and it had a profound impact individually and collectively. And so, I think it was kind of a spiritual awakening of our people" (*Mankiller* documentary, 2017). The Pit River tribes' efforts were not successful, largely due to their isolated location and the fact that they were battling a large corporation such as PG&E. (Pacific Gas and Electric Company returned 786 acres to the Pit River tribes on November 5, 2021.)

During the Pit River years, Wilma and Hugo grew further apart. She often visited Lou Trudell and the Oakland Indian Adult Education Program, where many Indian activists gathered. Lou and John Trudell were divorced by this time. She felt increasingly suffocated at home with Hugo and often went to her friend Lou's house in Oakland. The talks at Lou's house involved their children, the emerging women's movement, the role of the American Indian women, Indigenous rights, the environment, and politics (Mankiller 1993, 211). Wilma's friends Justine Buckskin Moppin (Klamath), Susie Steel Regimbal (Pomo), and Linda Aaronaydo (Creek/ Filipina) gathered around Lou's kitchen table at least once per week. Lou was a warm and generous person, and her home became a gathering place for her friends. From Susie, Wilma learned the traditional female leadership role and the importance of Indigenous value systems, as Pomo women are spiritual leaders. Wilma recalled how she and her close female friends survived "a battle to gain control of our own lives and create our own paths instead of following someone else's" (Mankiller 1993, 212). It was among these female friends that Wilma found the personal strength to dissolve her marriage and seek a different life for herself and her two girls. Lou and John Trudell were divorced. Wilma knew many working single mothers. Plus, she had the extended kinship system with her siblings in the Bay Area.

By the mid-70s, San Francisco had the third largest urban Indian population in the United States. Just as Wilma had encountered harassment and discrimination in the urban schools, new generations experienced the same. With the advances that came from Alcatraz, the next focus became education, with the creation of the National Indian Education Association in 1970. Wilma, too, shifted her focus toward education for American Indian children. A great need for Native social workers emerged by the early 1970s as Indian children were removed from Indian homes in great numbers and—along with juvenile delinquents—placed in foster homes. This need led to the creation of survival schools as a way of keeping Indian youth in school, out of trouble, and learning about their culture. Wilma learned much from these alternative schools.

The Heart of the Earth Survival School was based in Minneapolis, where AIM was established. The Red School House was created in St. Paul. The leaders, largely volunteers, taught kindergarten through twelfth grade with traditional curricula as well as Native American–focused courses. Embodying a grassroots effort, classes were held in different locations until grant funding materialized and a permanent location was created in Minneapolis. The Red School House closed in 2008.

The creation of an alternative school required organizing experience, fearlessness, motivation, and commitment. The Rough Rock Demonstration School established by the Dine' (Navajo) in 1966 is a good example. Practicing local self-determination, AIM founded a legal rights center, a health facility, a housing facility, and survival schools. The schools had a common mission: to give opportunities to at-risk youth and keep families together. Many of the kids struggled with problems similar to those found on the reservations, namely poverty, discrimination, substance abuse, and domestic violence. The schools were community schools. Bill Wahpepah provided the vision and leadership for the survival schools and assisted Wilma in creating the youth center in Oakland.

The members of AIM lobbied for the 1972 Indian Education Act and succeeded in gaining federal money for Indian education and for funding Indian children attending public schools. One of AIM's missions was to reinvigorate extended family relationships and rebuild community support systems by challenging the major differences between the values propagated by mainstream educational systems and Indian traditional values. The AIM teachers focused on student identity development and

Indigenous language revitalization. The survival schools had an emphasis on culture and identity, similar to the Black Freedom Schools. The circle with the four directions was ever-present. The circle signified the interdependence between people and nature, the interconnectedness of all living beings, and the infusion of spiritual development and growth in all areas of life. AIM education activists believed the value systems of Indians and non-Indians were too divergent.

Maintaining tribal sovereignty requires control over lands and resources and requires native languages and value systems. The Red Power movement had three main objectives: self-determination and an end to the trustee-ward relationship between the federal government and tribes; federal support for tribal traditions and sovereignty; and improved living conditions and justice for all Indian people. Vine Deloria Jr. urged Indian leaders to ground their leadership in the traditional values of their tribes and communities. "The more the Indians discovered about themselves and about American history and the history and fate of the other peoples of the world, the more they have sought refuge in the tribal customs, beliefs, and traditions that have remained" (Deloria 1974, 250).

All women had a tremendous impact on Western cities at this time in American history. These cities were filled with newcomers lacking community connections or obligations to extended family. Women, such as Wilma, were able to devote time and energy to political activity. The cities were still developing and had immediate community needs to solve, such as parks and schools, considered "women's work" as opposed to "man's work." The inner city and the growing suburbs provided many opportunities for women to volunteer and develop skills in governance. Some people called neighboring Santa Clara County the "feminist capital of the world" (Abbott 1993, 112). Australian musical artist Helen Reddy released the song "I Am Woman" in 1971 as the women's movement continued to expand internationally. Out of this movement, journalist Gloria Steinem and like-minded women created *Ms. Magazine* in 1972 as a mainstream, national magazine. With the women's movement gaining national attention, more women entering the workforce, and the popularity of the Helen Reddy song, the divorce rate in the nation skyrocketed.

By this time, Wilma had learned to play her guitar and still enjoyed R&B music. Redbone, an American Indian rock band formed in the early 1970s, had a No. 5 hit on the top 100 songs with "Come and Get Your Love." Political activist and rap pioneer, poet, and jazz musician Gil Scott-Heron released "Pieces of a Man" in 1971 and the arresting "The Revolution Will Not Be Televised" in 1970, and he became one of Wilma's favorite artists. On the African American experience, social injustice, and political hypocrisy, Heron was heavily influenced by Langston Hughes and often referred to as the Black Bob Dylan, a label and comparison Heron did not enjoy. In May 1971, Marvin Gaye released "What's Going On?," "Inner City Blues," and "Make Me Wanna Holler." In 1972, The Temptations released "Papa Was a Rolling Stone." These songs all had an urban edge that Wilma could relate to.

President Nixon called for a new relationship between the federal government and Indian communities as AIM grew and held protests in Plymouth Rock, Massachusetts, in Mount Rushmore, South Dakota, and in the Great Lakes; led the Trail of Broken Treaties; and finally, protested on the Pine Ridge reservation at Wounded Knee, South Dakota. A schism emerged between traditionalists and progressive Indians over control of reservation services. In January 1973, racist whites fatally stabbed a young Lakota named Wesley Bad Heart Bull. His white killers served only one day in the local jail and were then allowed to go free. AIM protesters clashed with police in nearby Custer, South Dakota, over these events and the Pine Ridge tribal chairman, Richard "Dick" Wilson, banned AIM from the Pine Ridge reservation. The next month, Dennis Banks, Russell Means, and 20 others (including Wilma's younger brother Richard) took over the small church in the village of Wounded Knee. As it was the site of the 1890 massacre of Big Foot's Band, AIM leaders selected it for its symbolism.

The U.S. military arrived in Wounded Knee on the Pine Ridge reservation with tanks, and they fired over half a million rounds of ammunition into the AIM-occupied building. Wilma followed the events here closely as she was constantly concerned for her brother's safety. After 71 days of the standoff, federal soldiers killed two Indians, Buddy Lamont (Lakota) and Frank Clearwater (Eastern Cherokee), and wounded many others. The activism surrounding Alcatraz and Wounded Knee began during the grassroots movement called the White Roots of Peace, as Tom Porter reminded the people of their responsibility to uphold their tribal traditions. Wilma had met Porter at the IFH as the caravan had traveled through San Francisco and Oakland four years earlier. The events at Wounded Knee galvanized the activists supporting Indian rights and interest in tribal traditional values continued.

By the end of 1974, Wilma and Hugo's divorce became final. Wilma and the girls moved to Oakland because the cost of living was much cheaper on that side of the bay. Not being able to afford their own place, they moved into a house with another Native woman and her child. It was a rough neighborhood. Wilma became director of the Native American Youth Center in East Oakland, and she claimed her enthusiasm made up for her lack of skills as she learned on the job to develop a curriculum, hire teachers, and locate a building for an after-school program. Wilma often played music by Paul Ortego (Mescalero Apache) and Jim Pepper (Caw) who she saw as positive Native role models. She also taught the girls to make dance shawls, and the boys learned to drum and dance. She planned field trips and created a curriculum and cultural program with skills learned at the San Francisco Indian Center. The curriculum included cultural lessons linked to spiritual discovery and growth (Davis 2013, 142). Instilling Native pride became a primary objective for Wilma, and she wanted the youth to use that pride for individual strength. She also discovered firsthand what self-help could accomplish (Mankiller 1993, 203).

Justine's sister owned a nearby bar called Chicken's Place. Wilma recruited volunteers from the bar to help with renovations at the youth center and raised money for other projects. Many Native activists who were involved with Alcatraz settled in East Oakland and gave the area a feeling of hope and optimism for the future. The East Oakland Native people never let her down when Wilma requested help with the youth center.

The next year, 1975, Wilma met Ross Swimmer, who had been in Oakland campaigning for the office of Principal Chief of the Cherokee Nation. This may have been one of the things that motivated Wilma to return to the Cherokee Nation lands. Also, Grandma Sitton passed away in 1973 and her death became another factor in Wilma's decision to return to Mankiller Flats. Not only Wilma, but many urban Indians returned to their homelands with plans to strengthen their tribal communities and government.

The early activist years of the late 1960s and early 1970s inspired a new generation of urban Indians toward a community-minded sense of working for the collective good of the Indian people. Despite the Watergate Scandal and his resignation in August 1974, Nixon is considered a friend of the Indian as he called for an end to the federal Indian policy of Termination and began creating conditions favorable to American Indian communities determining their own future with their specific tribal needs and goals (Smith 2012, 111). Indian activists captured mainstream media attention and that played a critical role in garnering public support. Wilma learned the city skills of relating to a diverse population, learning to go between Indian and non-Indian worlds, and maintaining pride in her heritage. American Indian identity became simultaneously maintained and transformed in the urban, multitribal region of the San Francisco Bay Area. "All the time spent in the fight for Alcatraz, at the youth center, with the Pit River people, gave me precious knowledge. All of the people I encountered, the militants, the wise elders, the keepers of the medicine, the storytellers, were my teachers, my best teachers" (Mankiller 1993, 205).

Already planning a return to Oklahoma, Wilma also began working as a social worker with the Urban Indian Resource Center. She worked on Indian child abuse and neglect cases and on foster care and adoption (Edmunds 2001, 213). For almost two years, Wilma raised four foster children of ages 18 months to 14 years, besides Felicia and Gina (Allinder 1985). She started creating legislation to prevent Indian children from being removed from their culture and this eventually passed as the Indian Child Welfare Act. After Felicia's best friend, an 11-year-old boy, committed suicide, Wilma knew it was time to move back home to Oklahoma (Solomon 2002, 64).

One day in 1975, Hugo took nine-year-old Gina to see the circus in San Francisco and instead of returning her home, he called Wilma and told her he was keeping Gina unless Wilma told him she loved him. Wilma refused. With his child support payments becoming sporadic, Hugo kept Gina for almost a year, taking her to Chicago, Berkeley, and Ecuador. While Gina enjoyed fancy dresses and learned Spanish, she became terribly homesick and began losing her hair. She also developed an ulcer. Once Hugo and Gina returned to San Francisco, Gina wanted to stay with her mom and Felicia. Frightened that Hugo might attempt to take either of the girls again, Wilma took them to visit Oklahoma in the summer of 1976, and it was on that trip that she definitely decided to move back home to Mankiller Flats.

Wilma became involved in traditional ceremonial dances while back home that summer. She and the girls attended a Four Mother's Society gathering for their once-a-month stickball game and a feast of the summer fruits and vegetables which was followed by all-night ceremonial Cherokee dances. During that brief summer visit, Wilma decided she would return to Oklahoma the following summer. "I was delighted to be back on our ancestral homelands. I wanted to come home and raise my kids and build a house on my land" (Mankiller 1993, xxi).

Returning to Oakland for the 1976–1977 school season, Wilma continued working at the school and working on tribal issues. On a trip to the Standing Rock Sioux reservation in Wakpala, South Dakota, Wilma attended the Third International Indian Treaty Council Conference from June 15–17, 1977. She helped prepare tribal delegates for the 1977 United Nations Conference on Indigenous Rights in Geneva, Switzerland. It was here that Wilma came to realize there was a historical period when Cherokee spiritual leaders conducted council meetings to help prepare the people for issues affecting the communities, whereas in the modern era, there was a separation of political and spiritual leaders.

Returning from the South Dakota conference, Wilma began making plans to move back to Oklahoma. She then traded her much-loved little red Mazda for her brother's buffalo robe, went to her friend Lou Trudell's house where they packed lunches, rented a U-Haul moving truck, packed their belongings, and left California with her two daughters plus their dog and guinea pig. They traveled as far as Salt Lake City, borrowed some money from a friend they knew there, then drove to Denver, borrowed some more money from a friend there, and finally made it to Oklahoma with $20 left. Arriving at her mom's house, where Irene had been since Charley's death, Wilma had no car and no job. There were some things about living in the Bay Area that Wilma was going to miss—like sourdough bread, live theater, the distinct neighborhoods, the ocean, and the intriguing people—but she was home and that made her happy.

4

Return to Oklahoma

Mankiller Flats was the first stop when Wilma and the girls moved back. Although her childhood home had burned down, there were still the familiar trees, wildflowers, and the spring that ran through the property, and Wilma needed to be among them. The spring on the property was where Wilma often used to collect water and where her parents and grandparents kept a springhouse for melons, milk, and butter to stay cool above the rushing water. This spring, with mint and watercress-covered banks, became her favorite place to pray. A Cherokee ceremony known as "going to the water" during the falling leaves time was said to promote healing. One of Wilma's first actions while visiting the family land included jumping in and bathing in the ice-cold water of that spring.

Wilma, Felicia, and Gina camped at Cherokee Landing State Park, on the banks of Caney Creek. When Wilma was a young girl, people used to camp there for a couple of days and cook freshly caught fish in cast iron skillets over an open fire. That summer of 1977, Wilma felt a great sense of freedom and the happy childhood memories of her Cherokee homeland. She and the girls swam, fished, learned to tell time by the sun, played Scrabble by lantern light, and listened to music from a portable radio by the campfire. Wilma was uncertain about the direction of her life, but after her experiences in Alcatraz and Pit River, she knew she wanted to do more.

Wilma turned her life and the lives of her daughters upside down when she moved, much as her parents had done to themselves and their children when they moved to San Francisco. Felicia and Gina were 12 and 10, respectively, and they missed their friends and social lives from the Bay Area. While they were used to camping from the Pit River days, the rural setting of eastern Oklahoma required considerable adjustment. It was as much a culture shock for them as it had been for 11-year-old Wilma when she moved from Oklahoma to California in 1956. Taking care of her girls was always an imperative for Wilma. After returning to Oklahoma, she drew upon the traditional values and tribal history of the Cherokees for guidance in her political career and personal relationships, as she looked for work and began making friends. She had much to catch up on due to the tremendous changes that had taken place among the Cherokee people since she left.

Between 1940 and 1960, Adair County, Oklahoma, had the largest Indian population and the lowest per capita income in the state. Members of the Cherokee Nation communities also had below-average educational attainment levels and a high unemployment rate. While the Cherokee Nation had experienced major changes in Wilma's absence over the past 20 years, two things had not changed—the traditional, mostly full-bloods stayed out of tribal politics, and most Cherokee people remained conservative Republicans.

The Indian Claims Act of 1946 created the Indian Claims Commission (ICC) to hear long-standing claims by American Indians against the U.S. government. In 1961, the Cherokee tribe in Oklahoma gained a windfall of $2 million as working capital remaining from the $15 million settlement for the sale of the Cherokee Outlet in the upper portion of Oklahoma.

Wilma recalled, "In the late 1940s and the 1950s, the visible Cherokee population had been predominately mixed blood for some time, and the mixed blood element included many well-to-do people and some prominent individuals. Because of this, a faulty belief arose among some Cherokee leaders that all Cherokees had become happily assimilated into the mainstream of American society. That was not the case. In reality, there were many full-bloods, half-bloods, or other mixed-blood Cherokees with more traditional lifeways" (Mankiller 1993, 33). These people lived in extreme poverty in isolated Cherokee communities, such as Wilma's, scattered throughout the hills; these settlements did not appear on any of the maps at the time and many were not visible from the road to travelers passing through the area. The communities consisted of traditional Cherokee families living on their individual allotments of land.

The families in the communities gathered at the churches or at tribal ceremonial grounds for fellowship, for ceremonies, and to arrange *gadugi* crews. *Gadugi* crews remained as traditional work groups who came together when there was a need to help someone for the common good of all. Wilma's ancestral lands existed among traditional Cherokees near the community of Rocky Mountain, approximately 15 miles from the town of Stilwell, and she became convinced that the continued survival of traditional Cherokee communities like Bell, Christie, Cherry Tree, Bull Hollow, Oak Hill, Kenwood, Rocky Ford, Chewey and others was key to the cultural survival of the people.

The United Keetoowah Band (UKB) formally organized under the Oklahoma Welfare Act of 1936 and served as a channel to bring industry into the Cherokee area (Summary Report Cherokee Tribe of Oklahoma, May 24, 1963). The UKB is a federally chartered corporation developed in 1950 by former chiefs Milam and Keeler, with the main purpose of organizing economic development for the Cherokees. The Keetoowah Society, the Nighthawk Keetoowah Society, Inc., and the Four Mothers Society are cultural organizations completely separate from the UKB (*Cherokee Advocate*, 1994d). New chief Keeler's initiatives created dissention in 1963 between the youth and elders and town and country, between the few Cherokees willing to work with Keeler and the more traditional "nationalistic" Cherokees who were content with their own institutions such as the *gadugi*.

Anthropologists Alfred Wahrhaftig and Bob Thomas, of the 1955 NIYC Denver workshops, conducted research on the Oklahoma Cherokees in the late 1960s and early 1970s. As a project of the Carnegie Corporation Cross-Cultural Education Project, Wahrhaftig studied economic development and identity issues for the Study of Man Institute at the Smithsonian Institute. Wahrhaftig found that those who controlled the regional systems of cultural definition and manipulated identity held the local political and economic power. Initially, the traditional Cherokees were very suspicious of these strange city men always watching them. Then, once they began reading the newsletter, they slowly started to accept the Chicago researchers and became angrier with the Office of Economic Opportunity on local matters, as they continued to feel left out and that their needs were ignored. By the summer of 1965, the Chicago researchers, including Clyde Warrior, became fully embedded in the communities. Businesses in Tahlequah began employing Cherokee-language speakers and Tahlequah and Stilwell merchants began displaying signs in the Cherokee Syllabary.

Chief Keeler and the Cherokee executive committee created an 11-point economic development program, which included the creation of new businesses in the Cherokee Nation restaurant, the Arts and Crafts Center, and the service station, apart from a warehouse. They equipped 851 homes with sanitation facilities and fresh water and established a revolving credit program. They also purchased 20 acres near Pryor, Oklahoma, for low-rent housing (Executive Committee Meeting, Cherokee Nation, September 30, 1965). In 1966, the committee established three training schools in Adair and Delaware counties, a bulldozer training program in Bull Hollow and another in Candy Mink Springs in Stilwell, and a welding school in

Stilwell. The committee built the Bull Hollow Community Center, deep in the hills west of Kenwood and sponsored by the Cherokee Foundation and the Cherokee Soil Conservation Committee, a part of the Manpower Development Training Act (MDTA) federal program. Greasy Rock, Hulbert, and Spring Valley soon wanted community buildings as well.

The continuing tribal divisions that had begun around the allotment process became evident once again in the spring of 1966. The Five County Cherokee Movement, led by Finis Smith, emerged from the hills of eastern Oklahoma with a declaration against community development actions by what they called the "Cherokee establishment." The member counties included Adair, Cherokee, Delaware, Mayes, and Sequoyah, which were largely populated by full-bloods. By the summer, hundreds of Cherokee men armed with rifles and pistols descended on the courthouse in Jay to witness the trial of John Chewey, a fellow Cherokee arrested for killing a deer on tribal lands without a hunting license (Steiner 1968, 42). An intense feud continued to develop as the Five County Cherokees also protested the Cherokee cultural center. A portion of the declaration of the Five County Cherokees of Oklahoma in 1966 was, "Now, we shall not rest until we have regained our rightful place. We shall tell our young people what we know. We shall send them to the corners of the earth to learn more. They shall lead us" (Wahrhaftig, "In the Aftermath of Civilization," 1975).

In 1967, the Five County Cherokees changed their name to the Original Cherokee County Organization (OCCO) and asked Bob Thomas to work with them. They established a local radio broadcast and published the bilingual newsletter, *The Cherokee Report*. Both were funded by the Field Foundation in New York. Chief Keeler accused the Carnegie researchers of being communists and creating division.

Under the Keeler administration, the Cherokee tribal government built 10 mutual housing units in the Briggs community and 16 in the Baron-Wauhillau community. They also constructed 25 low-rent housing units near Pryor and 16 in Tahlequah. Resources, labor, and tools circulated throughout the community through sharing or through the *gadugi* work crew. Men over 40 years of age made up the *gadugi* crews who built and maintained churches, stomp grounds, and cemeteries. They also built houses for needy families left homeless from fires, chopped and stacked wood for the elderly and invalid Cherokees, and transported families to distant hospitals (Wahrhaftig, "More than Mere Work," 1975, 328). Except for the community of Hulbert, each traditional Cherokee settlement comprised 20 to 50 households, with each household sharing and cooperating with their kin groups. The settlements were organized around churches or stomp grounds.

Community representatives served as pipelines of information and by 1970, they voted in executive committee meetings. In July 1970, President

Nixon cited the groundbreaking role of the War on Poverty program in fostering Indian autonomy, which led to the creation of the Indian Self-determination and Educational Assistance Act of 1975 (ISDEA). Passed as Public Law 93-638, this momentous legislation provided authority to Indian tribes to regulate their own services, similar to those among municipalities. Tribes assumed administrative authority over public services that affected them, which were previously administered by the Bureau of Indian Affairs.

In 1971, Chief Keeler became the first popularly elected principal chief since Oklahoma statehood in 1907. Wilma recalled, "When tribal leaders began rebuilding the Cherokee Nation in 1971, operating from a small storefront, they had no marketable natural resources, no funds, nothing but will power and a tradition of what Cherokees call gadugi, or sharing and working collectively" (Gaines 1996). One to three kin groups existed in each community, still practicing the *gadugi* when a specific need arose. Those without community centers had the place of worship at the center of the settlements, which also served as educational, political, and economic meeting places. The *gadugi* became an occasion as opposed to an organization—called upon as needed. It is important to understand the land masses involved as the *gadugi* is associated with land held and maintained by kinship groups and clans within each Cherokee community.

The Keeler administration drafted a tribal constitution and began restructuring the tribal government. The executive committee was dissolved, but Keeler appointed a new committee. Traditional Cherokees still did not participate because the Cherokee establishment continued to promote an assimilationist agenda.

Ross Swimmer, a Republican and former tribal attorney and president of the First National Bank of Tahlequah, became the next elected chief in 1975. The tribe also adopted a new constitution with provisions that a principal chief election and a deputy chief election be held every four years. The new constitution enacted three branches of government with a legislative 15-member tribal council and a three-member tribunal judiciary branch. The new constitution and governing structure were ratified in June 1976.

Wilma first learned about the tribal bureaucratic process when she went to the Adair County courthouse inquiring about the process of building a house on her family's land at Mankiller Flats. The process was approved but it would take longer than Wilma had imagined because of the bureaucracy. A few elder Cherokee men sat nearby, and Wilma overheard one say, "That's John Mankiller's granddaughter." She knew she was home, and it felt good. While in town that day, Wilma ran into her cousin Maudie Wolfe who invited her and the girls to a Stomp Dance at the Flint Rock Ceremonial Grounds. Maudie's husband, Jim, presided over it as head and chief of the Four Mothers Society. The Four Mothers Society had begun in the 1890s as a religious and social movement to oppose allotment.

Wilma and her daughters also visited the Stokes Smith dance grounds, where they met other people of Cherokee faith, many of whom were also Baptist preachers. Outwardly, traditional ceremonial practitioners and Christian Cherokees differ very little. Many Baptist preachers deliver the service in the Cherokee language and many credit the Cherokee Baptist Association with saving the language by continuously using in the church (Mankiller, *Every Day Is a Good Day*, 2004, 21). Many Cherokee people are tolerant of religious differences and most are people of faith.

Spiritual people had always attracted Wilma's attention and that continued when she returned home. She enjoyed being around people who prayed and reminded her of the quest to be a good person. During the Green Corn ceremony there is always a prayer recited at the beginning: "First, let us remove all negative thoughts from our minds so we can come together as one . . . ." Cherokee healers treated negative thoughts as equal to other physical illnesses and believed that if left unchecked, these thoughts could manifest into negative actions (Mankiller, *Every Day Is a Good Day*, 2004, 17).

Wilma and the girls arrived at the ceremonial grounds in the late afternoon in time to see a stickball game between the men and women. Rival Cherokee settlements once played stickball to settle disputes. The game was played in conjunction with a dance and other ceremonies. Called Anesta, the Cherokee stickball game is similar to Lacrosse. It involves two teams and the object is to catch the small, round ball and throw it up toward the top of the tall pole at either end of the field. Hitting the pole gained points. That day the women were victorious. As they teased the men about their win, everyone gathered for an enormous meal. After that, the elder men withdrew from the others and sat facing the east until the dance was about to begin. Once it was night, a few men prepared a central fire and Jim Wolfe walked onto the grounds near the fire and addressed the crowd in Cherokee. Then the dance began. Soon drawn to the dance circle, Wilma danced all night and as she danced, she felt whole again for the first time since her childhood. Wilma, Felicia, and Gina became members of the Four Mothers Society that evening.

Soon after that evening, Dorothy Wolfe, Jim's daughter, invited them to stay in an old house on her property, just behind the stomp dance grounds, while they built their new house on Mankiller Flats. "We were part of a community where Cherokee was spoken, traditional medicine was a part of everyday life, people talked about and tried to interpret dreams, and Cherokee knowledge was preserved in stories. We felt like the wealthiest people in the world" (Mankiller, *Every Day Is a Good Day*, 2004, 21). Living in that house without electricity or running water, Wilma slowly reestablished a connection to the natural world. She and the girls gathered wild grapes, hickory nuts, and walnuts and picked apples. After living on Dorothy's property for a while, they moved in with Wilma's mom as the girls prepared to start school in September.

Staying with Irene, Wilma searched for a job during the day and played her guitar and sewed ribbon shirts and clothes for her brothers and sisters and other relatives in the evenings. Most of her siblings slowly returned to eastern Oklahoma shortly after she did. Finally, she got an entry-level position with the Cherokee Nation.

In October 1977, Wilma began her new job as Economic Stimulus Program Director, responsible for training people at the post-secondary level in environmental science and health. The grant-writing skills Wilma had acquired while assisting in the Alcatraz and Pit River occupations helped her obtain the job. The bureaucratic system within the Cherokee Nation differed greatly from the grassroots activism Wilma had been involved with in California. Wilma's duties entailed expanding employment opportunities and programs leading to permanent jobs. There were seven programs in the areas of paramedical and health training; paralegal training; on-site management training; agriculture training; emergency vehicle operation training; apprenticeship and outreach; and waste disposal training. Within the vast bureaucracy that is the tribal government, Wilma sought grassroots democracy supporters, and she saved enough money to purchase a used station wagon. Within two years, Wilma became the program development specialist for the Cherokee Nation. With the increased funding arriving from grants, Wilma caught the attention of the tribal council and Chief Ross Swimmer for her good work.

Wilma often worked longer than others in the office. "My secretary would often find me sitting on the floor of my office trying to collate a grant proposal while my colleagues were worrying about the state of their bouffant hairdos." She knew then "that a distinct and vibrant Cherokee culture which should be more fully supported existed in some historic Cherokee communities" (Mankiller, *Every Day Is a Good Day*, 2004, 50). To get through the painful time when she began working with the Cherokee Nation and so many of Chief Swimmer's staff opposed her, Wilma participated in a ceremony to help cleanse her mind of feelings of resentment toward those who opposed her, and after that, she could work with them in a good way.

In addition to her extensive grant-writing and social services work with the community-based Native organizations in northern California, Wilma served on the board of directors of the Vanguard Foundation in San Francisco, the board of directors of Rainbow TV in Los Angeles, and the American Indian Community School in Oakland (*Cherokee Phoenix and Indian Advocate*, 1978c). Wilma and her brother Richard appeared in the 1978

Native Filmmakers Directory as a reference source for networks and film production companies interested in making authentic American Indian films. Richard was a former producer for KQED in San Francisco and Wilma served on the advisory boards of educational television stations in Boston and Los Angeles. She also served on the advisory board of a children's television show, REBOP, starring Levar Burton and produced by WGBH in Boston. The show aired from 1976 to 1979 on PBS stations and focused on promoting social understanding and diversity among young people. Wilma's interest in television and movie production continued throughout her life.

Wilma also completed her degree in social science in 1978 through a correspondence program from Stilwell Flaming Rainbow University Without Walls. This school provided college education to isolated Indians and rural whites and was awarded its degrees through the Union for Experimental Colleges in Washington, D.C. (Allinder 1985). Wilma was determined to demonstrate to Felicia and Gina that persistence and perseverance were worthwhile. Likewise, Wilma worked hard for the tribe to illustrate to her daughters what could be achieved with dedication and hard work.

Once the FBI had imprisoned or killed many of the AIM members and leaders, Indian women decided to continue the movement to advocate for Indian rights and recognize the important contributions women made to the Red Power movement. After the persecution and prosecution of many male members of AIM, and believing the male leaders of AIM did not adequately address their issues, several Indian women created Women of All Red Nations (WARN) in 1978. Madonna Thunderhawk, Lorelei DeCora Means, Phyllis Young, and many others formed the organization. WARN members focused on improving educational opportunities; health care and reproductive rights for American Indian women; combating violence against women; bringing an end to the stereotyping and exploitation of American Indians; working to uphold treaties over Indian lands; and protecting the land and the environment where American Indians lived. They also protested against the involuntary sterilization of Indian women by Indian Health Service workers during the early 1970s and campaigned on behalf of Native men and against prison culture. The group of activist women championed the restoration of treaty rights, eliminating Indian mascots for sports teams, and combating the commercialization of Indian culture. Wilma was actively involved in this organization.

As part of her new duties with the Cherokee Nation, where she was Economic Stimulus Program Director with the training centers, Wilma began soliciting applications from both trainers and workers, to have workers trained in a Department of Labor agricultural training program for orchard management and nursery production businesses. Building trades training—in carpentry, plumbing, electricity, and masonry—was also made available in the fall of 1978 for those workers interested in residential housing construction (*Cherokee Advocate*, 1978e). In addition, a training program in wastewater technology began in 1978. "The lack of modern treatment facilities and waste disposal sites in many communities is detrimental to the basic standard of good health and although federal assistance is available to communities to build modern facilities or upgrade existing plants, there are not enough professionally trained personnel to operate and maintain these facilities," said Wilma. The new training program, in coordination with the Department of Labor, intended to provide skilled entry-level workers and aid in maintaining the state of Oklahoma's environmental quality (*Cherokee Advocate*, 1978e).

The traditional community of Bull Hollow in Delaware County in the Cherokee Nation opened a community center six miles north of Twin Oaks. There were two similar facilities at Cherry Tree in Adair County and Belfonte in Sequoyah County, funded by a $7.6 million local public works construction Economic Development Administration (EDA) grant that the U.S. Department of Commerce gained through Wilma's grant-writing work. Chief Ross Swimmer dedicated the new building and expressed hope that it would help to unify the community. The new community centers contained 3,000 square feet of space, including a large community meeting room with a wood-burning fireplace, a modern kitchen, reset rooms, a storage area, and an office. The Tribal Council members present were Deputy Chief Perry Wheeler, Goodlow Proctor, Don Crittenden, Hiner Doublehead, Houston Johnson, Leo Fishinghawk, and Joe Ragsdale (*Cherokee Phoenix and Indian Advocate*, 1978a).

Next came a community center built in the Cherry Tree community, four miles south of Stilwell on Highway 59. Chief Swimmer declared that the current tribal leadership was a good team and included Wilma within that group. Her grant-writing skills produced another EDA grant of $700,000 for a Head Start program in the new Cherry Tree Community Center (*Cherokee Phoenix and Indian Advocate*, 1978a). These community centers became gathering places for the *gadugi* crews and other community activities and programs previously held at the local churches. Importantly for Wilma, she got to know her community members and the larger Cherokee Nation tribal members while working for these new community centers. She may not have remembered the *gadugi* crews from her childhood, but she quickly got to know about them as she visited the communities.

In the town of Dahlonega in south Adair County, there were other tribal developments—a tribal orchard and poultry operation and the expansion of the Cherokee Nation Industries, Inc. and Cherokee Nation Industrial Park. Tribal officials built a new day care center in Stilwell and also the Stilwell Tribal Complex, Stilwell Academy, a Licensed Practical Nursing School, and a new youth shelter. They also built and renovated 50–75 new homes within one mile of the new Twin Oaks community center because of Wilma's skill and talent in grant writing for federal funding.

Twenty-six tribes from across the United States attended the Second Annual Indian Industrial Development Workshop, held at the Tahlequah Tsa-la-Gi Motor Inn on December 5 and 6, 1978 and sponsored by the EDA's Indian Industrial Development Office which began in 1973. "The EDA was a godsend to the Cherokee Nation," remarked Chief Swimmer. Yet, he also warned against abuse and emphasized the importance of having a stable tribal government that knows industrial development and business. The two-day workshop had sessions on how to plan industrial development programs, how to finance projects, and what industries are looking for. Wilma received a crash course in the Cherokee Nation's economic development efforts during those two days.

Wilma's additional duties included transitioning the tribe's contracting services. Previously held by the BIA, the Cherokee Nation Social Services Department contracted directly with the federal government. President Nixon's Indian Self-Determination and Educational Assistance Act of 1975, or Public Law 638 (P.L. 638), commonly referred to as 638 programs in Indian Country, made this contracting possible. The tribe had over 40 separate programs ranging from health education to employment assistance, and the 638 contracting program provided a central point for people to learn about these programs and become self-sufficient. Contracts previously administered by the BIA were now controlled by the tribe, and Wilma devoted a great deal of time and energy into this alternative method of contracting. Chief Swimmer stated, "The individual has to become self-sufficient. It is the duty of every Cherokee person to get out of the stream of federal employment. It is your responsibility to go out there and find meaningful, productive work, whether it is helping someone else to get that work or to get the work yourself, because these programs aren't going to be around forever" (*Cherokee Phoenix and Indian Advocate*, 1981b).

The tribe became divided over degree of blood quantum and residency status as current tribal members required a one-fourth degree blood quantum for tribal membership with those living outside the Cherokee Nation not being allowed to vote in tribal elections. Tribal members also opposed voting among the Delaware and Shawnees, Cherokee freedmen, and intermarried whites living within the nation's boundaries. When the OEO programs became available, local struggles for power and control emerged. Most tribal members claimed to be members of the Republican party and many viewed Democrats as being associated with Jacksonian Democracy and Confederates. For many, Republicanism was ingrained into being a Cherokee in America. So, whether the Cherokee Nation was divided over politics or the degree of blood someone had, differences continued. Most Cherokees believed a person needed to have some cultural knowledge about the Cherokee people, such as knowing the language, in addition to the degree of Cherokee blood they possessed.

As mentioned earlier, Wilma was a member of the board of directors of Rainbow TV Workshop, a Los Angeles–based minority television corporation. In July 1979, the corporation received a $1.3 million award from the Public Broadcasting System to produce 10 episodes of a teenage-focused series entitled *The Righteous Apples*. The show, set in an east coast high school, revolved around a group of teens in a band who resolved conflicts as they maneuvered around people of other racial heritages and tried to figure out life. The first season turned out to be a success and the Corporation for Public Broadcasting awarded Rainbow TV another $1.3 million for a second season. The show was aired during the years 1980 and 1981.

Rainbow TV promoted, fostered, and encouraged a multicultural view of society and sponsored other projects for public television from the Communications Institute of New England, a Boston group that trained minority people for entry-level jobs in television (*Cherokee Advocate*, 1979).

Also in 1979, Wilma became director of the newly created Cherokee Nation Community Development Department, implementing renewal projects. By this time, Wilma was comfortable in her role within the Cherokee Nation, and the girls were doing well in school and making new friends. Felicia and Gina were teenagers at this time and busy with all the things associated with being teenage girls, so Wilma decided to return to school again. She enrolled at the University of Arkansas-Fayetteville, finished her degree, then continued toward her master's degree in community planning. She also began building a new house on Mankiller Flats, becoming reacquainted with relatives, and making new friends.

Among Wilma's new friends were a young non-Indian couple, Mike and Sherry Morris, and their three-year-old daughter, Meghan. Mike served as the new director of education for the Cherokee Nation, and Sherry was a homemaker. Sherry had been first runner-up Miss Mississippi at the Miss America beauty pageant. Wilma and Sherry became fast friends in spite of their cultural differences. Sherry was a true "Southern Belle," but had little self-confidence in her appearance. Wilma took pride in watching her friend become more self-confident as Sherry became interested in rural health care and early childhood development education. Getting more serious about her education and less concerned with her outward appearance, Sherry told Wilma how she was tired of wearing makeup all the time and exercising obsessively and how she was over all that. Life was good for Sherry and Wilma and they made plans to go to Arkansas the week of November 8, 1979, in search of antiques. Then everything changed.

The evening of November 8, Wilma's second cousin, Byrd Wolfe, and his wife, Paggy, visited Wilma. Byrd and Paggy were traditional ceremonial

dancers, and they sat around Wilma's kitchen table and discussed Cherokee medicine people. There were two kinds of traditional medicine that
were still being practiced among certain Cherokees—one involved using
herbs, roots, and other natural items for healing and the other used songs,
incantations, or other thoughts or actions. They discussed medicine used
to cause harm or to settle old disputes. Then, the three of them heard a
loud commotion outside and, peering through the curtains, saw at least a
dozen owls, some flying around and others sitting on treetops. Wilma's
family believed owls were a sign of bad luck; they believed that if owls came
close to the house, it meant bad news was coming. (There are other Native
people who view the sighting of an owl as a sign of coming death.) Owls
surrounded Wilma's house that night, and they made their presence
known. No one knew what the owls meant that night, but they would soon
find out.

Wilma attended the University of Arkansas full-time while supple-
menting her meager tribal income with a graduate assistantship, so these
were lean times. She asked Chief Swimmer if she could do some consulting
work for the tribe to pick up some extra money, and he agreed. The next
day, Wilma drove onto Highway 100 about four miles from her home. She
was headed to Tahlequah for a meeting with the personnel director to discuss the consulting work. Wilma drove up a steep hill with a blind spot, so
she did not see the car coming from the other direction, passing two cars.
When she did, she tried to veer to the right, but it was too late. The driver
of that car collided head-on with Wilma's station wagon. What Wilma did
not know until weeks later was that Sherry was driving the other car. The
impact broke Sherry's neck and she died on the spot.

The impact of the crash pushed the edge of Wilma's car-hood into her
neck. While being pulled from the wreckage, her injuries were so severe
and there was so much blood that it was unclear to the ambulance workers
whether she was male or female. She was severely injured and rushed to
Stilwell for stabilization before being transported to a larger hospital in
Fort Smith, Arkansas. During the 50-mile ambulance ride, Wilma faded in
and out of consciousness and had the most "tremendous sense of peaceful-
ness and warmth" (Mankiller 1993, 223). She described it as an over-
whelming and powerful feeling of flying fast and a sense of calm deeper
than she had ever known. Then, she remembered Felicia and Gina and
made a decision to live.

Arriving at the hospital, Wilma immediately went into surgery that
lasted six hours. Her x-ray revealed she had no whole bones between her
left knee and ankle. Her injuries also included a crushed face, crushed ribs,
and a broken right leg. Wilma remained in the hospital for eight weeks and
required 17 surgeries on her legs and face. An orthopedic surgeon at the
Fort Smith hospital had developed a proprietary method of sewing bones

back together using stainless steel thread and Wilma attributed her ability to walk again to the surgeon's skill. Three weeks passed before Mike, Sherry's husband, visited Wilma in the hospital and told her Sherry had been the driver of the other car and had not survived. When Wilma learned this, she began crying so uncontrollably that her face started hemorrhaging and doctors had to rush in to control the bleeding.

After surgery and being placed on a life-support system, she became angry and wanted to be off the machines and out of the hospital. The doctors thought it would take her three weeks to come off the life-support machine, but it took her three days instead. "Once I took charge of my life, my body gradually began to heal" (Awiakta 1993, 115). Wilma remained incapacitated for almost a year. Home alone for most of that period, she had time to examine her life in a new way and to refocus her life.

Cherokee medicine people, or healers, helped Wilma during her year of convalescence by teaching her to approach life from a positive and loving perspective. Her spirit changed as her car accident forced her to slow down and pay attention. This period in Wilma's life was the turning point in terms of her health and the vision behind her work. The healers taught Wilma the Cherokee truths of life: To be of good mind; to consider all as our relatives; to not be judgmental; to be positive (Awiakta 1993, 115). Wilma grew determined to bring the Cherokee people together. She believed in collaborative government and in leadership through persuasion rather than coercion. The pattern of restoring harmony from the inside out and of extending that concept from the individual to the community is a classic example of the Native American ability to adapt and survive. It is the ability to think purposefully, with mind, heart, and soul (Awiakta 1993, 283).

During her period of convalescence at Mankiller Flats, Wilma had casts on both legs and suffered enormous pain. Her sister Linda came every day for six months to help take care of her. Wilma had to learn to walk again, often aided by a cane, and had to wear a steel brace from her knee to her ankle on her left leg for the rest of her life, which often caused pain and swelling. Because of this experience, Wilma was no longer frightened of death. She also began writing more after the accident. Wilma refused to become negative or depressed and reevaluated her life, beginning a Cherokee approach to life and being of good mind. Cherokee elders proclaim one must think positively and take what life gives us and do what we can to make it better.

The 1979 car accident was so life-changing that Wilma viewed her life in terms of "before the accident" and "after the accident" (Awiakta 1993, 113). She stated that her hard edge developed in the late 1960s and early 1970s from growing up Indian in an urban environment and witnessing injustices committed against her family, Cherokee people, and all Indian people. She had an "us" versus "them" mentality. Alcatraz cemented these beliefs (Awiakta 1993, 114). "It was an ongoing process; growing up Indian in an urban environment, feeling my family members were victims of ill-advised federal policies, and realizing the government had not honored treaties or policies for health and education" (Awiakta 1993, 114).

Wilma recalled, "That accident in 1979 changed my life. I came very close to death, felt its presence and the alluring call to complete the circle of life. I always think of myself as the woman who lived before and the woman who lives afterward. I was at home recovering for almost a year, and I had time to reevaluate" (Mankiller 1993, xxi). It was a deep spiritual awakening, what Cherokees call "being of good mind." She thought a lot about what the rest of her life would entail and realized how short and precious life is. "The reality of how precious life is, enabled me to begin projects I couldn't have otherwise tackled" (Mankiller 1993, xxii). The car accident was as life-changing for Wilma as the experiences at Alcatraz had been. Her entire personality changed after her recovery, from that of a shy but angry social activist to a calm and measured leader. "She often wore long flowing skirts to conceal the brace and her calm concealed the pain" (Steinem 2015, 229).

Just a few months after the car accident, Wilma began experiencing muscle control issues. She lost her grip while holding objects such as a hairbrush, a coffee cup, or her toothbrush. She also developed severe double vision. She grew weaker, had trouble speaking and chewing, and lost 40 pounds. Then, she fell and rebroke the bones in her face. It was not until Labor Day 1980 that she discovered what was happening to her. She switched on a television channel broadcasting the annual "Jerry Lewis Muscular Dystrophy Telethon" and realized a woman on the program was describing her symptoms exactly. The next week, Linda took Wilma to a Tulsa physician, who diagnosed her with moderately severe systemic myasthenia gravis, a form of neuromuscular dystrophy.

Resolved to fight and grow stronger, Wilma drew on her internal strength to remove all negativity and focus on healing. She also drew on the strength of her ancestors and Cherokee healers and what she had learned from her good friend Justine Buckskin. She finally quit smoking cigarettes and underwent surgery to remove her thymus. The high doses of steroids that followed caused her to gain much weight. Through most of her adult life, Wilma believed it was wrong to focus on all the things that were wrong, be it her work, her health, her marriage, or her children, or the whole world in general. She came to understand that humans do not have much control over what the Creator sends their way in the course of their lifetimes, but they do have control over how they think about events. She made a deliberate decision to be of good mind.

The long healing and recovery process also inspired Wilma to begin writing more. She still felt great anger, but it was a "righteous" anger caused by her frustrations at the dehumanizing practices of Western medicine which she had personally experienced after the accident and the muscular dystrophy diagnosis. The short story she wrote to channel her anger while convalescing was titled, "Keeping Pace with the Rest of the World." It was originally published in 1985 in the magazine *Southern Exposure*.

The story revolves around a young Cherokee woman named Pearl and her Cherokee grandmother, *Ah ni wa ke*, "laughing water or bright eyes." Pearl takes her grandmother to the Indian hospital, where the doctor wants to amputate the grandmother's foot due to her diabetes. They immediately leave as the grandmother is appalled by the idea and prefers traditional Indian healers. While Pearl drives to locate a Seminole doctor, who is among the best, her grandmother worsens and slips into a diabetic coma. Pearl immediately takes her back to the Indian hospital, where she dies of a heart attack that night. Pearl slaps the doctor in the face and returns home. Staring into the fire that evening, Pearl sees her grandmother, and she looks so happy reunited with her husband, Levi Buckskin. Pearl decides to do all she can to "restore and revitalize the traditional Cherokee way of life as a tribute to Ahniwake and to the lives of other Cherokees who are not yet born" (Bruchac 1995, 216).

While the car accident was as life-altering as the Alcatraz occupation had been, the accident required physical as well as emotional strength to persevere. Wilma exhibited enormous strength during her recovery and emerged with a newfound sense of calm. Additionally, Wilma learned about the *gadugi*—a remarkable surviving institution of the Cherokee—during her two years with the Cherokee Nation prior to her accident. Her work experience, combined with her personal challenges, led to her future creative work with the communities and her belief in working together for the good of all.

5

Community Building

"Before (Bell, OK) I think that a lot of people thought life just happened to them, and after the project, they began to say, this is my family and this is my community and I am responsible for it."

Wilma Mankiller

Growing stronger each day and eager to help, Wilma returned to work for the Cherokee Nation in January 1981. After the physical and emotional challenges of the past two years, Wilma wanted to work closely with rural communities on self-help projects. Part of that desire arose as she helped create the Cherokee Nation Community Development Department. The new department became necessary so she could apply for and receive federal funding as well as private foundation grants for renewal projects in Cherokee communities. She secured a Health and Human Services (HHS) grant in April 1981 for $1,127,557 to improve the health of the Cherokee residents by building waterlines for running water, refurbishing housing, and building new houses. She procured another grant from HHS in September that year, for $65,000, to promote services among the elderly in the Cherokee Nation. These were substantial grants and Wilma became a highly valued employee for her grant-writing skills.

In October 1981, Chief Swimmer published his annual State of the Nation address in the local newspaper. He spoke of the present and future of the Cherokee Nation and specifically outlined all the progress made over the past two years. Speaking on the collaboration with the BIA Social

Services Department to implement the P.L. 638 contracting to tribes, he specifically singled out Wilma for her hard work. "I can't name them all, but in the planning area of the Cherokee Nation, people like Wilma Mankiller, that has really done a lot to help put this together" (*Cherokee Phoenix and Indian Advocate*, 1981b).

A 1982 study of poverty levels in four eastern-Oklahoma counties— Adair, Delaware, Mayes, and Cherokee—declared Adair and Delaware counties as the poorest in the state, with Tahlequah and Pryor as the two largest towns in the Cherokee Nation and the rest of the counties being rural. Cherokees comprised just over 20 percent of the population in eastern Oklahoma. While Wilma was in California for 20 years, two things that had not changed were the lack of running water in the mostly full-blood rural communities and the high level of poverty.

A power struggle arose within the Eastern Oklahoma Development District (EODD) over special interests within the 34-member board from Muskogee, Cherokee, Adair, McIntosh, Okmulgee, and Wagoner counties. Deputy Chief Perry Wheeler, a former funeral director and mayor of Stilwell from Sallisaw, and a member since the EODD's formation 15 years ago, stated that the differing opinions in development priorities could result in the loss of federal money to those counties. Deputy Chief Jackson, who had served as chairman of the board of the EODD since 1973, opposed the Bell project, which has been explained in the following paragraphs.

A recent grant procured with EODD assistance had financed a water system for 300 rural residents in northeastern Sequoyah County. Wheeler stated, "We have an axe to grind, except for an interest in seeing that the funds go out to the communities where they are needed. We also feel that we can better coordinate what we are doing at the Cherokee Nation, if we are aware of what programs are being implemented in the communities through EODD" (*Cherokee Phoenix and Indian Advocate*, 1981a). Determined to maintain control over the local projects and ensure the utilization of funds, tribal leaders needed cooperation from local residents.

The lack of local services failed to motivate people, and Chief Swimmer said, "We are going to reverse that trend and help people take control of their lives. Instead of being 'service providers,' employees of the Tribe will be 'enablers' who help people who want to change their living conditions make that change." He established a new client center within the Community Development Department and Wilma Mankiller directed the department's early stages of activity. "The community development department is, for me, a dream come true," stated Wilma. "I have long felt that the Cherokee Nation needed to involve itself more in full-blood communities. We are building understanding on both sides by helping the community members develop their organizing skills so they can help themselves" (*Cherokee Phoenix and Indian Advocate*, 1982). The department worked closely with the Institute on Man and Science, a nonprofit organization that helps organize projects in rural Appalachian communities.

Chief Swimmer selected Bell as the first area in which to implement this project. He knew the people there had a strong sense of community, a desire to help their neighbors, and a determination to maintain their traditional values. The Bell project had physical goals of improved housing and freshwater supply for the residents of Bell, Oak Ridge, and Kirk Mountain. Next came the social goals, involving community revitalization and helping one another. The Kerr Foundation provided $37,000 to cover the organizing costs; the Indian Health Service designed the water line and contributed septic tanks and drain fields; a Housing and Urban Development (HUD) community development block grant covered the costs of the materials and renovating the homes; the tribal housing authority paid for the materials to renovate the remaining homes; and the HUD mutual help housing program financed the construction of 25 homes. The people of Bell had to supply the labor. The Bell project was another influential event in Wilma's life, as the success of this project influenced her perspective on community development and tribal politics. Just as importantly, she met her future partner for life, Charlie Soap.

Charlie Lee Soap, a full-blood bilingual Cherokee, worked for the Cherokee Housing Authority. He and Wilma met when she inquired about a housing issue. Born just a few months before Wilma, on March 25, 1945, in Stilwell, Charlie had 10 siblings. Famous among the Oklahoma powwow circuit for his traditional ceremonial Plains-style dancing, Charlie often visited local schools in his maroon-and-white Chevrolet truck, which he had named Montana; dressed in his ceremonial regalia, he entertained the children with his dancing and stories. Above all, he always encouraged the students to continue their education.

Powwow Circuit

The Algonquin word "pau wau" was the Native American word some of the first Europeans associated with dancing. Although, pau wau meant "he dreams" to the Algonquins, the term was eventually accepted by Europeans to refer to dancing, and later began to be spelled "powwow." Having emerged in the 1910s, the powwow circuit is a series of social gatherings among Native Americans who come together for a one-day event or multiday events where they sing, dance, eat, socialize, and celebrate cultural traditions. The events have drum and dance competitions, with cash prizes and colorful tribal regalia. Nonpolitical in nature, they could be public or private and are often multitribal. They can vary in duration from hours to days.

Charlie was raised in a traditional Cherokee language–speaking home in Bell. His family later moved to the Starr community. His father, Walter Soap, once very active in the Keetoowah Society, taught Charlie the value of hard work at a young age, and Charlie often helped the family earn money. Charlie and Wilma became good friends as they worked together for the Cherokee Nation. He told her about his traditional childhood with his parents Walter and Florence and how hard they worked and how they spoke mostly Cherokee and very little English. Being a farmer, blacksmith, and carpenter, Walter, like many men in the area, also worked on the railroad. He learned to make horseshoes, plows, and several other things. Charlie also told Wilma about the traditional tribal value of *gadugi*, which entailed people in the communities—families, kinfolk, neighbors—helping one another. When his parents got older and their health declined, they could no longer work the farm. "We had to move to town, away from the lifestyle we were accustomed to, and everything changed, and we began to drift away from the gadugi way of life" (Soap 2002, 64). They no longer attended stomp dances nor could they interact with other traditional Cherokees in rural communities. They also began attending church in the town of Starr.

Charlie was a deeply spiritual man. He thought people should abide by what the elders always say about knowing who you are, knowing the ways of your people, and especially knowing your Creator. "One of the most important things is to know your Creator and reach out to the Spirit World" (Soap 2002, 65). While earning a degree at Northeastern State University in Tahlequah, Charlie also excelled as an athlete. He served for four years in the Navy, from 1965 to 1969. Twice divorced, Charlie was married to his third wife when he met Wilma in 1977. After Wilma began working for the Cherokee Nation, Chief Swimmer assigned Charlie to work with her on the Bell project as a coorganizer. His fluency in the Cherokee language helped in communicating with the Cherokee-language speakers in the more traditional areas and especially in the community of Bell, where Charlie grew up.

Wilma and Charlie went door-to-door conducting surveys in these communities, asking people about their housing and water needs. Next, the communities elected representatives from each neighborhood to serve in the Bell Water and Housing Committee, and then they began work. Besides the residents working, the younger people of the communities volunteered to provide their labor to the elderly members of the neighborhoods. Charlie and his older brother, Johnson, held community meetings in the Cherokee language to ensure everyone understood what was happening (*Cherokee Phoenix and Indian Advocate*, 1982). Wilma shared responsibilities with Bill Reid, an experienced sanitation engineer with the

Indian Health Service. Bill handled the daily crews while Wilma used her talents to search for funding and motivate people.

Wilma procured another HUD community development block grant of $650,000 for the Cave Springs-Bunch-Henderson communities' waterline in Adair and Sequoyah counties. That waterline was 34 miles long and supplied to 210 families. The Kenwood community in Delaware County also rehabilitated 25 homes with the grant money." A new vitality existed as residents increased activities for the elderly and worked together to create a volunteer fire department and remodel their community building.

An economically poor community comprising 95 percent Cherokees and Cherokee-language speakers, with a great need for water and housing improvements, Bell had a population of around 300 people in the early 1980s. When Chief Swimmer and Wilma began considering the Bell community for the first development project, Wilma received two warnings: the people would never consider doing the work, much less volunteer, and Wilma would need to leave Bell before sundown or she could face violence. Generations of broken promises had led to skepticism in Bell about outside help, especially from a tribal council that had previously ignored their needs for decades.

Before HUD provided funding for home improvements, a waterline was necessary to move the current status of the homes to standard level. Wilma and Charlie traveled to Bell intending to ask the residents of the community what they would like to see as an improvement in their lives. At first, it was no small feat to gather a group together. Wilma and Charlie posted notices in Cherokee and English asking the community to come and discuss what they would like Bell to be like in 10 years. As they held their first community meeting, only Charlie's brother Johnson showed up. It took three additional attempts at organizing a community meeting to collect a dozen people curious enough about what the two from the "nation" wanted with them. Then, they began telling Wilma they wanted a water connection in every house and indoor plumbing. So Wilma made a bargain with the community of Bell: if they did the work, she would get the supplies and tribal support.

Those involved in the project recruited local volunteers and constructed a 16-mile waterline for the Bell residents. Wilma claimed this was a "shining example of community self-help at its very best. The local residents were able to build on our Cherokee gadugi tradition of a physical sharing of tasks and working collectively, at the same time restoring confidence in their own ability to solve problems" (Mankiller 1993, 234). In Bell, while other people, especially in the tribal government, saw the dilapidated housing, the lack of indoor plumbing, and the settling of disputes with violence, Wilma and Charlie saw something else. They saw people who still helped one another. They saw people who hunted and fished and took what they caught or captured and gave it to older people in need. They saw people cut wood and deliver it to older people in the winter. They saw people come together and help one another. They saw something those from outside the community did not see—the sense of reciprocity and interdependence that Wilma had known as a child in her community of Rocky Mountain. The residents still fought when a dispute arose, but they also helped each other, showing that the traditional tribal value of *gadugi* still existed.

The group of volunteers named themselves the Bell Water and Housing Project, and the work began under the local leadership of Thomas and Sue Muskrat. Wilma and Charlie assigned each family a two-mile section, and when they completed that section, another family tackled the next two-mile section. Jim Coffman, who directed the Cherokee Water District, attended one of the community meetings and trained people on how to put the pipe together and put it in a ditch. Johnson Soap had some experience with working on waterlines. and he volunteered throughout the project. Shorty McChristian, a neighboring white man who operated the backhoe, always volunteered to repair the machines whenever one of them broke down due to their dilapidated state. Some people in the community remained skeptical of tribal leaders and on learning they had to register with the Cherokee Nation to get the waterline, many were hesitant. It became an issue of being able to trust what Wilma and Charlie told them. Many of the traditional Cherokees still had fresh memories of the allotment days and did not rush to sign anything associated with the government.

Local CBS-affiliated news stations visited the Bell work sites a few times over the next 14 months to report on the progress. These visits created excitement among the local residents as they saw themselves on the nightly news and felt less isolated. The national television program *CBS Sunday Morning with Charles Kuralt* documented the success of the Bell project, and it is referred to with great pride locally as the "town film." A great source of pride for Wilma was observing her fellow Cherokees revitalized once more. She knew the project would be successfully completed when families began competing with one another over who could complete their two-mile section the fastest.

Wilma had started working for the Cherokee Nation in 1977 with absolute faith that the Cherokee people could do things for themselves. She had faith in the *gadugi* concept. They elected their own local leadership, and they rose to the occasion. Once the housing in Bell had been renovated, the members of the steering committee involved in the waterline project managed a senior citizen education project, an annual fundraising powwow, and a bilingual education program to help preserve the Cherokee language and culture ("Leaders as Guides of Return: Wilma Mankiller," 2010).

The men and women of the Bell community also rehabilitated 20 homes and built 25 additional energy-efficient homes in coordination with the Cherokee Housing Authority. Wilma later said, "It was a community few people believed in and most people's attitude at that time was, well most of those people are living on welfare, they're sure not going to get out and work as volunteers" (Steinem 2015, 228). Wilma and Charlie knew the only place nearby where the Bell residents could work was a chicken factory across the state line in Arkansas, so they did not have many options in terms of places to work for wages. On July 4, 1984, the HUD department awarded the tribe the National Merit Award for the self-help waterline and housing rehabilitation in Bell, which served as a major model for other tribal projects throughout Indian Country (*Cherokee Phoenix and Indian Advocate*, 1985a).

A new spirit of *gadugi* emerged among the residents after the self-help projects. After the completion of the Bell project, the communities of Burnt Cabin, Wild Horse, and Briggs began work on their own projects with the help of community development block grant monies and Wilma's grant-writing skills. Originally part of the War on Poverty programs under the Johnson administration, the community development grants allow rural and low-income community development to improve the quality of their lives through local programs in health, education, and housing. As part of the HUD department, tribes became eligible to participate after the passage of the Indian Self-Determination and Educational Assistance Act.

Other community organizers emerged in Briggs, where Lil Perry over-saw construction of a 29-mile waterline across rough terrain and at a total cost of $561,159, with the monies coming from HUD and IHS grants. Briggs, four miles east of Tahlequah, developed a new spirit of community building. According to Perry, "The friendship and cooperation developed among the residents during the work on this project is pumping new life into the community. Working together on the waterline has made them realize they can do other worthwhile things together" (*Cherokee Phoenix and Indian Advocate*, 1985a). The Briggs community waterline project began in March 1984 and was completed in summer 1987. As Wilma and Charlie continued working together on these waterline projects, they connected on a more personal level.

The relationship between Wilma and Charlie did not become romantic until the completion of the Bell project in 1984. On their first date, Charlie picked Wilma up in his truck, Montana, and they drove into Tulsa, about 50 miles to the west. They watched the Sylvester Stallone movie *Rambo* and then ate Coney Island hot dogs. On the drive back to Mankiller Flats, Charlie commented positively on the movie and the good hot dogs. Wilma replied that she did not care for either. Still, she did like Charlie and came to discover him as the most secure man she ever knew. Comfortable with himself and in being with Wilma, Charlie asked her out again. Wilma later recalled this period of her life, in the early 1980s, as comforting to her soul.

The pair's next community development project became the Kenwood community, another traditional Cherokee area. Seven hundred community members lived in rural west-central Delaware County, mostly full-blood Cherokee-language speakers. The Kenwood community incorporated and elected a water board to update and run the water system. The Cherokee Nation hired community organizer Johnny Backwater, who was also the fire chief. With Wilma's grant-writing assistance, the community received an award of $100,000 from the HUD department to rehabilitate 20 homes (*Cherokee Phoenix and Indian Advocate*, 1985e).

Efforts to improve communities did not end there. Beginning in 1976, the Cherokee Nation invested $4.2 million in community infrastructure such as waterlines and parks and on home rehabilitation and business development projects. Funding came mainly from community development block grants in competitive department of HUD programs and mainly because of Wilma. Of the $2 million allocated regionally, the Cherokee Nation received a grant of $475,000 to remodel homes near the Henderson and Cave Springs waterline. Cherokees received funding in all four areas—facilities (roads and water), community centers and health clinics, home rehabilitation, and economic development—with the tribes' own community development programs. Wilma was the first to introduce the concept of using self-help on block grant projects. She had written the Bell proposal to build a waterline using only volunteer labor.

Cherokee Nation Industries, Inc. (CNI), as the third largest employer in Adair County, had 120 employees with 80 percent of them being Cherokees. Gary Chapman, chairman of the CNI board of directors stated, "At a time when a lot of industries are failing, we have a successful, growing business. Part of the reason for that is the company's management: they stay on top of economic and industry conditions and are willing to seek other markets when their bread and butter business falls off." Radio Corporation of America, RCA, moved production of the wire harnesses to Mexico and Taiwan and CNI began producing military electronics, subcontracting from the Vought Corporation. CNI expanded from assembling one wire harness to producing 42 separate parts for the multiple launch rocket system. Also, CNI negotiated contracts with the Brunswick Corporation to make additional wire harnesses and the FMC Corporation to make electronic assemblies, printed circuit broad illuminators for urban buses (*Cherokee Phoenix and Indian Advocate*, 1982).

Wilma emerged from these projects with a reputation as a person active in the communities and capable of completing projects. Seeing the progress of the Bell project, Chief Swimmer asked Wilma to run for the office of deputy chief in 1983. Swimmer asked her to join his campaign because of her dedication to the tribe and the fact that she could be trusted with money. At first, Wilma declined to run for tribal office. Then one day, she saw a family living in a car and another living in a bus. They had been there so long they had even erected a clothesline. Seeing those situations changed her mind. She knew the dire need for housing improvements in the rural communities and felt sure she could do more as deputy chief. She thought of the poor housing, high medical costs, and educational needs and decided she may be able to create positive change working within the tribal government system. Wilma's motivation overcame her own reticence at getting involved in tribal politics, which could be brutal. She knew she had the fortitude and thick skin to be able to withstand the long bureaucracy-filled days. Wilma reshaped the role of a politician in the tribal government because of her experience in creating programs.

Wilma knew that candidates held political rallies, so she placed an announcement for a rally on the local radio station, had the event catered, and held a reception at a historical house in Tahlequah. "So, I go on the evening of the event and I'm prepared to answer questions from tribal members and the whole evening only five people showed up, and I think three of them were my relatives" (Mankiller, Keynote Address 2002 at the University of Utah Women's Week, 2002). Her friend from Alcatraz, Grace Thorpe, also came to lend her support for her old activist friend. Wilma recalled, "I think it was really clear to me then that things could only go up from that point forward" (Mankiller, Keynote Address 2002 at the University of Utah Women's Week, 2002). Wilma was always optimistic.

During the 1983 campaign, after Wilma realized CNI board chairman Gary Chapman had begun actively working against her, she enlisted volunteer help from her mother, her daughters, and her brothers and sisters. Agnes Cowan, the first female tribal council member, and J. B. Dreadfulwater, a popular local gospel singer, became Wilma's two greatest challengers. They both criticized her lack of tribal government leadership but ignored her years of experience as a community organizer in California. A tireless campaigner, Wilma traveled throughout the 14-county area, going door-to-door campaigning in Cherokee communities against Cowan and Dreadfulwater. Wilma barely defeated Dreadfulwater and, ultimately, Cowan to emerge victorious after a run-off election. The community development work Wilma and Charlie had conducted in Bell aided in her campaign work. Many rural Cherokees, older Cherokees, and some who supported Chief Swimmer helped decide the election in her favor. "In a way, my 1983 election was a step into tribal tradition as well as a step forward for women," Mankiller said (Conley 2005, 221).

Throughout the campaign, she stayed focused on the issues instead of whether women should be in leadership. She described herself as an extreme liberal Democrat. She also thought her liberal activist background might be her greatest hurdle to overcome around the Cherokee Nation, but the fact was that her female gender became her biggest challenge. All 15 tribal council members opposed her running for deputy chief because she was a woman and a Democrat. Many people did not care for the way she dressed, often in jeans and cowboy boots. They also opposed her because she lacked previous tribal council experience. Some opposed her because she had only minimal experience in Cherokee governance and due to the fact that she had lived away from the communities and the Cherokee Nation for 20 years. Seven women ran for the tribal council that year and the three who won included Barbara Starr Scott, Wathene Young, and Patsy Morton. Both Scott and Young opposed Wilma and never became supportive of Wilma's political career.

When she first decided to run in the 1983 election, Wilma expected people to challenge her due to her previous activist background or because she was always going around talking about grassroots democracy. When she and Charlie began the waterline projects and began organizing the rural communities, Wilma assumed people in the towns would challenge her ideas. Describing that election as the most hurtful experience she had ever been through, she said, "I decided to simply ignore it and continue on, and I thought that the idea that gender had anything to do with leadership, or that leadership had anything to do with gender was foolish, and I could see no point in even beginning to try to debate that non-issue with anybody, so I just continued on" (Mankiller, Keynote Address 2002 at the University of Utah Women's Week, 2002).

On August 14, 1983, Wilma became deputy chief. The newly elected tribal council proved most difficult to work with, as many of them had opposed her election and remained openly hostile to her in tribal council sessions. Wilma's additional duties included supervising the daily operations of over 40 tribally operated programs in housing, education, and health care. Chief Swimmer being a Republican banker with ultraconservative viewpoints and Wilma being a Democratic Liberal, social worker, and community planner who had previously worked for Indian and treaty rights, they made an interesting team. A primary focus for Chief Swimmer and Deputy Chief Mankiller was creating an environment for the full-bloods and mixed-bloods in Cherokee communities to live together in peace. Deep divisions existed among communities and families because of the economic and community development issues.

The sexism Wilma experienced early in her political career came from a minority of people seeking to discredit her. People told Chief Swimmer of the political suicide he committed by endorsing a woman for election, but once they got used to her and realized her competence, most of them desisted from sexist behavior. Perhaps some people understood that the times were changing for women in leadership positions. After all, President Reagan appointed Sandra Day O'Connor to be the first female Supreme Court judge during his administration. Geraldine Ferraro became the Democratic vice-presidential nominee in 1984. These were good actions for the nation and for all women in America, but it did not mean rural communities were ready for female leaders.

The Cherokee Nation rarely received any good news from the federal government, but it did in February 1984. The U.S. government conceded that $2.5 million was owed to the Cherokee Nation for nearly 815 acres of tribal lands transferred to railroad companies in 1866 and later sold to the cities that sprung up around the station grounds. The tribal council approved the settlement on February 11, 1985. On March 3, 1984, Chief Swimmer and Deputy Chief Wilma broke ground in Briggs with a number of water board members and continued blasting through rocks for the 22-mile waterline project. On March 10, the tribal council approved a $650,000 waterline for the Cave Springs-Henderson area.

Chief Swimmer met in April 1984 with Secretary of the Interior William Clark and explored contracting remaining BIA functions. The Cherokee Nation had not solely managed tribal affairs since pre-Oklahoma statehood. At the time, the Cherokee Nation handled 90 percent of the services formerly implemented by the BIA for $4.5 million, including tribal development and training, adult education, employment assistance, adult vocational training, registration, communications, fiscal management, tribal services, and tribal economic development.

Also, more recently, the tribe had begun directing Johnson O'Malley educational programs, natural resource development, and Indian child welfare programs. Only 10 percent of tribal funds remained under BIA control—including credit and finance controls, all land-related programs, and the Sequoyah High School Indian boarding school—amounting to a budget of $23 million. Thinking they would surely become unemployed, many BIA workers opposed tribal contracting. However, as the Cherokee Boys Club demonstrated among the Eastern Band of Cherokees, good government employees were hired by the tribe to continue employment. If money was saved from BIA services contracted, the surplus funds were reallocated to begin or improve other programs (*Cherokee Phoenix and Indian Advocate*, 1984f).

The historic first joint tribal council meeting between the Cherokee Nation and the Eastern Band of Cherokee Indians took place in April 1984 at Red Clay, Tennessee. As a symbol of unity and cooperation among the Cherokee people, both tribes created a base from which to work together on problems and issues. In 1838, the federal Indian policy of Removal had destroyed the Cherokee Nation. At the time, the elders had stated, "In seven generations, the Cherokee will rise again." Seven generations later, the Cherokee Council East and West reunited in 1984 and Wilma was in attendance at the historic occasion.

Wilma was a shell shaker for her clan, the Wolf Clan, and stated that the Cherokee survived because they kept dancing. They held the center and maintained connection. Dr. Tom Holm, American Indian studies instructor at the University of Arizona, says the Sun Dance, the Green Corn Dance, and the stomp dances of the Creeks, Cherokees, and Seminoles "reaffirm group cohesion, reassert the individual participant's value in the community, and attest to the tribal obligation to the Creator" (*Cherokee Phoenix and Indian Advocate*, 1985b). The Cherokee Nation was beginning to rise again and the stomp dances and traditional institution of the *gadugi* crews still existed.

Deputy Chief Wilma traveled to the traditional lands of the Cherokee Nation in eastern Tennessee, joined by Chief Swimmer and other delegates from eastern Oklahoma. The occasion brought thousands of Cherokee descendants to the reunion. This meeting served as a time for the tribal leaders to learn from one another those aspects of their tribal programs and businesses that worked effectively and those that needed improvement. The council meeting continued annually after that first year, alternating between sites in eastern Oklahoma and western North Carolina, the site of the Eastern Band reservation lands.

No one expected the nearly 20,000 people who came to the council meeting that spring in 1984. Many were Cherokee and Cherokee descendants, many were not. Cherokee writer Marilou Awiakta described the atmosphere at the event: "The most striking image is the ceaseless current of men, women, and children, moving peaceably among the knolls, over the meadow. The Cherokee set the tone for the crowd. Though visually they often may be distinguished only by a deeper tint of skin or hair, a bit of beaded jewelry, an occasional ribbon shirt or dress, they are still, as an observer of the 1837 council described them, 'the decorous Cherokee,' and they behave in keeping with the dignity of the occasion" (Awiakta 1993, 102).

Chief Robert Youngdeer, representing the Eastern Band of Cherokee Indians, was the great-grandson of a Cherokee man who had abandoned the Removal march at the Mississippi River and made his way back to the southern Appalachian Mountains to live there. A decade later, the historic tribal council meeting provided a remembrance that "for more than a century the federal government subjected the Cherokee to a killing winter; divided the nation; forbade the teaching of language and culture; imposed the Dawes Act of 1890, which linked blood quantum to entitlement to land and federal services and which had the avowed purpose of fomenting selfishness, which is at the bottom of civilization" (Awiakta 1993, 105). "Blood, however, flowed east and west and also into remote coves and valleys in between, secluding itself in the genes of families (some of whom have married outside the tribe and back since 1540) and biding its time" (Awiakta 1993, 105). This historic Red Clay meeting gave rise to a new pride in Cherokee identity not seen in the southeast since the time of Removal. Back home in Tahlequah, in an additional Cherokee Nation tribal council meeting the following week, the council introduced a proposal making the Cherokee Nation a "model tribe," a term drawn up by U.S. Secretary of the Interior William Clark.

One of the biggest issues Wilma dealt with as deputy chief and then as chief was the Arkansas Riverbed case. In July 1984, the Cherokee Nation won the first round in court for the U.S. government to repay the tribe for the extraction of sand, gravel, and coal from the Arkansas Riverbed, a 96-mile stretch owned by the Cherokee Nation. A June 8 ruling declared the government must pay damages to the tribe for mineral extracted, for lost interest income, and for a hydroelectric plant constructed without tribal consent.

Chief Swimmer, serving as cochairman of the Presidential Commission on Indian Reservation Economies (PCIRE), released a report at the end of 1984 concluding that there were two major obstacles to Indian economic development. First, there were too few Indian entrepreneurs and they lacked experience in creating and operating businesses. Second, tribal staff lacked an understanding of business principles. President Ronald Reagan created the PCIRE to determine ways to eliminate the experience and knowledge barriers. Comprising a nine-member task force, the PCIRE tribal and business leaders focused on lessening tribal dependency on the federal government in tribal affairs. The Indian Tax Status Act was renewed and worked with the Department of Defense (DoD) to strengthen "Buy Indian" language in DoD appropriations bills. Over nine years of Swimmer's tenure as principal chief, collective tribal assets grew from $6 million to $28 million (*Cherokee Phoenix and Indian Advocate*, 1984a). The tribe continued growing at a phenomenal rate.

Under the Swimmer and Wilma administration, CNI's annual sales increased to $8.7 million with an annual payroll of more than $3 million. Cary Wyatt, president and CEO of CNI, stated that success was far above national averages in the electronics industry with profits having increased by 111 percent for 1983. CNI employed 270 people in 1984, creating major electronics assemblies for army and navy defense suppliers, Vought, FMC, and Texas Instruments (*Cherokee Phoenix and Indian Advocate*, 1984a).

To be effective in all aspects of her new position as deputy chief, Wilma quickly learned about all the people and all the issues of the tribal businesses and the edicts arising from Washington, D.C. Her two years as deputy chief challenged Wilma as she continued her community development work. "Her measured criticism and calm demeanor made her welcome among national politicians" (Awiakta 1993, 218). Her time as deputy chief was tough because of the many tribal council members who opposed her. Among her first actions were plans to improve tribal services in housing and health care. The tribal council opposed the request so Wilma began a series of columns in regional newspapers explaining the tribal services and her goals.

During the Cherokee National Holiday in September 1984, Chief Swimmer spoke on the advances of the communities over the past several years. "It takes all of us working together, mixed-bloods and full-bloods, the elderly and the young, the communities, the employees of the tribe and its supporters. If we are going to break the dependency on the BIA and the federal government, it takes all of us working together" (*Cherokee Phoenix and Indian Advocate*, 1984b). Joined by Deputy Chief Wilma and Crosslin Smith, tribal cultural advisor and descendant of the Original Keetoowah Society leaders, Chief Swimmer stressed that the heartbeat of the nation lay within the communities. Crosslin Smith was also a traditional practitioner and available weekly at both Claremore and Tahlequah Indian hospitals to see patients.

By 1985, Wilma was on the board of directors for the Women of Indian Nations, a political action committee, and she represented the tribe in the National Tribal Chairmen's Association. She was also a member of the Native American Indian Women's Association and the National Organization of Native American Women. She was also a founding member for the Seventh Generation Fund and a task force member for Save the Children, Inc. Wilma also served on the board of trustees for Bacone College in Muskogee and served on the Bill Willis Skills Center administrative advisory committee. The Bacone College board of trustees consisted of 30 elected members, including approximately 10 American Baptists, 10 American Indians, and 10 representatives from Oklahoma. Finally, she was a member of the board for directors for the Oklahoma Academy for State Goals. Wilma believed the state must investigate its tax structure to understand why other states were attracting industry on a much wider scale that Oklahoma. "The immediate goal of the organization is to gather accurate information independent of state government and use that information to influence the elected leadership" (*Cherokee Advocate*, 1985).

By 1985, almost all the Cherokee Nation community development projects involved volunteer labor. Deputy Chief Wilma stated that the HUD department appeared receptive to trying alternative ways of doing projects. Seeking additional grants from private foundations, Wilma organized the Bell Community and received a $500,000 HUD grant. After that, three other waterline projects installed a 33-mile waterline in Adair County. Julie Moss, tribal grant specialist involved in grants of $2.3 million for Cherokee Nation, explained the process: "Community expressed need for water, housing, roads and Charlie Soap, Community Development Director, organizes the community into a committee who later organizes local residents into work parties" (*Cherokee Phoenix and Indian Advocate*, 1985a). Wilma's theory on economic development projects included many omitted social aspects of a community and she stressed that Community Development Block Grant (CDBG) money be used for economic development using the approach of self-help (*Cherokee Phoenix and Indian Advocate*, 1985a).

Five Cherokee full-blood communities gathered from January 14 to 17, 1985, to share community development lessons learned from the recent self-help projects each completed. Leaders participated from Kenwood (Delaware County), Bell (Adair County), the Henderson-Cave Springs area (Sequoyah/Adair County), Burnt Cabin (Cherokee County), and Briggs (Cherokee County). The Cherokee Nation sponsored the workshop at the Tsa-La-Gi Lodge in Tahlequah. With the goal of revitalizing caring communities within the Cherokee Nation, community and church leaders asked residents from the five communities to identify a collective vision for the tribe. Wilma stated, "There is a definite need for community leaders to develop more of a sense of independence from the Cherokee Nation community development staff. They are independent at this point but this workshop should nurture that sense of independence and move it along even further" (*Cherokee Advocate*, 1985).

By this point, Kenwood had remodeled 20 dilapidated homes, volunteers in Bell had completed a 17-mile waterline, Briggs was halfway done with its 22-mile waterline, and the Burnt Cabin community had completed a five-mile waterline and a water treatment plant. Plans were also made to take self-help to the Henderson-Cave Springs communities and complete a 33-mile waterline project. The objectives for this workshop included having each community's leader focus on the strengths and relevance of the Cherokee culture and its impact on their work, developing leadership at the community level, and teaching participants to conduct similar workshops in their communities (*Cherokee Advocate*, 1985).

In February 1985, the tribal council established a commission to oversee and supervise the codification of general Cherokee laws into a set of tribal statutes, much like federal and state laws. Lance Hughes, the tribe's data specialist, was in charge of the project. Once it was completed, it made the Cherokee Nation the first tribe in the United States to have its own set of codified laws (*Cherokee Advocate*, 1985). Cherokee Nation received more national attention for its tribal programs. In February 1985, an NBC news team visited Cherokee Nation and videotaped segments portraying economic development projects that ensured a tribal income for future generations. The news crew visited the Cherokee Nation Industries, Inc. in Stilwell, the Kenwood Ranch, and the Lodge of the Cherokees in Tahlequah; they interviewed Chief Swimmer and Bob Hathaway, the general manager of the Cherokee Gardens nursery business. Mike Jensen, NBC financial correspondent, reported on *The Today Show* on April 12, 1985, that "the old stereotypes of Indians 'sitting around' and being lazy has been broken by the Cherokee Nation" (*Cherokee Phoenix and Indian Advocate*, 1985f).

Wilma organized the joint tribal council meeting held in Tahlequah in June 1985. With the theme of "United We Stand," Wilma stated that Red Clay marked the beginning and "now we're picking up where we left off last year by making sure the lines of communication stay open." Adding to that, Wilma said, "In some ways the Tahlequah meeting adds to the importance of Red Clay. The seeds sown in Tennessee last April have sprouted and we'll be reaping the fruits here in June and for years to come" (*Cherokee Phoenix and Indian Advocate*, 1984c).

Chief Swimmer's Annual State of the Nation Address in the summer of 1985 related the theme, "The Present and Future of the Cherokee Nation." The Cherokee Nation, along with the Indian Health Service and the BIA, was the largest employer in eastern Oklahoma. With a payroll of over $14 million a year, for the first time since statehood, Cherokees had educational and employment opportunities that were previously not available. The Cherokee Nation Industries, Inc. employed 200 people with over $4 million a year in sales. The Cherokee Housing Authority created over 500 new housing units becoming the largest Indian Housing Authority in the United States, with 3,000 units under management. Since passage of the Indian Self-Determination and Educational Assistance Act (ISDEA), or P.L. 638, tribes largely operated their own programs by contracting services from the BIA. Before the ISDEA, the Cherokee Nation operated 40 separate programs, and since passing the law, the BIA and the federal government allowed control and provided aid to make it more self-sufficient. When Swimmer spoke of his work with the BIA he named Wilma Mankiller for also doing a lot of work to put things together (*Cherokee Phoenix and Indian Advocate*, 1981b).

In addition to learning about the tribal businesses and federal Indian policy for contracting tribal programs previously operated by the BIA, Wilma also gained a quick education in Cherokee identity and tribal membership. The Cherokee Freedmen controversy erupted during Wilma's tenure as deputy chief. Some Cherokees within the Southeast owned slaves and during the Removal period, these slaves traveled with the tribe to their new homes in Indian Territory. The slaves often spoke Cherokee and practiced Cherokee tribal traditions. The controversy that erupted during the 1990s was about their rightful place within the tribe. Wilma remarked that the descendants of former Cherokee slaves "should not be given membership in the Cherokee tribe. That is for people with Cherokee blood" (Sturm

2002, 179). Others were of the opinion that if someone is culturally Cherokee, then they are Cherokee, so this issue became a point of contention for
her. In March 2006, the Cherokee Supreme Court ruled that the Freedmen
descendants were entitled to enroll in the Cherokee Nation.

The next joint tribal council meeting between the Cherokee Nation and
the Eastern Band of Cherokee Indians occurred from June 27 to 29, 1985,
near Tahlequah, marking the first meeting west of the Mississippi River.
Chief Robert Youngdeer and Chief Ross Swimmer both agreed to develop
culturally sensitive curricula to improve tribal learning. As part of a resolution for educational committees to make long-range plans, the chiefs
approved a resolution protesting any attempt by the BIA to prohibit
Cherokee-language training. They also requested that the national Job
Corps office amend their policy to allow recruitment of students from
North Carolina to the Talking Leaves Job Corps Center in eastern Oklahoma. This program, one of only two in the country operated by Indians,
allowed students to earn a high school diploma and learn a vocational skill
(*Cherokee Advocate*, 1985).

The joint tribal council approved a committee to exchange business
information between the two tribes and supported continued funding of
Community Development Block Grants and Small Business Administration programs. Each tribal council also expressed appreciation for the University of Arkansas for giving in-state tuition to several tribes once
inhabiting the state of Oklahoma, east and west included. The joint tribal
council additionally recognized Billy Walkabout, a Western Cherokee who
was among the most highly decorated Vietnam Veterans and received the
Congressional Medal of Honor. The council also adopted Col. James F.
Corn as an honorary member of both tribes and gave him the name
Waguli, meaning Whip-poor-will. Corn purchased the land in Red Clay,
Tennessee, for the Cherokees; it was where the tribe had held its last meeting before the Trail of Tears in 1838 (*Cherokee Phoenix and Indian Advocate*, 1985b). "In 1929 Colonel James F. Corn of Cleveland saved Red Clay
from becoming a factory site by buying the land and giving it to the state"
(Awiakta 1993, 110). These joint tribal council meetings intended to "build
one fire," or put away differences, come together as a people, and work for
the common good of the Cherokee people. As Wilma took part in these
joint tribal council meetings, she continued to learn about what worked
and what did not for both of the tribes, east and west.

At an education conference in the summer of 1985, Wilma said, "The
spoken Cherokee language is not an anachronism. It is not relegated to the
distant past. It is a vibrant part of everyday Cherokee life, particularly in
rural areas. The written language, however, is not in widespread use and
needs considerable attention to be revitalized. It pleases me greatly that
the Cherokee Nation Education Department is beginning to take an active

role in the revitalization of Cherokee literacy. The retention and growth of Cherokee literacy is crucial to the cultural survival of the Cherokee people" (*Cherokee Advocate*, 1985). The American Indian Movement placed great importance on revitalizing the Native languages, and these actions within the Cherokee Nation made Wilma proud.

The National Congress of American Indians, with approximately 100 member tribes, met in Tulsa in October 1985 to elect new officers and discuss economic and sociopolitical issues affecting member tribes. Wilma urged member nations, "As federal dollars diminish, don't rush into things, don't panic." Because all the tribes were so different there was no national solution to the problem of federal budget cuts to Indian programs during the Reagan administration. "If there is a solution it has to come from within our tribe. Tribes must sit down and define economic development because every tribe is very, very different." She recommended that economic development be appropriate since community and members would better support a business they liked. She also added that more economic development could come from Indian individuals rather than from big businesses. Also, she urged Indian organizations to showcase successful tribal businesses so other tribes could learn what it took to be successful. Finally, she stated, "We have to think of things that are indigenous, things that we are already doing for economic development" (*Cherokee Phoenix and Indian Advocate*, 1985a).

Wilma's new political career took up most of her time. While at home, she lived simply with three dogs and lots of books on economics, literature, and philosophy. Her house was just down the road from her mom's house. Felicia and Gina had moved out by this point and begun their own lives. Both had graduated from high school, enjoyed hanging out with their friends, and had steady boyfriends. Wilma and Charlie continued working with other communities on waterline projects. The largest of the five waterline projects extended 33 miles, with over 200 families volunteering thousands of hours. This project ran through the rugged hills of four rural southeast Adair County communities in Cave Springs, Henderson, Bunch, and Marble City, providing running water to 204 families. The ground breaking ceremony for this multicommunity waterline project took place at the Cave Springs School on August 8, 1985. The $1.2 million project also included $475,000 for the rehabilitation of 36 homes for Cherokee families in those communities.

By 1985, the traditional Cherokee people had completed projects in Bell, Burnt Cabin, Wild Horse, Kenwood, and Briggs. Between 1975 and 1985, the Cherokee Nation utilized $4.2 million of CDBG funds to build waterlines, homes, and businesses (*Cherokee Phoenix and Indian Advocate*, 1985e). The success of these community self-help projects reminded

Cherokee communities that they had the power within themselves to shape their own lives and make their own decisions.

Even with the strides women made in the workforce during the late 1970s and early 1980s, the efforts of Conservative homemaker/law student Phyllis Schlafly highjacked the passage of the Equal Rights Amendment, which Wilma wholeheartedly supported. Schlafly created a Conservative newsletter and tirelessly campaigned against the Equal Rights Amendment. Her actions associated with the Supreme Court ruling legalizing abortion in *Roe v. Wade* garnered the support of Conservative women across the country. On June 30, 1982, three states failed to provide the ratification necessary for passage of the ERA. In March 1983, nearly one-fourth of all Native households, including Wilma's, were led by single mothers, which was more than twice the national average. As times changed, Deputy Chief Wilma had her work cut out for her.

6

Chief Wilma, First Term

Wilma experienced a big shock in December 1985, when Chief Swimmer announced that he had accepted President Ronald Reagan's nomination of him as the new assistant secretary of the interior for the Department of the Bureau of Indian Affairs in Washington. By proclamation of the new Cherokee constitution of 1976, the deputy chief automatically replaced the resigning chief. So, on December 5, 1985, Wilma became the principal chief of the Cherokee Nation. She was 40 years old, and with the birth of Felicia's first child, Aaron Swake, a new grandmother. This was an exciting time for Wilma, her family, and the Cherokee Nation.

The inaugural ceremony for principal chief took place on December 5, 1985, in the tribal council chambers in front of two large poinsettias. Wilma wore a black suit as she placed her left hand on a Bible and took the oath of office. Wilma reminded the tribal members in attendance that in traditional Iroquois society, from which the Cherokees descended, leaders considered the past seven generations and the future seven generations when making major decisions. She declared economic growth as the primary goal of her administration. Hoping to eliminate fears over her gender, Wilma explained to her audience that the Cherokee people she spoke with worried more about jobs and education than whether or not a woman should be chief (Reinhold 1985).

Wilma's 1985 inaugural address also stressed how the current Cherokee Nation programs worked effectively and how she planned to continue on that path. Her belief in a separation of powers between the executive branch and the tribal council illustrated one of the greatest changes from the way the tribal businesses previously operated. Wilma described her guiding principle as bubble-up economics, in which the people of the communities served as the planners and implementers of the projects they selected as most beneficial to their specific communities.

Knowing President Reagan planned to implement more budget cuts to Indian programs, Wilma realized that Cherokee Nation tribal leaders had to respond with the most logical way of developing the economy. "I think we can better meet those challenges if the Office of the Chief, if the tribal council, if the employees and the Cherokee people themselves, all join hands and work together" (*Cherokee Phoenix and Indian Advocate*, 1986b). Wilma had a formidable challenge ahead of her as she inherited Swimmer's staff, many of whom had not supported her. It was another delicate balancing act between herself and the 67,000 registered tribal members of the Cherokee Nation, as she settled into her new position, due to those who did not support her or think a woman should hold the high office of chief.

Just 29 days after taking office, Wilma met a great environmental challenge that was to last for the next 36 years. On January 4, 1986, the Sequoyah Fuels plant in Gore, Oklahoma, experienced a major accident. Sequoyah Fuels Corporation, a subsidiary of the Kerr-McGee Corporation of Oklahoma City, came to the Cherokee Nation under the Keeler administration and began processing uranium. The construction of the plant began in 1968, and it became operational in 1970, converting yellowcake uranium into uranium hexafluoride. Uranium Hexaflouride (UF_6) is a compound used for the enrichment of uranium to produce fuel for nuclear reactors and nuclear weapons. In 1986, Sequoyah Fuels had 17 percent of the world's uranium hexafluoride production capacity. Its customers shipped natural uranium yellowcake to the Sequoyah facility so it could be processed into uranium hexafluoride.

The explosion at the facility killed 26-year-old James Harrison. The accident involved a ruptured overfilled cylinder containing 29,500 pounds of gaseous uranium hexafluoride. Of the 42 workers, 37 were hospitalized, and 21 people were from the Gore area, where the factory stood on 75 acres near the confluence of the Illinois and Arkansas rivers. Sequoyah Fuels president Reau Graves Jr. claimed the uranium had been contained within the plant site and thus posed no danger in terms of contaminating the water used for farming or drinking. In contrast, the Nuclear Regulatory Commission (NRC) investigators reported that uranium had seeped into the ground of the Gore facility. Sequoyah Fuels officials later claimed that 21,000 pounds of uranium existed in the soil. The plant was the largest employer and biggest taxpayer in Sequoyah County, and its management held a strong position with regard to keeping the plant open to avert a significant loss to the local economy (Schneider 1992). Wilma began to follow this accident, the response of Sequoyah Fuels, and the NRC closely.

During Wilma's first term, her long-term goal involved developing the tribal economy in the 14 counties of northeastern Oklahoma. She hired Ira Phillips to head the business development programs and watched business programs develop into sources for people to resolve their problems at the community level. This became more important to Wilma because she believed working with local leadership resulted in the best outcomes for the needs of the residents. Based on tribal traditions and Cherokee history, the tribe had international integrity and controlled its own destiny without going through times of severe unemployment. Wilma consistently stressed that the Cherokee people had to figure out ways to rebuild themselves at the community level. Wilma wanted to focus on what the Cherokee Nation was already doing right and build upon that.

Due to necessity, most tribes operate both as a government and as a conduit for federal funds and provide needed services to tribal members very professionally. Intervention in the cycle of poverty rarely occurs and Wilma hoped to organize the communities to resolve problems themselves. She believed the federal approach made people too dependent on the views of outsiders and she planned to tap into the creativity and strength of the community leadership. Wilma believed she was leading the Cherokee Nation in a positive direction and hoped that would continue as long as the office of the chief, the tribal council, and the employees, and the Cherokee communities kept working together. On the Bell project, Wilma said, "Driving to that community, rounding the bend, and seeing all the volunteers who had shown up and were ready to go to work was the most significant moment of my work I've ever experienced, far more significant than being elected chief" (Mankiller, *Continuum: The Magazine of the University of Utah*, 2001).

At the regional level, in February 1986, Wilma replaced Choctaw chief Hollis Roberts as president of the Intertribal Council, a compilation of the five southeastern tribes, Cherokee, Chickasaw, Creek, Choctaw, and Seminole. It was formed so that the five southeastern tribes could work together on common problems and projects. During her time as president, Wilma reinstated the Arkansas Riverbed Authority to investigate several trespass cases along the Cherokee and Choctaw and Chickasaw owned Arkansas River. This was necessary since a federal court had ruled that people and entrepreneurs were trespassing and could be forced to lease property from one of the Indian nations.

On October 4, 1986, a massive flood event occurred along the Arkansas River from Kansas to Muskogee, Oklahoma. Flood waters reached almost 40 feet by October 6, inundating over 2,000 homes and businesses and resulting in over $68 million in damages in the Tulsa area and the western portion of the Cherokee lands along the Illinois river. Wilma later recalled how few people blamed the government. The communities came together to work with the health clinics and emergency management centers so people had access to medical care, pharmaceuticals, and essential services. *Gadugi* crews helped deliver water, cut trees, moved debris, and checked on the welfare of the elderly and handicapped. Many Cherokees understood the great richness and depth of the spirit of *gadugi*, coming together for the benefit of the community and selfless public service.

This flood must have been on Wilma's mind as she entered a partnership between the Cherokee Nation, the Army Corps of Engineers, and Southwestern Power Association. Following the Supreme Court ruling in *United States v. Cherokee Nation* (1987) that granted the Cherokee Nation title to the Arkansas Riverbed, Wilma became determined to bring jobs to the citizens of the Cherokee Nation and knew this was a good opportunity. "She merged the Native ideal with the pragmatism of ownership, time and time again incorporating Cherokee traditions with the political will to bring a better life for her people" (Longo 2018, 13). The resulting hydroelectric power plant along the Arkansas River near Bell, Oklahoma, generated electricity and economic opportunities for the people of eastern Oklahoma.

The Cherokee Nation joined the Council of Energy Resource Tribes (CERT) cofounded by Dine' president Peter MacDonald in 1982. CERT became an important consultant during the hydroelectric project. The Cherokee Nation's hydroelectric power project began at the end of 1987 and was completed by early 1992. The tribe financed and constructed the plant, while the U.S. Army Corps of Engineers operated it, and the Southwest Power Administration marketed the power. Power-generating turbines were constructed on the W. D. Mayo Lock and Dam No. 14 on the Arkansas River near Sallisaw. Chief Wilma stated, "This project ensures the tribe a substantial income well into the 21st Century" (*Cherokee Phoenix and Indian Advocate*, 1986a). The tribe expected almost $300,000 per year in revenues until retirement of the debt, then the Cherokee Nation could realize as much as $3 million per year.

Wilma also formed a task force to study a proposed Indian Health Service plan to cut health care funding to patients with less than one-quarter degree of Indian blood (*Cherokee Advocate*, 1986). In April 1986, Wilma—representing the Cherokee—and the chiefs of the other (southeastern) tribes, Creek, Choctaw, Chickasaw, and Seminole, attended a meeting in Washington, D.C. As president of the Intertribal Council, Wilma inquired about the Reagan administration's 17 percent cut to the Indian Health Service funding. Reagan approved $809 million for the Indian Health Service in 1985, a decrease from the $831 million approved in 1984.

One of Wilma's greatest moments of pain and sadness came as congressional representatives heckled her on the floor of the U.S. Congress because of her last name. This bothered her because it reminded her of the pain from being bullied for her last name and country accent back in school in San Francisco. Women in power, and especially American Indian women, experienced an alarming amount of sexism and racism throughout their political careers in the late 20th century. At 41, Wilma acknowledged that most feminists would love to have a name like hers, and the name Mankiller had served her well while in tribal government. She knew, even then, that her role as a tribal leader of the second largest tribe in America broke new ground for women—not only American Indian women but all American women seeking leadership positions.

Whereas in previous years water and housing had been priorities, with the Community Development Block Grants (CDBG), economic development became the new focus for tribal business projects. Because of continuing budget cuts in the Reagan administration, tribes became emboldened to seek other sources of revenue and employment. Wilma believed the dwindling federal funds would not affect the Cherokee Nation as much as other tribes, but the federal government needed to understand the many problems Indian communities—including the Cherokees— faced. "We have been very successful at making the federal dollar go further, but we have a lot more resources in our communities that we're tapping into" (*Cherokee Phoenix and Indian Advocate*, 1986b). Part of her community development work included convincing the poverty-stricken Cherokee communities that it was not their fault they were poor and their condition was the result of countless failed federal Indian policies. While the Cherokee Nation remained interested in attracting industry to their area, the priority became to promote small, local businesses and offer technical assistance to existing Indian-owned businesses.

In 1986, Wilma founded the Private Industry Council, bringing government and private businesses together to identify ways to bring businesses to northeastern Oklahoma. She hoped to attract responsible businesses with good environmental records. While Wilma became more focused on economic development than water and housing, with the goal of more self-sufficiency (*Cherokee Phoenix and Indian Advocate*, 1986a), Charlie became more focused on the water and housing issues for the tribe. As the community development director, Charlie began enlisting community organizers throughout the rural communities to lead their respective communities in the waterline projects. Like the water board created for the Bell project, other communities created their own water boards and that made a significant difference in the completion of each project.

Wilma soon learned how to deal with her opposition in tribal council meetings. As she entered her first tribal council meeting, one man on the tribal council thought it was the worst thing possible for a woman to be conducting the meeting. He kept interrupting Wilma throughout the meeting, stating she was violating some rule or that she was not following some procedure—obscure rules and procedures that Wilma had never heard of. Wilma decided at that moment that she had to become assertive or she would deal with those types of interruptions and that kind of disrespect for the next four years. She then had a great idea of how to handle the interruptions. Between the first and second meeting, Wilma had all the council members' microphones changed so the president of the tribal council controlled the microphones. During the second tribal council meeting, when the same rude man began interrupting the meeting, she cut off the sound from his microphone so no one heard him. The meetings became smoother and more productive.

Away from tribal council meetings or Cherokee Nation business, Wilma began giving more interviews. She often discussed the depictions of American Indians by mainstream society and the negative stereotypes in films and popular culture. She remarked on the degree to which it was a major problem. "Western movies always seemed to show Indian women washing clothes at the creek and men with a tomahawk or spear in their hands, adorned with lots of feathers. The image has stayed in some people's minds. Many people thought Indians were either visionaries, 'noble savages,' squaw drudges, or tragic alcoholics" (*U.S. News & World Report*, 1986). Wilma repeatedly declared that Indian people have a much greater tenacity to maintain their traditional culture and value system than most people believe.

Wilma's issues with men's resistance continued. United South and Eastern Tribes (USET) is a nonprofit intertribal organization providing a forum for the exchange of information and ideas among the 33 federally recognized USET member tribes. The organization enables the tribes' joint interaction on a government-to-government level with state and federal agencies. When Wilma attended her first USET meeting in spring 1986, she found that no one had provided a chair for her, so she found a chair for herself and pulled it up to the table. She next discovered that her name did not appear on the agenda. At the end of the meeting, she stood up and told the men who she was, why she was there, and what they could expect to see from her. Impressed with her character, the USET members elected her president of the organization two years later.

Although the main goal of the Mankiller administration was economic development, Wilma devoted a good deal of energy to educational improvements. To preserve the Cherokee language, a Summer Institute of Cherokee Literacy began in June 1986, with Durbin Feeling as a Cherokee-language specialist. Chief Wilma remarked about the program, "The Summer Institute of Cherokee Literacy is an example of the tribe's diversity. We are aggressive in business development and just as aggressive in the retention of our culture. Language is essential to the retention of a tribe's culture" (*Cherokee Advocate*, 1986). "I've often referred to Durbin as 'this generation's Sequoyah' because of his determination to perpetuate the Cherokee language. He recently stated that the Cherokee language is growing, not dying as are the tribal languages of some North American tribes. I can attest to that. My two-year-old grandson, Aaron Swake, speaks Cherokee and understands it extremely well" (*Cherokee Advocate*, 1986). Wilma understood the need to preserve the Cherokee language given that it is a valuable part of the Cherokee culture.

Continuing her travels in the fall, Wilma spoke at the September 1986 meeting of the Seventh Generation Fund economic development conference at Navajo Community College in Tsaile, Navajo (Dine') Nation. The topic was "Investing in our People and Land: Community and Land Based Economic Development," and she emphasized on small-scale development relying on the local people and existing in a culturally and environmentally sound manner. Between 1978 and 1986, the fund provided financial and technical support to over 85 Native communities working to build their economies on renewable resources (*Indian Country Today*, 1986). The Seventh Generation Fund was a nonprofit, public foundation established by the late Daniel R. Bomberry in 1977 for tribes and American Indian organizations who were committed to making sovereignty a political and economic reality. As BIA budget cuts continued, economic development was more pressing than ever and Chief Wilma became more active with the Seventh Generation Fund.

Wilma and Charlie married on October 13, 1986. The couple made a powerful team and Charlie was Wilma's greatest champion as she advanced the concept that Cherokees could be in control. They had a solid marriage based on equality and respect. They did not, however, share the same interests always. Wilma enjoyed opera music and the radical musings of jazz poet Gil Scott-Heron while Charlie did not. Wilma proclaimed in her sly, witty way, "We are living proof that similar political views and taste in food and music are not the keys to a long-term relationship" (Mankiller, *Every Day Is a Good Day*, 2004, 130).

Charlie emphatically encouraged Wilma to run for principal chief in the upcoming 1987 election. He also resigned from his position as director of the community development department so there would be no appearance of impropriety after he and Wilma married. Yet, criticism and claims of nepotism occurred after Wilma delayed Charlie's resignation until he qualified for retirement benefits (Steinem 2015, 220). Overcoming the criticism together, Wilma and Charlie merged innovation and persistence with knowledge of traditional Cherokee values to facilitate community empowerment. He created the Gadugi Project in 1987. This organization provided funding for supplies and technical assistance to continue waterline projects. Wilma and Charlie also learned more about successful economic ventures from the Eastern Cherokees.

They traveled to Cherokee, North Carolina, and visited the Qualla Arts and Crafts Cooperative searching for ideas and information about how the cooperative had maintained success since the 1960s. Focusing on traditional Cherokee art, the Mankiller administration partnered with the Cherokee National Historical Society, Inc. to create the Lost Arts project, with the goal of preserving and reviving Cherokee cultural arts, as was being done among the Eastern Cherokees. Wilma began collecting Native art because, just like the language, she understood its importance in Native cultures.

At the January 1987 tribal council meeting, the council voted unanimously for a resolution supporting a local environmental group, Native Americans for a Clean Environment (NACE), in its efforts to stop pollution of the Arkansas River. The group's chairperson, Jesse Deer In Water, talked about how supportive the Cherokee Nation, and specifically Wilma, had been in the Kerr-McGee/Sequoyah Fuels decision to abandon their plans for a waste disposal site at the Sequoyah Fuels plant. Deer In Water said, "The Nuclear Regulatory Commission has ordered Kerr-McGee to find a new way to transfer waste from the plant to the river because the ditch they've been using is contaminated. It's our contention that if the waste is contaminating the ditch it's flowing in, it will contaminate the river too" (*Cherokee Advocate*, 1987). The tribe and the state of Oklahoma joined together and sued Sequoyah Fuels and kept them from disposing off 50,000 tons of nuclear waste from the plant location.

Following the remediation efforts of the uranium plant, Wilma began working with NACE. Just a year after the accident, in 1987, the plant started converting depleted uranium hexafluoride into depleted uranium tetrafluoride. Uranium tetrafluoride is used to make depleted uranium metal for military applications. Depleted Uranium, U238, is the waste portion of uranium that comes from the enrichment process used to remove fissionable U234 and U235. The Department of Energy transports nuclear waste all over the country (Dr. Doug Rokke, Nuclear Physicist, Major (retired) United States Army Reserves, 32-year service. Jacksonville State University, personal interview, April 1998). In 1988, the Nuclear Regulatory Commission, NRC, fined Kerr-McGee just $310,000 for safety violations and the company settled out of court with 13 plaintiffs. The same year, General Atomics Technologies, Inc. of San Diego bought the plant from Kerr-McGee. In 1990, the NRC reported that groundwater analysis reflected uranium contamination 10,000 times higher than permissible limits when operations ceased for seven months. Once the plant reopened, another accident occurred in late 1992. A reaction in a digester created a massive contamination in the facility soil and groundwater. In 1993, the NRC ordered the plant to immediately cease operation and the facility was decommissioned.

Wilma had a successful first term and she accomplished many projects, as she advanced the concept that Cherokees could be in control of their own lives. Wilma encouraged first-term councilman, John Ketcher, a World War II veteran and tribal council member who shared her priorities of unity and economic development, to run for deputy chief. Running for chief in the spring of 1987 was a very different experience from her 1983 deputy chief campaign. While campaigning in different communities, Wilma had sugar poured in her gas tank, had the tires on her car slashed, and received threatening phone calls with the sound of a gun being cocked on the other end of the receiver. However, the same sexism emerged that Wilma had experienced during her 1983 campaign. Wilma's three opponents were Perry Wheeler, Dave Whitekiller, and Bull McGee. Whitekiller filed a complaint with the tribal elections committee that Wilma should use her husband's last name because Whitekiller and Mankiller sounded too similar and the voters may become confused. Tribal politicians continued to oppose her, and Swimmer discouraged Wilma from running in the 1987 election due to a lack of support from the tribal council. Those who opposed Wilma sought any excuse to discredit her, and the fact that she was a woman seemed the easiest justification for not embracing her leadership.

Throughout the campaign, Charlie visited the Cherokee-speaking traditional communities and reminded them of the traditional leadership role of Cherokee women prior to the coming of the white man. Speaking of her campaign, Wilma declared, "My ideas were way more liberal than those of the people I was asking to elect me" (*Boston Globe*, 1988). Charlie helped assure the elders that Wilma was not too radical and emphasized that before the white man arrived, Cherokee women played a major role in tribal government. Voting registration was at record levels as Wilma and Charlie traveled throughout the nation encouraging people to register.

The central issue in the 1987 campaign for chief was whether or not gender affected leadership. Wilma's health also became an issue in this campaign. Wilma's previous kidney problems returned, and for the last weeks of the campaign, she was hospitalized in Tulsa. An opponent launched a telephone campaign telling voters Wilma was going to die. So, she held a press conference from her hospital bed to convince voters she was very much alive and recovering nicely. Yet, her doctors could not determine the exact location of her infection, which caused irreversible kidney damage. For the next two years, Wilma endured repeated infections and hospitalizations.

In a run-off election, Wilma received 4,034 votes to challenger Perry Wheeler's 3,251 votes. Wilma used her national platform as the principal chief of the Cherokee Nation to educate the American public on the traditional roles of Cherokee women. She also used the media attention and the interest in her life to discuss Cherokee history and correct many misconceptions. Because of her personal illnesses and her experiences with the health care system, increasing access to health care became another of her main issues while in office.

Delivering her 1987 inaugural speech, Wilma highlighted that her priorities in office for the upcoming term included breaking the cycle of poverty and helping to revitalize rural communities while retaining the Cherokee sense of culture, history, and tribal identity. Under Wilma's tenure—from 1985 to 1987—CNI profits rose to approximately $2 million. She improved the Head Start facilities and the administration of the Sequoyah High School. She also revived the Talking Leaves Job Corps and saved it from being closed in 1987 due to a lack of operational space. She established a youth shelter and advocated for improvements for Cherokee children in foster care, gaining more tribal control over health care and education.

The 1987 election led to favorable publicity for the tribe, with Wilma at the helm. During Wilma's speaking engagements, she championed Cherokees and other tribes and urged women to assert their rights. The public had been very curious about a woman serving as chief, but she desired to affect policy and worked toward that goal. Advising women to be patient, to rise above negativity, and to forge ahead, Wilma said, "I think there's practically nothing in the world a woman can't do" (*Cherokee Advocate*, 1986). Throughout her tenure, Wilma's opponents cited her lack of leadership, yet she always stressed cooperation at work.

Continuing to represent the Cherokee Nation and its leaders by associating with national organizations, Wilma joined the board of the Ms. Foundation for Women in 1987. This association began when noted feminist-activist Gloria Steinem called Wilma and asked her to serve on the foundation's board. That call was the beginning of a 23-year friendship between the two women. On the Ms. Foundation board, Wilma became the go-to person for bringing women together. Her contributions made American Indian women much more visible to those who otherwise would not understand them and their issues. Wilma became a role model for other Native women as well. Elouise Cobell (Blackfeet) said of the pioneer, "She shared that women could aspire to and achieve major leadership positions in our Native communities" (Radical Profeminist Blog, 2010).

Wilma served on the board of the Ms. Foundation until 1991 and she and Gloria grew closer during those years. Wilma also told Gloria about an incident from her life that she had not shared with her family or her other friends. According to Gloria, Wilma had confided in her after a Ms. Foundation meeting that became sad and painful because of the large number of proposals to assist rape crisis centers and the fact that there was not enough money to go around. "Wilma told me the story of something she hadn't dealt with herself. In a movie house near her housing project in San

Ms. Magazine Foundation

Ms. is an American liberal feminist magazine cofounded by second-wave feminist and sociopolitical activist Gloria Steinem and Dorothy Pitman Hughes. The original editors were Letty Cottin Pogrebin, Mary Thom, Patricia Carbine, Joanne Edgar, Nina Finkelstein, Mary Peacock, Margaret Sloan-Hunter, and Gloria Steinem. *Ms.* first appeared in 1971 as an insert in *New York* magazine. The first standalone issue appeared in January 1972, with funding from editor and journalist Clay Felker. From July 1972 until 1987, the magazine appeared on a monthly basis. It is now published every quarter. The mission of the Ms. Foundation for Women is to build women's collective power in the United States to advance equity and justice for all. "We achieve our mission by investing in and strengthening the capacity for women led movements to advance meaningful social, cultural and economic changes in the lives of women."

Francisco, she was sexually assaulted by a group of teenage boys" (Steinem 2015, 229). This story helps explain why teenage Wilma despised her new environment in the city, why she felt so unhappy and alienated living in San Francisco, and why she ran away from home numerous times and lived for a year with Grandma Sitton. It is typical that Wilma never shared that story with any of her sisters or other female friends. In the late 1950s, young women did not feel empowered to speak out against sexual assault, thinking they would be blamed or that no one would believe them.

Wilma believed Indigenous female leadership was collective, collaborative, compassionate, and courageous. American Indian women had been consistently involved in leadership throughout Indigenous history. Female Indian leaders shared characteristics such as patience, humility, grace, determination, listening skills, the ability to contemplate a situation, independent thinking, and the ability to develop innovative strategies to accomplish the needed task (Hoxie 2014).

At her inauguration speech, Wilma reminded her detractors and others in attendance that prior to the arrival of the European colonizers, Cherokee women determined the qualifications and chose the candidates for chief. Wilma again stressed, "We need to really trust our own selves and our own thinking and not allow others to convince us that our thoughts, ideas and plans and visions aren't valid" (Robbins 1987). She managed 1,000 tribal government employees and a budget of $47 million for the 75,000-member tribe.

When not traveling to Washington to lobby for Indian issues or serving on the board of directors for several organizations or being occupied with speaking engagements to educate others about American Indian issues,

Wilma worked long hours in her office in the tribal complex. A typical day began at 6:00 a.m. and ended between 8:00 and 9:00 p.m., during which time she would be engaged in a mix of duties that ranged from tribal council meetings to meetings with Oklahoma's governor or other important state officials and the supervision of the Cherokee Nation's many programs and businesses. Wilma also enjoyed visiting the Cherokee communities throughout the tribe's 14 counties so she could stay in touch with the people. In an interview with Wilma in 1988, Cherokee author Marilou Awiakta described Wilma as staunch and sturdy, nurturing and deeply calm, and possessing a great sense of humor. Cherokee people say, "While other people get agitated and jump up and down, Wilma moseys on through and gets the job done" (Awiakta 1993, 112). "The chief has an open-door policy and a philosophy of building programs from the grassroots up—helping people define their own needs and then developing systems to meet them" (Awiakta 1993, 113).

During her first term, Chief Mankiller worked in community development and helped those who most needed it. This led her to change from having an attitude of no federal funding to being an astute grant writer. She found great joy in increasing the standard of living of fellow Cherokees. She encouraged them to become active in the community. Wilma figured out how to work with the Indian Health Service and Congress to get things built. The Cherokee Nation built a clinic in Stilwell and another clinic in Sallisaw, apart from purchasing the hospital in Jay and converting it into a health clinic. Wilma also established an ambulance service. Her expansion of the Stilwell Health Clinic led to the Cherokee Nation having the largest tribal health care system in the country at the time (*Cherokee Advocate*, 1987).

The Trail of Tears National Historic Trail Bill passed through Congress and was signed into law by Reagan in December 1987. The passage of the bill allowed the Department of the Interior to establish a nine-state trail marking the Cherokees' march to eastern Oklahoma, ending in Tahlequah, which came to be known as the Trail of Tears. Wilma served on the advisory board and remarked, "The Trail of Tears is a dark chapter in the history of our tribe and our nation. Today, as we prepare our people and the tribe for challenges of the future, we cannot dwell on that period in our past. But we do remember—we all must remember as part of the crucial preservation of our heritage" (*Cherokee Advocate*, 1987). Given that her ancestors had been forcibly removed and sent on the Trail of Tears, Wilma felt proud serving on the board commemorating the historic event.

In 1988, 10 national Indian organizations formed a Coalition for Indian Development to gain more strength and lobbying power. The member organizations included the First Nations Development Institute, the Council of Energy Resource Tribes, the Seventh Generation Fund, the Native

American Rights Fund, Americans for Indian Opportunity, the National Center for American Indian Enterprise Development, the American Indian Resources Institute, the National Congress of American Indians, the Native American Fish and Wildlife Service, and the Council of Tribal Employment Rights Offices. The combined reports of this coalition reflected the fact that development projects conceived by Indian people in their communities have a greater chance for success than those imposed from outside the communities. Rather than focusing on short-term gains, successful Indian community projects reflected a vision of what Indians wanted their communities to look like in the future, and Wilma enjoyed this kind of collaboration and alliance (Ambler 1990).

In May 1988, the Cherokee Nation Community Development Department and the residents of Kenwood received a national award for the rehabilitation of 25 homes in the Delaware County community. This was part of the national recognition program of HUD for Community Development Excellence. It was the second national award for excellence received by the tribe in a span of three years, the first being for the Bell waterline project. From 1983 to 1988, Cherokee traditional communities built 91 miles of waterlines and rehabilitated 432 homes in 17 communities. Wilma contributed her time and considerable skill to each project.

In September 1988, Congress passed the Indian Gaming Regulatory Act. This law provided a legislative basis for the operation and regulation of Indian gaming, thereby protecting gaming to generate revenue for the tribes and encouraging economic development of the tribes. Wilma was no fan of gaming, as least initially. The decision about launching gaming proved a tough decision for her. She listened to opposing views and asked community members what their fears were. She intentionally located the first bingo hall in a fairly isolated location because she wanted to appease those who opposed the action. She considered the opposing views and incorporated them into the whole (Olaya 2015). She knew all the good that could come from the gaming revenues, including infrastructure projects and improvements in health care and education. Bingo came first, in 1993, and then Cherokee gaming grew into a thriving industry with over 5,000 jobs.

Allowing gaming in eastern Oklahoma was not an easy path. The Cherokee Nation considered purchasing the Will Rogers Downs horse track in Claremore to allow betting on horse races but decided against it. One of Wilma's greatest skills was her ability and willingness to listen, and she heard from many in the communities about the pros and cons of gaming among them. Needing additional sources of revenue, she reluctantly allowed Cherokee bingo parlors. Wilma had begun her path to tribal leadership in California, where she had learned the value of listening to differing opinions and finding common ground. This came in handy when negotiating the gaming issue in the Cherokee Nation.

President Ronald Reagan attended a summit with Russian president Mikhail Gorbachev and, in a news conference, proclaimed that the United States made a mistake in allowing Indians to pursue their "primitive life-style" rather than becoming citizens along with the rest of the Americans. In 1988, President Reagan said the federal government was "humoring" American Indian people by putting them on reservations rather than inte-grating them into the rest of society. He later denied that remark and stated that the American Indians "should have the right to choose their own life" (*Boston Globe*, 1988). On December 12, 1988, Wilma met with President Reagan and other tribal leaders and stated that the administra-tion's policy of self-determination works and should continue. She told Reagan, "We are looking for a federal partnership, not a handout." She asked for the transfer of federal resources to the tribal level for determina-tion on the allocation of funds (Reagan Presidential Library). She responded to Reagan's Moscow remarks in the *Cherokee Advocate*, saying, "It is safe to say that our tribal members did not feel that they were being humored when they were forcibly moved to Indian Territory. It is also safe to say, that the thousands of American Indians who presently reside on reserva-tions do not feel humored. The darkest pages in American history contain the stories of the treatment of American Indian people. For President Rea-gan to make light of this situation is appalling. American Indian history is an important part of United States history. It is sad that the President of the United States knows so little about the history of the United States" (Landry 2017)). The issue of federal control of Native nations became more acute as the tribal trust money case emergd out of Washington, D.C.

This issue continued to garner much attention and soon exposed a mas-sive bureaucratic fraud over the mismanagement of tribal money.

A Special Senate Investigation Committee convened in February 1989 to hear testimony about alleged abuse and corruption in federal programs for Native Americans. The *Arizona Republic* newspaper uncovered much of the alleged abuse involving the infiltration of organized crime into reservation-run bingo games, sexual abuse at government-run schools for Native children, and scams from contractors working on reservation proj-ects. The committee also heard evidence that the BIA had mismanaged trust funds totaling $1.8 billion and oil and gas companies had scammed tribes out of billions of dollars. These actions of fraud resulted in the Elou-ise Cobell case. In 1996, Elouise Cobell, a Blackfoot Indian baker from Montana, filed a class-action lawsuit against the federal government over its mismanagement of funds for tribal lands. With over 500,000 plaintiffs from across Indian Country, the case became the largest class-action law-suit against the U.S. government in American history. After over 15 years of litigation, the defendant and the plaintiffs both agreed that an accurate accounting was impossible. In 2010, a settlement was reached for a total of

$3.4 billion (the Claims Settlement Act of 2010). It was divided into three sections: $1.5 billion was used to create an Accounting/Trust Administration fund (to be distributed to Individuals Indian Money Accounts [IIM] account holders), $60 million was set aside for Indian access to higher education, and the remaining $1.9 billion was used to create the Trust Land Consolidation Fund, which provides funds for tribal governments to purchase individual fractionated interests, consolidating the allotments once again into communally held land.

The report from the Senate investigation concluded that there was a need for dismantling the federal government's $3.3 billion per year programs for Indians and replacing them with direct grants to tribes. This proposal allowed tribes to take part in a new system of self-government grants. Wilma wholeheartedly supported the committee's recommendations and planned to organize Indian support for them. Working toward those goals, in February 1989, the Mankiller administration and tribal council formed the Cherokee Nation Police Department, who began patrolling Cherokee tribal lands. At the state level, Wilma began serving a three-year term on the Oklahoma Indian Affairs Commission. At the national level, she began a two-year term on the U.S. Small Business Administration Region IV Advisory Council.

In April 1989, Wilma underwent elective surgery to end her recurring urinary tract infections. The surgery took place at the University of Oregon Medical Center and helped for a while. Her schedule was relentless. She appeared on the 1989 Labor Day Muscular Dystrophy Association Telethon with Jerry Lewis and shared her story. She hoped that sharing her experience with myasthenia gravis could help others. On a happier note, Wilma's second grandchild was born that year—Gina gave birth to her son, Kellon Quinton.

By 1990, the tribe took the lead in self-governance through the enactment of a tax code, the reestablishment of the tribe's district court, law enforcement, and judicial systems. By this time, Cherokee Nation Enterprises (CNE) operated three Cherokee casino facilities, two convenience stores/gas stations, and a Cherokee gift shop. The tribal self-governance agreement for direct funding was signed on February 10, 1990. The agreement allowed the tribe to plan, conduct, and administer programs and receive direct funding to deliver services to tribal members. Among the actions of the new tax code were a tobacco tax and sales tax on goods and services sold or created on tribal lands. Ten tribes received block grants and used the funds for local needs. These grants also extended to the Indian Health Service, which was so important to Wilma as her kidney problems persisted and worsened.

Misdiagnosed for her kidney problems in Tulsa, Wilma sought help in Denver, then underwent an experimental procedure at the University of

Oregon, but to no avail. Through her close friend Gloria Steinem, Wilma connected with a top kidney transplant surgeon in Boston. Her eldest brother Don, who lived in California, donated his kidney. Wilma underwent the transplant procedure on June 20, 1990. She recovered at the home of friends Bill and Suzanne Presley for several weeks. The transplant was a success and she returned to work by August 1990. She was also anxious to return home for the birth of Felicia's second child—who would be her third grandchild—Jaron Swake.

Wilma worked as hard as possible for the tribe and other Native people. While recovering in Boston, Wilma negotiated with Washington officials for the Cherokee Nation to participate in allowing tribes to self-govern using federal funds. There was a constant struggle to maintain sovereignty.

Back home at Mankiller Flats, Wilma often recalled her past and the history of the Cherokees. She remembered the oral tradition of a great Cherokee prophet named Charley, who carried a message from the Creator to the Cherokee people. Charley emerged from the deep woods flanked by a wolf on each side and told a group of Cherokees that the Creator was unhappy they had given up the old traditional ways for the new ways of the white man. Charley told them to return to the Great Spirit in their dreams and that if they ignored this message, death would come to them. Those who ignored the prophesy did not die, so the power of the prophet diminished. Wilma and others realized that Charley may have been referring to the death of the spirit. This story was one of Wilma's favorites. It served as a lesson to always keep the Cherokee language, ceremonies, and culture alive. Wilma also had a painting that depicted Charley and the two wolves in a place of prominence in her home (Mankiller 1993, 257).

Cherokee culture remained alive as the Gadugi Project and Kenwood residents organized the Kenwood Community Arts and Crafts Cooperative in August 1990. The Kenwood Cooperative developed from the trip to Cherokee, North Carolina, that Wilma and Charlie had taken a few years earlier. Joining with Charlie's organization, the Gadugi Project, the Kenwood Cooperative allowed community artisans and craftspeople to work together and negotiate a better price for their wares. There was little interest initially, but this changed once the wares were sold out at the National Indian Education Association in Tulsa in 1988. They then organized a marketing collective and Julie Moss coordinated the Cherokee Community Loan Fund, working to assist micro businesses, or home crafters. The Seventh Generation Fund became key in the project because of its capacity to build community, self-sufficiency, and support for the informal economy and the links between local people. The Kenwood residents rebuilt their communities via their traditional philosophies. Kenwood became a model of how Indian people organize alternatives to governmental directives to strengthen their culture, promote traditional arts, and make a living on their own terms.

In November 1990, the Mankiller administration and the tribal council established the Cherokee Nation District and a criminal and procedural code, and three months later, in February 1991, the tribe approved four legislative acts for cooperative law enforcement within the Cherokee Nation. These laws allowed the Cherokees to raise revenue to provide governmental services to Cherokee people and promote economic development, self-sufficiency, and increased tribal sovereignty.

Also, in the fall of 1990, Chief Mankiller authorized the tribal police to raid and close 14 of the 22 United Keetoowah Band (UKB) smoke shops in Tulsa, Cherokee, Adair, Sequoyah, and Delaware counties (Edmunds 2001, 224). The federal courts ruled that UKB shops were not exempt from state taxes. In the first case, *Sonny Buzzard v. The Oklahoma Tax Commission*, the UKB filed legal proceedings against the tax commission after the state of Oklahoma seized tobacco products and ordered Buzzard's smoke shop to be closed for failure to pay taxes. Buzzard and the UKB claimed that the shop was in Indian Country territory and the state had no jurisdiction. The U.S. District Court, Northern District of Oklahoma, ruled in February that the plaintiff had no recourse—as the land was under the jurisdiction of the state—and that the Cherokee Nation had sovereignty over the lands. Increasing tension emerged as Wilma fought against fraud by those not having federal recognition yet claiming individual Cherokee identity. She received much criticism for distributing a list of illegal groups claiming to be Cherokee (Janda 2007, 120). She also faced backlash over a compact with the state of Oklahoma for the Cherokee Nation to pay a 25 percent tax on all tobacco purchased for resale. Wilma viewed it as an expression of tribal sovereignty, but to others it represented just the opposite (Janda 2007, 127).

In a second case, *The United Keetoowah Band v. Secretary of Interior*, the UKB claimed they were the successor to the Cherokee Nation and the Secretary of the Interior should provide them with grants and contracts for services to their tribal members. In 1990, the UKB filed a case against Chief Mankiller, the tribal council, and various employees claiming the defendants acted illegally and denied the UKB rights to operate smoke shops on lands the Cherokee Nation claims jurisdiction over (*Cherokee Advocate*, 1992c). A circuit court later dismissed the land claims on all issues as UKB received services from the Cherokee Nation. The UKB filed an additional suit against the Secretary of the Department of the Interior, laying claim to lands held in trust for the Cherokee Nation and saying the Cherokee Nation ceased to exist at Oklahoma statehood. The UKB sought funding from the Department of the Interior and $10 million in damages for funds withheld in the past. The U.S. District Judge Thomas Brett of Tulsa dismissed the case, finding against the UKB on all issues. The state of Oklahoma has recognized the UKB since 1946 as a band of Indians under the Oklahoma Indian Welfare Act who sought to break away from the Cherokee Nation. Because its members are also members of the Cherokee Nation, they receive services from the Cherokee Nation.

Wilma served on a special American Council on Education Task Force and they produced a report showing the decrease in minority higher education. There was also a focus on the underrepresented minority students and the value systems they grew up with. "In traditional tribal cultures, Native people are taught all things are interconnected to form a whole. Spirituality, for example, is not just something one expresses once a week by dressing up and attending Sunday morning services. Rather, spiritual values are incorporated into all aspects of daily life. The same holds true for education" (Mankiller 1991). Education in some tribal communities need not take place while one sits in a classroom memorizing specific facts. Wilma argued that education is an ongoing lifetime process that exists not in a vacuum but as a part of the whole. In many Native communities, there is a much greater emphasis on the collective achievements of the family or the community than on the achievements of the individual. Native people who have achieved great personal success are not held in the same esteem as those who have achieved great success in helping others. Wilma was a strong advocate of peer mentoring programs where senior students help incoming freshmen make the transition from tribal life to college life.

The 1980s provided a new, more accepting atmosphere for many women in America, once they proved their mettle, and Wilma Mankiller was no exception. Cherokee women enjoyed a greater freedom than many others. Traditionally, they had relatively more sexual freedom, could divorce easily, and had a women's council. The status of "war woman" or "beloved woman" is the highest honor for a Cherokee woman. A harmonious nature of gender relations existed among Cherokees, despite the changes wrought by European colonization. Into the 19th century, a traditional worldview existed with a gendered division of work yet sanctioning the autonomy, prestige, and power of Cherokee women (Janda 2007, 103). Because of the belief in balance and harmony, the gender roles complemented each other.

Wilma's path to leadership was a culmination of her Cherokee heritage, her awakening political consciousness, and her community development work. Her identity and the image she projected to mainstream society, as a feminist and as an advocate of American Indian rights, became two central themes in her career. Her exposure to Cherokee traditions and the discrimination faced by people of color influenced her identity. Wilma learned not to change her goals or the work that she did but to adapt the strategies and tactics involved in getting things accomplished for the tribe. In the 1960s, Indian activists used a certain tactic to bring attention to treaty rights and tribal issues, but in the 1980s, different tactics became necessary. "I think the fact that we were able to set out to plan over a decade – say we're going to build free-standing helath clinics, develop a prevention program and then actually stay focused on that and get it done. That sounds, you know, not that exciting – but at that time we had no gaming money. SO we just had to figure out how to work with the Indian Health Service and th Congress to get things built" (Voices of Oklahoma Interview, 2009, 26).

Wilma believed that in a leadership position, leading was not doing what everyone wanted her to do, it was listening to the concerns of everybody and assimilating those concerns and reaching some kind of consensus. She remarked, "The biggest danger for any leader is to surround themselves with people who won't speak up or argue with you when you're doing something wrongheaded. You've got to have people that will engage in a lively debate with you" (Hoxie 2014). Wilma enjoyed debating issues with other people who held differing opinions.

7

Chief Wilma, Second Term

In April 1991, Chief Wilma traveled to Washington, D.C., and met with President George H. W. Bush, along with other tribal leaders. She asked the president to publicly reaffirm the government-to-government relationship between the tribes and the United States and he agreed to that (*Washington Post*, 1991). Receiving confirmation of presidential support and commitment to the continuing sovereignty status of the Cherokee Nation became important to Cherokee leaders.

In the summer of 1991, Wilma won her campaign for reelection as chief with an impressive 82.7 percent of the popular vote. She had hoped only to avoid a run-off with one of her two opponents, William K. Dew and Art Nave. The high percentage of votes in Wilma's favor confirmed that the Cherokee Nation voters no longer considered a woman as an unsuitable leader.

Wilma continued to receive national media attention. *The Baltimore Sun* published an article on Wilma leading the Cherokee Nation. The reporter emphasized that while leading her tribe to greater self-reliance, Wilma drew strength from traditional Cherokee values. Wilma remarked, "My ability to survive personal crises is really a mark of the character of my people. Individually and collectively, we react with a tenacity that allows us again and again to bounce back from adversity." Her accomplishments in economic development, health care, and tribal self-governance made Wilma "a legend in Indian Country" (Gaines 1991).

Turning to environmental issues, Chief Wilma participated in the first National People of Color Environmental Leadership Summit, which was held during October 24–27, 1991, in Washington, D.C. Also participating in this summit were delegates of African American, Pacific Islander, Latino, Canadian, Mexican, and Central and South American descent. They submitted a call to President George H. W. Bush and Congress to stop all policies and practices that contributed to environmental racism. Environmental racism is any policy or practice of environmental injustice based on pollution or hazardous waste in a vulnerable community in a racialized context. Environmental attorney and cochair Gail Small (Northern Cheyenne) proclaimed, "Environmental laws do not protect our people. We have suffered through 1,500 years of colonization and oppression by people who set out to conquer Indians and our lands" (Taliman 1991). Small exclaimed that with less than 4 percent of the original land base left, the Department of Energy representatives were now asking tribal communities to accept white America's nuclear waste, trash, and poison. She argued that America's way of thinking about environmental laws must be challenged.

Small and the other summit leaders called on all leaders to refuse to accept the deliberate targeting of tribal land to be used as a dumping ground for hazardous wastes and radioactive materials. Cochair Dr. Benjamin Chavis from the United Church of Christ Commission for Racial Justice stated, "Environmental racism is racial discrimination in policy making, enforcement of regulations, the deliberate targeting of communities of color for toxic waste facilities and the history of excluding people of color from the leadership of the environmental movement" (Taliman 1991). Wilma spoke about the need to share the Native philosophy with other cultures and the need to educate Indian people about the dangers of economic development projects that involve hazardous waste. "We are a tenacious people who have maintained our cultures. We must take charge to make sure we have a presence in the environmental movement. By building a multi-racial, multi-cultural movement, we will be able to sustain our children and grandchildren" (Taliman 1991).

In 1991, Wilma traveled to Northeastern State University in Tahlequah to hear Alex Haley speak for the Galaxy of Stars series. He described his frustration that so much ignorance persisted in America about African American people and their contributions to American history. She considered Haley a role model for his work in bringing pride back to many African Americans following his book and television miniseries *Roots*, which aired in 1977. Wilma also wholeheartedly agreed that the same ignorance existed about American Indian people and their contributions to America. She was also happy to be back home to witness the birth of Felicia's third child, and her first granddaughter, Breanna Olaya.

David Leroy was the official negotiator for the Department of Energy Office of U.S. Nuclear Waste. His job was to offer tribes $150,000 to consider storing spent nuclear fuel rods on their lands. Wilma worked with her friend Grace Thorpe and the National Environmental Coalition of Native Americans (NECONA). The local group NACE also worked with Wilma to prevent the new licensing of a plant. Thorpe, the daughter of Olympic athlete Jim Thorpe, was a tribal judge for the Sac and Fox tribe in Oklahoma. She had been good friends with Wilma since the radical days of the Alcatraz occupation. After the deadly explosion in 1986 at the Sequoyah Fuels plant and the lack of action by the NRC, Mankiller dedicated much attention to the uranium facility, cleaning up the area. Seven years passed and it was still there. James Wilcoxin, attorney for the Cherokee Nation, stated a high level of cancer existed among the Indians in the immediate area around Gore, Vian, and Webber's Falls but there had been no real involvement of the Indian Health Service. The plant processed "yellow cake," refined from mined uranium ore to produce UF6, used in commercial nuclear power plants and military weapons (Savilla 1992b). Near the confluence of the Arkansas and Illinois rivers, the 600-acre site was located in Gore, Oklahoma. The facility operated as a uranium conversion facility and left more than 10,000 tons of radioactive waste on site.

Besides trying to get the depleted uranium contamination cleaned up in Gore, Wilma also became heavily involved in the Arkansas Riverbed issue with the Department of Treasury and the Army Corps of Engineers. In *Choctaw Nation v. Oklahoma* (1987), the Supreme Court ruled that the Cherokee Nation and other tribes owned the banks and riverbed of the Arkansas River. Three tribes, the Cherokee, Choctaw, and Chickasaw Nations, filed claims with the U.S. Court of Federal Claims in 1989 and the

---

ARKANSAS RIVERBED CASE

The Arkansas River follows a course nearly 1,400 miles long, from the headwaters in the Rocky Mountains near Leadville, Colorado, to Napoleon, Arkansas, where it spills into the Mississippi River. Along the way it crosses through Kansas and Oklahoma. Meandering across northeastern Oklahoma, the Arkansas River traverses the Cherokee Nation lands. It forms part of the boundary between the Cherokee Nation on the north and the Choctaw Nation on the south, for a total of 96 miles. Tribal ownership of the river dates back to the Treaty of Dancing Rabbit Creek (signed between the U.S. government and the Choctaw Nation in 1830) and the Cherokee Treaty of New Echota (1835). Chickasaw participation in ownership dates to the Treaty of January 17, 1837. The Cherokee Nation received $20 million for its Arkansas Riverbed property.

Arkansas Riverbed case began in April 1992. Wilma appeared before a congressional judiciary committee related to the Cherokee, Choctaw, and Chickasaw Nations of Oklahoma Claims Act of 1992 to direct the Department of Treasury to compensate the tribes for losses incurred in the federal construction of the navigation project on the Arkansas River. Wilma estimated she devoted at least one-third of her time as chief attempting to win a settlement on the loss of access to mineral rights owned by tribes in the Arkansas Riverbed.

Closely associated with her health initiatives became protection of the Cherokee Nation environment because of the Kerr-McGee uranium facility accident and the fact that the remaining waste was still not cleaned up. After the NRC finally admitted the presence of extreme contamination at the facility, they ordered the plant permanently closed. Wilma wrote, "Many tribal communities have made it a priority to recapture, protect, and maintain traditional tribal knowledge systems and lifeways that are often described as a whole or interconnected way of viewing things. The environment is not seen as a social justice issue but as an essential element of all life" (Mankiller, *Every Day Is a Good Day*, 2004, 146).

Wilma believed in the power of education and also the need to include teachers and curriculum that reflect the student population. "In the past few years, academia has become more and more aware of the fact that the minority population is increasing, while the corresponding numbers of minority students enrolling in institutions of higher education have declined" (Mankiller 1991). Wilma described the need for diversity in faculty, staff, and student body and advocated for a bottom-line commitment to minority education. "The crucial decade of the 1990s will determine whether we face this crisis head-on or allow the situation to worsen" (Mankiller 1991).

On November 22, 1991, Wilma and other tribal leaders met with Governor Bill Richardson (D-NM) and the HUD department in Santa Fe, New Mexico, seeking alternative approaches to address the severe housing shortage in Indian Country. This meeting resulted in the Indian Housing Demonstration Project Act of 1991. The Secretary of the Interior and the Secretary of HUD jointly agreed to carry out a program under this Act. The main purpose of this law was to allow Indian tribes to determine the housing needs of tribal members and the appropriate use of federal housing assistance provided directly to the tribes.

Wilma believed that all tribes should have a code of ethics and she created the Cherokee Nation Code of Ethics, which used the standard legal definition of conflicts of interest. The Cherokee code also barred tribal employees and tribal officials from using any information generated within the tribal government for personal gain. The code also required all tribal employees and officials to expose any corruption they may have knowledge of within the tribal government. As long as there was no separation of powers within tribal governments, it was difficult to enforce any code of ethics (*Sho-Ban News*, 1991). The separation of powers between the Cherokee Nation Industries and the tribal government proved a successful structure.

The following year, the Cherokee Nation operated enterprises as an internal operation, with system enterprises accountable to the tribal administration who in turn answered to the tribal council. This is not considered conducive to good business decisions, according to studies conducted by the Harvard Kennedy School. The Cherokee Nation also conducted its business enterprises under the direction of a semi-independent economic development corporation. This kept long-term, strategic decision-making in the hands of elected tribal leadership and daily business decisions came under the purview of managers and boards of directors, protected by the corporate structure from inappropriate interference in nonstrategic, short-term business matters. The Cherokee Nation managed its business enterprises under both systems.

The Cherokee Nation Industries operated under a corporate charter with a board of directors and business management separate from tribal government. The gaming enterprise functioned under a different corporate structure that blended the tribal operations with business functions in a unique arrangement. They conducted all other enterprises without the benefit of corporate structures. Wilma proposed establishing an Economic Development Corporation, which would ensure that funds invested in enterprises serve the interests of the tribe and that the enterprises have the flexibility and freedom from political pressures to be profitable, to seek and obtain capital, and to create and keep jobs (Wilma Mankiller Collection, Business Structure Proposal, October 21, 1992).

In 1992, America celebrated the 500th anniversary of Columbus's arrival in North America. Groups around the country sponsored festivals, parades, and seminars summarizing the monumental changes North America had undergone since 1492. Wilma doubted if Americans paused to reflect on the entire history of North America, including the Indigenous people who had been living there since time immemorial. On Columbus Day, Wilma took the opportunity to educate non-Indians about many pressing issues in Indian Country. In a national radio broadcast, she described how she was taught in the third grade about Christopher Columbus discovering this great and new world with abundant water and forests. "Well, you know, it certainly wasn't a new world to the millions of people that had lived here for thousands of years, and there's no discussion of that at all" (National Public Radio Interview, 2008).

Wilma became aware of this great lie in 1969. "You know, I think it was the first time I heard the story that the Iroquois Confederacy, which is a kind of international group, was founded before Columbus arrived." While acknowledging that wanting to know about other cultures is natural among some people, Wilma declared that using Columbus Day as an opportunity to have a discussion and provide more education about Indigenous people is a good start. She emphasized how important it is to acknowledge the genocide and political history and to talk about it in order to move forward in a good way together but not go around with anger in our hearts every day because of what happened (National Public Radio Interview, 2008). Wilma viewed the media attention she received as chief as an opportunity to speak out on the rights of Indians everywhere and she was not bashful in pursuit of that goal.

On August 11, 1992, Wilma and council members from the Cherokee Nation and the Eastern Band of Cherokee Indians held an annual joint tribal council meeting. Wilma admitted that education represented the weakest area for the tribe at that point in her administration. "We are not having the kind of impact that I would like to have, so our major emphasis during the next few years is going to be on education" (*Cherokee Advocate*, 1992b). Education became a majority priority as the two groups passed 15 cooperative resolutions. One resolution included a petition to Congress to fund Cherokee-language programs. This resolution intended to reverse the decision prohibiting Cherokee students from continuing their traditions and culture at the beginning of the 20th century.

Following through on her agenda to place education as the top priority for this period in her administration, Wilma attended the National Indian Education Association (NIEA) conference in Albuquerque in October 1992. Created in Minneapolis in 1970, the annual conference provides a national forum to share and develop ideas for cultural curriculum and influencing federal policy. The NEIA provides advocacy and resources to promote educational sovereignty, support the continued use of traditional knowledge and language, and improve educational opportunities in Native communities.

Wilma returned to Washington in December 1992 for a meeting with President Clinton to seek tax credits for private investors in Indian Country. She also wanted the right to issue mortgage bonds so Cherokee Nation tribal members could build their own homes and gain access to government guaranteed loans and insurance. She thought President Clinton's unprecedented level of involvement in minority affairs provided much-needed hope for the new administration to cooperate for constructive changes. These actions would represent a great step forward toward the benefits of home ownership, which were not currently enjoyed due to the nature of the allotted lands and the trust structure. Indians could not own land, so they could not build equity. Throughout Clinton's administration, however, his promises to Indian Country were largely broken.

Back in her office at the Cherokee Nation, Wilma exuded an unflappable self-confidence. Her confidence came from her ability to rebuild herself mentally and physically after daunting physical challenges. She was tenacious about rebuilding her people community by community, despite the poverty, low self-esteem, health problems, and unemployment that many Cherokees faced. She always tried to emphasize that the Cherokee people could do anything they set their mind to. The challenge arose in getting people to believe that, after 200 years of being told that others had the best ideas for them. She was a hands-on leader and her favorite community work was helping others help themselves. She stated that the trials she faced helped prepare her for the office (Spaid 1992).

One day in 1992, while Wilma was in her office at the tribal headquarters of the Cherokee Nation in Tahlequah, in walked her old friend from the Alcatraz days, John Trudell. He was barefoot, sported a half-Mohawk haircut, and wore one long silver earring in one ear. John landed the role of Jimmy Looks Twice in the 1993 film *Thunderheart* while also continuing his musical career. Musician Bob Dylan called John's 1985 album *Graffiti Man*—with the superb guitarist, the late Jesse Ed Davis (Kiowa/Comanche)—the best album of the year (Dylan often played it over the loudspeakers before his concerts). Wilma and John drank coffee and reminisced about the Alcatraz days and how they had both ended up where they did. Wilma called John one of the best thinkers she had ever met and one of her dearest friends. The two remained friends and presented at a conference together a couple of years later.

On the road once again, Mankiller gave the commencement address at Northern Arizona University in Flagstaff, Arizona, in December 1992. She spoke of treaty rights, the power of tenacity, tribal traditional knowledge, and leadership skills. She encountered many non-Indians who had visited tribal communities in Oklahoma or in other places and seen all the social indicators of decline, including high infant mortality and high unemployment. They always asked, "What happened to these people? Why do Native people have all these problems?" Chief Mankiller knew the only way for non-Indians to understand the contemporary issues and how Indians planned to reverse them was by having some understanding about tribal history. She related how the Cherokee Nation had a government long before there was a U.S. government. "We had treaties with England even before we had treaties with the colonies, and then later with the United States" (Mankiller 1992).

Wilma noticed several unique aspects of Cherokee communities. The first was their unbelievable tenacity. Although the Cherokee Nation was one of the most acculturated tribes in the country, there were thousands of people who spoke Cherokee. Also, traditional ceremonies that had existed since the beginning of time were still being conducted by many traditional tribal members. Once she and Charlie began visiting the most remote traditional communities, she realized they could build on that tenacity to improve the communities. Wilma also noted the Cherokee people's attention to culture, history, and heritage. She observed local leadership in the communities and remarked, "You could find the leadership just by seeing who people go to when there's a time of crisis in the community" (Mankiller 1992). Wilma also observed what she believed to be the single most important element of the community that had remained among the Native people—a sense of interdependence. "I've been very fortunate to be able to travel extensively in this country and abroad, and I can tell you that even though our people are very fragmented today, we still, in the more traditional communities still have a sense of interdependence" (Mankiller 1992). Because Cherokee people revere those who care most about others in the community and are always helping others, Wilma knew she could build on that traditional value and motivate people in communities to help their neighbor or the community. "Some tribal leaders and people in elected leadership positions build institutions, and they see that as a way of rebuilding a nation, and what we're trying to do is rebuild communities and families. We see that as a way of rebuilding our nation. So, there are many different approaches to doing that" (Mankiller 1992).

The tribe's ability to operate its own primary health care clinics, a fully accredited high school—which was a boarding school—a vocational education school, 24 separate Head Start centers, an extensive array of day care centers, adult literacy programs, and many, many other programs and businesses was a testament to the struggle for tribal sovereignty. Wilma exclaimed, "Anyway, we've grown, and the reason we've grown and rebuilt is because of our own hard work and our own determination to have a community, and to have a tribe again, and that's where we are today" (Mankiller 1992). Wilma thought tribal people needed to trust their own thinking and believe in themselves enough to articulate their own vision of the future and work to make the vision a reality. Native people had been acculturated to believe that their traditional ceremonies were pagan, that their language was archaic and useless, and that their history did not exist, or if it did exist, was distorted. Wilma advocated for Native self-sufficiency in most of her speeches.

For Wilma, the single most important task for the future became eliminating negative stereotypes. She stated, "We've started that on porches in eastern Oklahoma and in kitchens and in community centers. Yes, there remains an incredible array of negative stereotypes about native people in this country. The real fundamental change in eliminating stereotypes is going to have to be in the academic community" (Mankiller 1992). Wilma harkened back to her activist days in seeking curriculum changes to include more accurate and inclusive Native history and including more

Native professors within the universities (Mankiller 1992). She believed that American history cannot be taught truthfully and completely without including Native history.

During the tribal council meeting in April 1993, Wilma spent a considerable amount of time on housing, seeking ways to accomplish the goal of getting more Indian houses. She also devoted considerable energy to health care issues, gaming issues, and Cherokee language–revitalization efforts (*Cherokee Advocate*, 1993b). In her State of the Nation address in April 1993, she said she had shifted her focus away from education and toward housing and health care. After joining the National Indian Housing Commission that year, Wilma specifically sought alternatives for funding.

After meeting with Bruce Babbitt, secretary of the Department of the Interior, and Senator Daniel Inouye (D-HI) to discuss Indian gaming laws, at their request, Chief Wilma served on a committee to meet with state governors over Class III gaming issues affecting Indian Country. Wilma reported that she received community support for a bingo facility in the town of Catoosa and also for a new vocational technology center in Delaware County. The 1992 fiscal audit reported $71.6 million in tribal revenue, a 21 percent increase from 1991, due to the new construction projects.

Decentralizing services and moving tribal services closer to communities became another central goal for Wilma. Tribal administrators added two new field offices, in Pryor and Warner, bringing the total to 10 field offices, when eight years ago only 2 field offices had existed. Revenue from BIA grants and contracts increased from $4.5 million to $7.5 million over a period of three years since the new self-governance project. Wilma stated, "Many people said it was not a good idea when we decided to do things ourselves and not let the BIA control the allocation of our resources" (*Cherokee Advocate*, 1992a). She thought their record of managing the money and projects had proved otherwise. The Cherokee Nation tax code, enacted in July 1990, resulted in close to $1 million annually in additional revenue. To accommodate the growth in staff and revenue, Wilma issued a $2.9 million bond to construct additional space for the registration, health, personnel, and education departments as she planned a new tribal headquarters. The bond issue was one among a few to be undertaken by an Indian tribe with private sector underwriters.

Wilma passed a controversial law on November 6, 1993, establishing a residency requirement for the offices of principal chief and deputy principal chief within any of the nine districts of the Cherokee Nation. During the 1991 Cherokee Nation elections, two candidates for tribal council were disqualified from the race and their names removed from the ballots because of residency. Florian McKee Griggs, a candidate for tribal council, stated, "This amendment is just a tool of the Mankiller administration to control who gets to run for office in our tribe. Every Cherokee, who must live and work outside the Cherokee Nation, should be alarmed at this sort of disregard for our rights." James Gann, candidate for a council seat, stated, "I estimated the amendment requiring residency has effectively stripped nearly 80,000 Cherokees of their rights" (*Cherokee Observer*, 1994c). Wilma believed only those leaders who lived among the Cherokee communities could adequately represent them.

Wilma remarked, "We do better as a people when we can work on our own issues and concerns and problems. It is hard for people who don't know our history to understand that one of the powerful countries in history had a policy of wiping us off the face of the earth, then instituted a number of repressive policies to deal with 'the Indian problem.' We've had many low points. The Trail of Tears has to stand out for tremendous loss of life and land, but there have been many others. We almost have to reinvent ourselves and our government again and again. But it amazes me how we've always managed to land on our feet" (Koenenn 1993).

Wilma returned from an economic summit in Little Rock, Arkansas—an intense two-day session focusing specifically on how to stimulate the economy, both in the short term and the long term—with insight on increasing division in the country. Encouraged by the number and diversity of people there, Republicans and Democrats, Wilma witnessed people from every sector of the business community and every sector of society talking collectively about how to get the country moving again. She explained that a great need existed for bipartisan negotiations in the early 1990s. "In order to begin addressing specific issues like the economy, health care, education, inner cities, and other social issues, people must begin working together collaboratively if there is to be any progress in solving major problems facing the nation and all communities" (Mankiller 1993). She continued, "Sometimes I sit down with a diverse group of people in Oklahoma to work on some problem that we all have in common; it is almost like sitting down with people who have some kind of veil over their face or something. We all look at each other through this veil that causes us to see each other through these stereotypes. I think we need to lift back the veil and deal with each other on a more human level in order to continue to progress." As mentioned earlier, one of Chief Wilma's greatest talents as a leader was her ability to listen and to collaborate with others (Mankiller 1993).

Wilma's leadership style transcended political party lines as she consistently worked across the aisle to accomplish her goals—because that was the requirement to achieve results. A reporter from the *Los Angeles Times* described Wilma as a "prudent businesswoman with the tenacity of a bird dog." Wilma described her grassroots approach to leadership: "I'm an old '60s person, think globally and act locally. I'm only in an elected position because that's where you can allocate resources for things you believe in" (Koenenn 1993).

Wilma also devoted considerable attention to the issue of Cherokee identity. She became so frustrated by various groups around the country using the Cherokee name that in 1993, she circulated a list of groups claiming to be Cherokees. The Pan American Indian Association criticized her, and one member asked what gave her the authority to prevent anyone from using the Cherokee name. This episode reveals the complexities involved when it comes to Cherokee descendants without documentation and those whose families opted not to sign the Dawes Rolls and had no tribal membership. Although the Cherokee Nation determines membership criteria, the federal government decides the consequences of tribal membership.

Wilma discovered that the state of Georgia had recently passed legislation sanctioning three groups as state-recognized Indians. Wilma accused two of the groups, the Cherokee Indians of Georgia and the Georgia Tribe of Eastern Cherokee, of using the Cherokee name under fraudulent circumstances. Wilma included these and other offending groups in letters she wrote to governors in Florida and Georgia, complaining about the proliferation of groups claiming Cherokee heritage. "Perhaps more seriously, the reality is that many of these groups are causing an untold amount of confusion within the general public. Many organizations use various versions of the Cherokee name, adopt official seals, and issue membership cards." These groups are fraudulent in their presentations as some have people pay membership fees, provide them with membership cards or certificates, and then expect the members to participate in federal programs and services. "Only the Bureau of Indian Affairs and federally recognized tribal governments can certify whether or not a person has Indian blood and is therefore entitled to participate in federally funded programs for education, health, housing, food, and other benefits" (Tomas 1994). Since the 500th anniversary of 1492, an onslaught of those who would have themselves similarly recognized began, but they are not eligible for recognition either by the tribe or by the federal government.

Wilma's fight against the persistence of negative stereotypes garnered national attention in 1993 when she became one of the most vocal opponents of the hit song "Indian Outlaw," by country music star Tim McGraw. In a letter to radio stations across the nation, she wrote about the negativity in the song: "It is insulting to Indians, it perpetuates fraudulent stereotypes created by ignorance; it is exploitive commercialism at the expense of Indians, and it promotes bigotry" (*Red Sticks Press*, "Country Singer Up to Bootstraps in Controversy," 1994). At her insistence, many radio stations across the country stopped playing the song.

In 1993, Wilma also remarked on the popularity of Native American books. "It comes at a time when some orthodox religious hierarchies are undergoing a serious examination of their basic underlying principles. The present appeal of Native American spirituality may be that it is the antithesis of most orthodox religions. It may be just a passing fad; like the 1960s fascination with Far Eastern religions, or it may be an enduring attempt to understand the original people of this land. For me, the flagship book on Native American spirituality remains Vine Deloria's *God is Red*. He does an outstanding job of translating complex spiritual issues into very simple truths. Few, other than perhaps Silko in *Sacred Water* and Awiakta's *Selu*, have come anywhere near its clarity" (Tickle 1993).

Adding to the growing literature produced by Native American authors, Wilma published *Mankiller: A Chief and Her People* in 1993. The autobiography, coauthored with Michael Wallis, included a considerable portion on Cherokee History. Wilma wrote about the need to change the dialogue on American Indians approaching the new century. This accompanied her belief that public perception feeds stereotypes and vice versa and if Natives do not drive the narrative and the dialogue, then non-Indians will. She reflected on the knowledge of all the misery and suffering from the past that cannot be denied. However, she believed that positive events, actions, and occurrences in Indian Country needed to take center stage. "The United States government, one of the most powerful countries in the world, did everything it could to make sure our cultures did not continue. Among the Cherokee, there was a period when our ceremonies went underground. Now, when I see Cherokee women strap turtle shells on their legs and go out in the circle by the fire, I can't help but feel it is almost a revolutionary act" (Mankiller 1993, 57). Wilma wrote about the need for more Native leaders, heroes, and role models.

On the road again, Wilma delivered the commencement address at Sweet Briar College in Virginia in December 1993, focusing on community involvement, leadership, addressing negative stereotypes, and working together. It was an all-female college, and she encouraged the students in the audience to get involved in their communities no matter where they went or what they did in life with their new degrees. Wilma talked about how people wanted their problems to be solved for them by someone else, whether they lived in inner cities, suburbs, rural communities, or tribal communities. She explained that in American society people usually waited for others to assist them in problem-solving and said she thought that wrongheaded. "I always tell our own people that I don't know who they are referring to" (Mankiller 1993). Wilma implored the young women in the audience to personally take charge and solve community problems themselves. She explained that there was no great prophet who was going to come along and save this country.

Wilma's friends once told her she was a person who liked to dance on the edge of a roof. One piece of advice she gave the students that evening at Sweet Briar was to not live their lives safely but to take risks. She told them not to do things just because everybody else does them. Chief Wilma remarked, "In my generation someone who had a big impact on me was Robert Kennedy, who in one speech said, 'Some people see things the way they are and ask why, and others dream things that never were and ask why not?'" She advocated for the students to always question why things are and why they have to be done the way they always have been. She hoped they became active, took some risks throughout their lives, exerted some real leadership on issues. She also encouraged them to "dance along the edge of the roof as you continue your life from here" (Mankiller 1993).

Regarding the message she wanted to send to young women, Wilma stated, "Cherokee girls have the usual self-esteem problems of all American girls, plus the added problems caused by society's goofy misconceptions about them. So many Americans still think Indian women are down by the creek washing clothes. Women have to take more personal responsibility to turn the country around. When I was younger, I was full of anger. But you can't dwell on problems if you want to bring change, you must be motivated by hope, by the feeling you can make a difference. That's why my work is never done" (Merina 1994).

In 1994, Wilma created the Office of Indian Justice. She also accomplished much in terms of educational opportunities and Native curriculum and language programs, following the principle that Native students do better when they have the support and sustenance of other Native students, faculty, and staff. Wilma believed that educators need to know they are dealing with students from unique backgrounds and family value systems. She felt it is insufficient to think this is the American school system and the Native students just have to fit in, as that approach had proven to be a failure.

It was spring in 1994 when Wilma traveled to Ball State University in Indiana for a Women's Week lecture and discussed what it was like for female leaders. She began with the familiar barriers that still existed for women in elected positions. She stated, "1992 was supposed to be the year of the woman, that's ridiculous. When half of Congress and half of the Senate are women, then we'll have the year of the woman." Wilma described how there is still a male image of what a leader should be and women do not attract the funding that men attract. "If you are male, it is much easier to gain a leadership position and maintain it" (Mankiller 1994a).

Wilma explained in a 1994 interview, "Many native students in public schools have had wrenching experiences. They're teased about their names, called chief, or they're expected to be the authority on every Indian tribe and issue. That's a tremendous burden for a child." She said she was speaking from personal experience. "Absolutely, I was, like so many Native children, teased about my name my accent. I had a very tough time throughout my school years. I searched for role models in the history books but found very few. For years, I had no self-esteem" (Merina 1994). Wilma was a consummate advocate for teachers learning about Native culture and amending history texts to more accurately reflect the Native experience. "It's our responsibility to produce materials, curriculum, teacher's guides, and videotapes for the classroom. And I'm pleased to report that in Oklahoma there's a new program remitting high school students to fulfill their foreign language requirement by studying Cherokee" (Merina 1994).

All leaders have critics and Wilma was no exception. One of Wilma's harshest critics was David Cornsilk, editor of opposition newspaper *The Cherokee Observer.* Cornsilk wrote that the Cherokee people were slowly waking up to the harsh reality of the Mankiller administration and the damage done by them. He claimed there were persistent rumors that the people would vote Mankiller out in the next Cherokee election. According to Cornsilk, to "get all she can while the getting's good," Wilma would sell off the only valuable asset the Cherokee people had left, the Arkansas riverbed. Cornsilk accused Wilma of arranging for the Arkansas riverbed lands for other lands already under federal control. He proclaimed that Wilma had arranged for the state of Oklahoma to further steal from the Cherokee citizens to get paid back for what was stolen from them during the allotment period. He wrote, "It is a given that the Cherokee people have been cheated over the course of our relations with the U.S. and Oklahoma concerning the Arkansas riverbed, but that is no reason to cut off our nose to spite our face. By Mankiller's own admission, the Arkansas riverbed is full of natural resources, not to mention its potential for agricultural and business development" (*Cherokee Observer,* 1994a). Cornsilk then attacked the Mankiller administration's management of tribal businesses that failed during her tenure, including the Lodge of the Cherokees, the Cherokee Gardens Greenhouse operation, the Restaurant of the Cherokees, and the O-si-yo Club. "By trying to get rid of the Arkansas riverbed, Mankiller is admitting to us that she does not have the ability to manage our resources" (*Cherokee Observer,* 1994a).

Wilma's focus on social and family issues met with further criticism from those who watched other tribes invest heavily in casinos and tobacco stores. Wilma stated, "I'd like to see whole, healthy communities again, communities in which tribal members would have access to adequate health care, higher education if they want it, a decent place to live and a decent place to work, and a strong commitment to tribal languages and culture" (Sullivan 2010). In addition to the criticism Wilma received over her decisions in tribal businesses, she received criticism for her lack of involvement in the gaming industry.

Explaining a few of her accomplishments as chief, Wilma stated, "If you look at data over the last 20 years, we've had an impact on infant mortality and the educational attainment level. We're nowhere near where we need to be on any of those issues, nowhere near, but we're headed in the right direction" (Verhovek 1993). "I think the most important attribute of Cherokee culture is the sense of interdependence, of interconnectedness, of tribe, of family and community. It's a value system" (Jones 1999).

Ten tribal leaders from across Indian Country met with President Clinton on April 29, 1994, in a historic tribal leaders' summit and selected Wilma as one of the two emcees. The meeting was the first time a sitting president met with tribal leaders as they presented their concerns. President Clinton stated,

> There is a great yearning in this nation for people to be able to reestablish a sense of community, a sense of oneness, a sense of cooperation of shared values in spirit. There is a yearning for us to be able to live together so that all of us can live up to our God given potential. To be respected for who and what we are, I say to the leaders of the first Americans, the American Indian and Alaska natives, welcome to the White House, welcome home. In every relationship between our people our first principle must be to respect your right to remain who you are and to live the way you wish to live and I believe the best way to do that is to acknowledge the unique government to government relationship we have enjoyed over time. Today, I reaffirm our commitment to self-determination for tribal governments. (*Au-Authm Action News*, 1994)

Wilma dealt with another difficult issue when the Public Health Service determined that lump-sum payments to the Cherokee Nation violated the Treasury Department regulations dealing with transferring federal funds in the self-governance compact. Public Health Service is the parent branch of government of the Indian Health Service (IHS). The IHS is a federal agency within the Department of Health and Human Services that provides direct medical and public health services to members of federally recognized tribes of American Indians. Wilma argued that lump-sum payments required under the Cherokee Nation FY '94 Annual Funding Agreement with the IHS illustrated another example of departmental resistance to implementation of self-governance within the IHS.

In a letter to Senator John McCain, vice-chairman of the Senate Committee on Indian Affairs, Wilma emphasized how the IHS had conceded and how the IHS secretary had committed the department to make lump-sum payments in the annual funding agreements with self-governing tribes. She wrote, "We feel the Department's interpretation of the law lacks merit. Rather than interpret federal laws and regulations in a manner that facilitates the annual funding agreements as 303(e) of Title III expressly requires, IHS and PHS seem to be straining to interpret the law in a manner calculated to frustrate the agreements" (*Cherokee Observer*, 1994b). Wilma was successful in receiving more lump-sum funding from the IHS.

In the 1994 State of the Nation address, Wilma spoke of the consolidation of the BIA offices in Muskogee and Anadarko. "The problem with this consolidation proposal is they are proposing to consolidate the Muskogee and Anadarko area offices in Oklahoma, but they are not proposing to consolidate any other area offices anywhere in the country." The BIA intended to cut their budget, she said, yet it was not being executed fairly or uniformly. Oklahoma should not have to bear such an incredible burden. Wilma remarked, "The way they (BIA) went about the consolidation proposal is actually an outrage. They were way down the road on the proposal before even consulting us. They since told us they had a number of resolutions supporting it so we asked them to produce the resolutions. The only one they produced was a resolution from the United Keetoowah Band supporting the consolidation." The Muskogee office carried out the trust responsibility of the federal government for 18 eastern-Oklahoma tribes and provided services for those tribes (*Cherokee Advocate*, 1994a). Wilma stated, "I guess I agree with former Creek chief Claude Cox of Oklahoma, who said reforming the Bureau of Indian Affairs was kind of like rotating four bald tires on an old car" (Dyer 1993).

Wilma came to understand that the media had a significant amount of power and influence and could change the way people viewed American Indians. She understood the importance of using the media to teach non-Indians and other tribes about the story of the Cherokee people and to correct the persistent negative stereotypes. Wilma stated, "Sometimes I feel like wearing a pin that says, 'I am not the Mazola corn lady'" (Johnson 1994). She often answered stupid questions from people with no understanding of Native history in America and corrected the negative stereotypes they believed in.

On July 30, 1994, Wilma attended a gathering of tribal representatives from the Cherokee Nation and various minority journalists to honor the first Native American newspaper, *The Cherokee Phoenix*, and to celebrate the founding of Native American journalism in New Echota, Georgia. When she arrived, Wilma knew the area was on Indian land because she saw corn and beans planted there. Some people wonder why Native people are fixated on history. Wilma explained that to tribal people, history was not ancient. "History is a circle and we can reach out and touch 500 years ago because it's part of who we are." Wilma said many Cherokee people were still in a healing process with the state of Georgia because it was a bitter battle that removed the Cherokee people from their original land. She declared it was time to come together with all people and be inspired by those present. "Where my ancestors are buried, the general perception is that Native people have special rights. We gave up a lot of land and rights for those rights and we're not giving up one more inch" (Edmo-Suppah 1994). Wilma believed that just getting women into political office was not enough because some women do not do the right thing once they are there. She advocated for a revolution in thinking. "There has to be a revolution in thinking first or what good would it do if I support a Democrat or a Republican and they don't support Native issues" (Media Burn video, 1993).

In one of her final written statements before leaving office, Wilma discussed continued economic growth. She said there was a consensus in Indian Country that if tribes were going to improve their economic growth, they needed to achieve that improvement at the tribal level. Wilma also explained how the tribes have realized that federal resources were going to continue to decline, no matter who was in the White House. To address economic development issues in Indian Country, Rebecca Adamson (Eastern Cherokee) expanded on the concept of the First Nations Development Institute (FNDI) created in the 1980s. In 1992, she began the Eagle Staff Fund to funnel grants and technical assistance to community-based economic development projects.

The FNDI fund also supports a program called the Oweesta Fund, created in the 1980s, and it helped begin the Lakota Fund, a model for more recent tribal microenterprise funds. Primarily funded by the Ford Foundation, it is a venture similar to one operated by the Grameen Bank of Bangladesh. The Lakota Fund is separate from the First Nations group. FNDI also became instrumental in passing legislation making the BIA more accountable on managing trust funds (Fogarty 1995). Wilma supported Adamson and her vision for community-based economic development projects.

Describing the high points of her administration, Wilma said there were two—receiving an invitation to join the elders and having new medical centers built. At the memorial service for Key Ketcher, a respected tribal elder, another elder had spotted Wilma in the audience and asked her to join a group of tribal elders, all ministers, in the front row. Recalling that moment, Wilma said, "At an emotional level, it was better than receiving the Presidential Medal of Freedom or anything else." The second high point she spoke of was getting the Stilwell and Sallisaw medical clinics built. "The whole area of health is something I think I was particularly proud of. Being chief of the nation's second largest Indian tribe was like being a conductor of an orchestra and having lots of people playing lots of different instruments, and keeping them all playing the same song. There was a lot of give-and-take and I really enjoyed that" (Jones 1999). Wilma knew that revenue from gaming could be used to benefit health care, so, toward the end of her second term, three bingo halls emerged—in Fort Smith, Tulsa, and Siloam Springs.

During her second term as principal chief of the Cherokee Nation, Wilma continued her advocacy work educating the public about American Indians. She published her autobiography and began delivering speeches and lectures on understanding tribal histories and tribal sovereignty. Consistently, she spoke and wrote about the effects of negative Indian stereotypes on public policy, the need for Indians to trust their own thinking again, the role of women in traditional Indian cultures, and the importance of education at all levels.

The Wilma Mankiller Health Clinic became a reality thanks to the gaming revenues in 1994. An 80,000 square foot expansion was completed in 2021. Wilma spoke at the Indian Health Service Women's Health Initiative Steering Committee from June 22 to 24, 1993 (Willow 1993). She argued that the federal government acculturated tribal people believing that the BIA, or the Indian Health Service, or somebody else had better ideas for them than they had for themselves. She believed in expanding quality health care and creating new jobs for the people in and around Adair County. The expanded Wilma P. Mankiller Health Center has facilities for dental care, optometry, pediatrics, behavioral health, WIC, physical therapy, primary care, specialty care, and public health nursing. It also has an accredited drug rehab center, a pharmacy, a dialysis center, a conference and community room, and medical records and administration offices.

Wilma knew the time had come to retire when she began to sound like the people she used to protest against. When she served as chief, she tried to lead as a moderate and had to be the chief of all the people, whether they agreed with her politically or not. By the time she left office, there were fewer questions about whether or not a woman should be in a leadership position in the Cherokee Nation. Wilma proclaimed, "Cherokee people are more concerned about competency, about whether the Head Start bus shows up on time or whether they are properly diagnosed at the health clinics, than whether a woman is leading the nation. My elections were a step forward for women and a step into the Cherokee tradition of balance between men and women" (Meili, 2017). When Wilma left office, she set aside two days to meet with friends and colleagues. Those two days turned into two weeks as the people kept coming to wish her well.

8

Warrior Woman

After leaving office, Wilma became a scholar in residence as a part of the Montgomery Fellows Program at Dartmouth College in Hanover, New Hampshire. She taught Native American Studies and Law and Women's Studies. Because Charlie's son, Winterhawk, was still in high school, Charlie remained at home. Wilma enjoyed teaching, but in February 1996, she got sick. A doctor diagnosed her with pneumonia, another urinary tract infection, and second stage large-cell lymphoma. For the next five weeks, Wilma remained hospitalized while doctors sought the best treatment for her.

Gloria and Wilma began educating themselves on treatments and read books on nutrition. Kristina Kiehl, Wilma's friend from San Francisco, arranged for a weekly visit from a massage therapist for Wilma. There were no comparable treatment facilities back home in Oklahoma, so Wilma remained in Boston another eight months, alone, undergoing chemotherapy treatments. Gloria knew how much Wilma dreaded the regular outpatient treatments. "She had already spent way too much of her life in hospitals and she was not as invulnerable as she seemed" (Steinem 2015, 238). Charlie, Felicia, and Gina visited when Wilma underwent more biopsies and tests (Edmunds 2001, 227).

Gloria stayed with Wilma in Boston. "Of all the gifts she had given me, that was the greatest" (Steinem 2015, 239). "In our weeks of talk, movies, and friendship, I watched Wilma turn a medical ordeal into one more event in her life, but not its definition" (Steinem 2015, 239). Wilma taught Gloria the way of good mind. For several years after that, Gloria would join

Wilma at the end of summer for the Cherokee National Holiday, during which they attended all-night stomp dances together. "I watched as Wilma wrapped thick strips of cloth from knee to ankle, covering the steel brace that she could not walk without, adding the weight of tortoise shells and stones by her own choice" (Steinem 2015, 241).

In March 1996, Wilma began the first round of chemotherapy treatments, again staying with Bill and Suzanne Presley. The treatments were difficult for Wilma because of her 1990 kidney transplant. "I've had lots of health problems and lots of political battles, all kinds of things in my life, but I think if you stacked all of them one on top of another, nothing could equal what the last six months have been. It has been a huge enormous battle" (*Ojibwe News*, 1996b). Chemotherapy shrank the tumor in her intestine but her kidney function was not normal. She lost 80 pounds and still felt weak, but better than she had felt in several years. The chemotherapy treatments ended by August 1996, but her transplanted kidney failed. In October, Wilma started six weeks of radiation treatments in Fort Smith. She also began dialysis. The peritoneal dialysis caused severe anemia, so she began regular blood transfusions in spring 1997. By autumn, she was in the Bahamas receiving stem-cell treatments, which helped the anemia.

The disease strengthened Wilma, spiritually and emotionally. Wilma recalled, "Real serious illness is a very lonely journey. You have all kinds of people love you and be supportive and be helpful to you, but it's a journey you really take by yourself. My own nature as a person is to be positive, and even when everybody around me was very traumatized, I managed to stay level and mature and not fall into despair at any time, even when things looked pretty grim" (*Ojibwe News*, 1996b). Like a lot of critically ill people, she realized some friends were just "situational friends" who were around when all was well and disappeared when the going got rough.

Wilma beat the cancer. "When I was finally able to return to my home in Mankiller Flats, surrounded by the land that I love, the first thing I did was walk to the freshwater spring of my childhood, sit in my usual spot facing east, and say a heartfelt prayer of thanksgiving that I was able to come full circle to this special place where my life had begun" (Mankiller 1993, 118). Returning home was as healing for her as the treatments. Wilma was free of lymphoma symptoms and feeling better. "I'm a realist. I know the statistics for lymphoma, so I don't have this Pollyannaish idea that you can wish away these things and go merrily on your way. I just feel fine now" (*Ojibwe News*, 1996b).

Wilma continued her advocacy for American Indian sovereignty, treaty rights, and women's rights. Settled into her post-public service life, she enjoyed writing and delivering speeches and lectures on her mission to spread optimism about American Indians, as requests for speaking engagements poured in. Cherokees have a tradition of their leaders being excellent orators. Most notable among them were Attacullaculla, one of seven Cherokee delegates who traveled to London in 1767; former chief John Ross; actor, cowboy, and humorist Will Rogers; and Indian rights activist Ruth Muskrat Bronson. Attacullaculla was an 18th-century Overhill Cherokee leader who shaped diplomatic and trade relations with the British colonial government for over 50 years. John Ross led the Cherokees on the Trail of Tears and made several trips to Washington, D.C., on behalf of Cherokee tribal rights and sovereignty. William Penn Adair Rogers, known as Will Rogers, was born in the Cherokee Nation near Claremore, Oklahoma, in 1879 and became a popular radio personality, film actor, and writer. He traveled the world and the United States delivering his witty humor and social commentary. Ruth Muskrat Bronson was a Cherokee poet, educator, and Indian rights activist. She also became the first Guidance and Placement Officer of the BIA in 1931. Wilma shared their talent and skill in public speaking and advocating for Indian rights.

Wilma spread her message about American Indians through interviews, lectures, speeches, essays, and books. One of the key topics Wilma discussed was Indian sovereignty and its importance to all Indian affairs. Wilma's lectures over the next decade usually focused on American Indian and feminist issues important to her since the 1960s. She also continually corrected the negative stereotypes. Wilma stated that when she traveled outside of Indian Country, "People are always enormously disappointed when they meet me because I'm not handing out crystals or am not laden with Native American jewelry" (Nelson 2001).

Wilma delivered lectures locally and regionally. In a speech at Northeastern State University, in Tahlequah, Wilma urged the audience full of students, mostly Native students from the area, to complete their education and have Native pride. "We need a country full of young educated Native American people. Be proud of who you are as a native person." She said we should view barriers in life as challenges. "I've managed to survive cancer, I've managed to survive a kidney transplant, I've managed to get elected as a female chief of our tribe. I've failed of course, but I've never looked at the things that didn't work as failures" (*Ojibwe News*, 1996a). Wilma urged her audience to have a sense of community and to care for others. "There's no sense of community in the world. One of the few things we (American Indians) have left is we have that sense of community as Native people." She believed American Indian students were interested in getting a good education and urged colleges to become culturally diverse. "If your goal in this country is to provide higher education to all students, it's very important for minority students to look up and see faculty and staff and other students that look like them" (*Ojibwe News*, 1996a).

Wilma witnessed some improvements in Indian education. Students at the Native American Preparatory School in Rowe, New Mexico, received a rigorous college preparatory experience with an emphasis on appreciation for their cultural heritage. The 1,600-acre campus had a student body from 13 states. Wilma stated, "In essence, I think these children will have the best of both worlds: the best of the Indian world, the best of the non-Indian world. I love seeing Indian children who have always had the worst schools in America have access to the best education in America. That's a great thing for me to be able to say" (Next Step Magazine, 1998). Continuing to champion education, Wilma next attended a Johnson O'Malley Conference in Tulsa in December 2001 where 500 young children competed in a Cherokee-language-and-culture bowl. "It was one of the most inspiring events I have recently attended," she said. It thrilled Wilma that the language persevered and so many young people had an interest in learning it.

The different ways Native people described things in different languages intrigued Wilma. "Charlie and I were at a family picnic a couple of summers ago and this old tribal man told Charlie in Cherokee, 'There is a really angry man coming in the sky and he has long hair like you. He's very angry and is going to create a lot of trouble.'" That is how he described a tornado and a few hours later, after they returned home, her sister called and said a tornado just took down a tree in her yard (Mankiller 2001).

Traveling once again, Wilma appeared in Washington with Alice Walker, Angela Davis, actress Jasmine Guy, poet Sonia Sanchez, and Helen Rodriguez-Trias to benefit the National Black Women's Health Project at a conference on April 26, 1997. Each of the activists read an excerpt from Walker's latest book, *Anything We Love Can Be Saved*. Alice Walker is an American novelist, short story writer, poet, and social activist. In 1982, she became the first African American woman to win the Pulitzer Prize. She won the award for her novel *The Color Purple*. Walker deeply believed that mutual struggle had the power to surpass individual human effort. Wilma agreed with that worldview, given her background in activism.

Wilma was also honored for her many contributions in the areas of health, education, and housing for the Cherokee people. At the beginning of 1998, a "Women of Hope" poster series featured Wilma, along with 11 other Native women leaders in their fields. Study guides for educators accompanied the poster series. The posters focused on the women's accomplishments and struggles and provided guidance and philosophical Native American teachings (Whirlwind Soldier, 1997). The introduction to the series stated that the posters help overcome the sense of powerlessness that we often feel in the face of injustice and to find the circle of strength that exists within the classroom. One of the main purposes of the poster series was teaching K-12 public school students to appreciate the power of understanding cross-cultural issues in America. These cross-cultural issues became popular in the call for multiculturalism in the late 1990s.

On the morning of January 21, 1998, Wilma received the Presidential Medal of Freedom from President Bill Clinton. The ceremony occurred in the East Room of the White House. Wilma was accompanied by her mom Irene, Charlie, Felicia, and Gina. As she entered the White House, she reflected on how far she had come since her childhood in Mankiller Flats. Gloria later said, "As she stood there, strong, kind, and not at all intimidated by another chief of state, I was not the only one in the audience who thought she could be president" (Steinem 2015, 231). Two days later, Wilma sat on the front steps of a local Stilwell church playing with her nieces and nephews, seemingly unphased by the extraordinary award she had just received.

Although Wilma had not been in office for over two years, that did not end the criticism she endured about her administration's performance. The editors of the *Cherokee Observer* investigated the legal status of the 1975 Cherokee Nation constitution and that of the Mankiller government, with editor Robertson concluding, "Although the current government of the Cherokee Nation of Oklahoma (CNO) claims to enjoy the same sovereign powers as every other federally recognized tribe, the constitutional foundations of the CNO government are, in fact, dangerously deficient and will likely remain so until the Cherokee people decide to convene an authentic constitutional convention and reorganize under the Oklahoma Indian Welfare Act of 1936. From W. W. Keeler to Ross O. Swimmer to Wilma Mankiller, the modern chiefs of the Cherokee Nation have uniformly neglected the pressing need for constitutional reform in the interest of preserving their own power. They and the governments over which they have presided merely asserted the authority to govern without taking seriously the responsibility to ensure that their claims were based on secure constitutional foundations" (Robertson 1998).

In 1998, Wilma appeared with Gloria and political activist, author, and academic Angela Davis at the "Take a Stand" event sponsored by the Boston Women's Fund. Founded in 1984, this group of progressive women supported marginalized women and girls in achieving racial, social, and economic justice. Wilma and Angela Davis appeared together again at the University of Utah on March 6, 2001. Davis is a former member of the Black Panther Party and dedicated to the struggle for liberation and empowerment of oppressed minorities. After the chaotic year of 1968, which saw the assassination of Martin Luther King Jr., Davis became even more politically active and joined the Communist Party. She was involved in a shootout in 1970. She has published on topics associated with the emergent feminist consciousness of the interconnectedness of racism, capitalism, and sexism, the African Liberation Movement, the Cuban liberation, activism against the Vietnam War, and prison reform.

Also, that spring from March 18 through April 30, 1997, the Southwest Museum of the American Indian in Los Angeles presented an exhibition entitled "Native Women of Hope," featuring 12 women from across Indian Country of varying ages who played major roles in creating change in government, literature, law, medicine, science, and the arts. The photographer, Hulleah J. Tsinhnajinnie (Seminole/Muscogee/Dine'), spent 18 months traveling around the country discovering the lives of the women featured. Besides Wilma, the other women honored included Navajo surgeon Lori Arviso-Alvord; Oglala Lakota political and environmental activist Charlotte A. Black Elk; Western Shoshone Indigenous land rights activists Carrie and Mary Dann; Creek poet and musician Joy Harjo; Kuma Hula dance teacher and educator Pualani Kanahele; Anishinabe environmental activist Winona LaDuke; Kuna/Rappahannock actress and director of Spiderwoman Theater Muriel Miguel; Crow president of Little Big Horn College Janine Pease-Pretty-on-Top; Flathead Salish painter and printmaker Jaune Quick-to-See Smith; Oneida composer and performer Joanne Shenandoah; and Tlingit Thunderbird Clan anthropologist Rosita Worl. Wilma incorporated many of these women and their stories in her 2004 book, *Every Day Is a Good Day: Reflections from Contemporary Indigenous Women* (*Los Angeles Sentinel*, 2000).

Over the summer of 1998, Wilma again began experiencing medical issues and soon learned that the chemotherapy and radiation treatments she had undergone had caused her transplanted kidney to fail. On July 22, 1998, Wilma received a second kidney transplant, this time donated by her 32-year-old niece Virlee Williamson of Rogers, Arkansas. "I am absolutely overwhelmed by Virlee's generosity. She has to take a month off work to undergo a relatively serious surgery. She was a special person before she made this decision. Now she has moved herself into a rare category of compassionate people who act on their beliefs." Virlee stated, "In a way, it seems like I'm giving something to her that will enable her life's work to continue. She has accomplished so much in her life already, there is no telling what else she will do when she is healthy again" (*Indian Country Today*, 1998). The operation took place at Beth Israel Deaconess Hospital in Boston, where Wilma had undergone her first kidney transplant in 1990, operated on by Dr. Anthony Monaco. Dr. Monaco was the surgeon for her second kidney transplant as well. While Wilma was in Boston recovering from her second transplant, Gloria again stayed with her. They ate Hershey's Kisses and watched the television series *Prime Suspect*. Wilma loved the strong, brilliant, and highly competent female lead character played by Helen Mirren.

Just over a year later, in 1999, Wilma experienced additional medical issues and learned the diagnosis was breast cancer. She entered the hospital once again and had a double lumpectomy, followed by radiation treatments. Gloria, having survived breast cancer, took care of Wilma again during this time. Wilma remembered, "She filled prescriptions for me, took me to the bathroom when I needed to throw up, would sit with me during chemotherapy treatment. It's a very close, a very personal relationship. I honestly don't know the famous Gloria Steinem at all. I only know this other Gloria. She's so tiny, and I'm a pretty big woman, and there she was, under my arm, lugging me around when I was really sick" (Jones 1999). People often asked Gloria how two very different women came to become "chosen sisters." She stated, "It seems to me quite simple. We just in every way became a part of each other's lives" (Jones 1999).

Gloria sought Wilma's advice in 2000 when she contemplated getting married for the first time at age 66 to David Bale. Bale was a South African human rights advocate and father of actor Christian Bale. Gloria met David at a fundraising event for the Voters for Choice organization in Los Angeles in 1999. Wilma considered the union for a while and then called Gloria and told her he was "the real deal." That was one of Wilma's favorite sayings (Snell 2010). Gloria and David married at dawn on September 3, 2000, at Wilma and Charlie's house. Then they all had a lovely breakfast and went back to bed. David passed away after a battle with brain lymphoma in 2003.

Wilma continued her writing and in 2000 published an essay in a book called *Woman: A Celebration to Benefit the Ms. Foundation for Women*. This collection included essays by various authors—Carol Gilligan wrote on "Childhood," Byllye Avery on "Adolescence," Wilma Mankiller on "Womanhood," and Letty Cottin Pogrebin on "Maturity." It also featured photographs of women from around the world throughout the ages. In Wilma's essay on womanhood, she stated, "To live life on our own terms, women have been—and must continue to be—unafraid to take risks and to stand up for what we believe in" (*Woman: A Celebration to Benefit the Ms. Foundation for Women*, 2000, 66). This decade became one of her most productive ones in terms of writing and lecturing, with her health issues seemingly behind her.

Wilma's next keynote speech occurred in Tulsa at the Ninth Annual Business Leadership Program in March 2000. She spoke of how American culture discourages leadership qualities in women and how the stereotype of what women should be must change. She remarked, "Some people think that women like myself and other women leaders started out that way. I didn't. What happened to me is that I began to care more about the issues I was involved in, than I did my own concerns" (Tiernan 2000). She said she had learned to type because she and others were interested in creating a legal defense fund and they needed a typist. She had learned to write grants because she wanted to create a Native American youth center and preschool program in Oakland and needed funding.

Wilma's public speeches and lectures developed to include more details about tribal governments. Commemorating the 20th anniversary of the University of Arizona American Indian Studies program in 2001, Wilma delivered a speech entitled "It's Hard to See the Future with Tears in Your Eyes," a quote she borrowed from Mohawk teachings. Wilma remarked, "What I am trying to do at this point in my life is talk about the things we share with you, and some of my own experiences, talk about things that I have thought about or have feelings about for our common interest." Wilma focused on the many tribal societies and the importance of the involvement of women in local communities and governments.

She described the lack of accurate information about Indian people. "It's absolutely amazing that after all these years of interaction and all these years of living on our traditional lands, after stocking their pharmacies with our medicine, after using our corn, after using ceremonies for pleasure, after all of that, people know very little about us. And what happens to us is we go to their institutions, we go to their schools, we go to their colleges, we copy their culture, we read their literature and their magazines, and we learn everything about them, we learn everything about the people around us, but they don't know anything about us" (Mankiller 2001).

Throughout her lecture at the University of Arizona, Wilma described the importance of honoring treaty rights and the exercise of tribal governments and tribal sovereignty. "Equally important is the issue of trying to figure out how we hold on to a strong sense of who we are as Native people. Tribal elders tell us how to be as people—to be respectful, to speak peace, to be good to one another, to never hurt children, or men not to harm women—all of the things that people think are important values to our communities. Help each other, that's a big one at home in Oklahoma" (Mankiller 2001). People who are most respected among the Cherokee people are not those with great wealth and many possessions, but those who help others in need.

> To be born an indigenous person is to be born with an identity, to be born knowing who you are and knowing where you belong. There are so many in the world that don't have that feeling. For us to be able to know our history through our lives and our ceremonies connects our past, our present, and our future. History is a part of who I am. I am a product of history. We know our problems, we live with them every day. Our strength lies in the fact that despite the fact that the most powerful force in the world once tried to wipe us off the face of the earth and then instituted a set of policies designed to make sure we no longer existed as cultures and as peoples, we are still here. (Mankiller 2001)

On November 30, 2001, Cornell University honored Tom Porter (Mohawk) and Wilma for their decades of work with Native communities. The forum presentation examined the trends and challenges facing

American Indian communities in the 21st century. The forum was hosted by Cornell American Indian Program's Akwe:kon Press/*Native American Journal*; Lifeway, a project of Tides Center; and *Indian Country Today*. In the late 1960s, Porter and the traveling group of elders, White Roots of Peace, carried a message to remind Indian people to value their traditional language, ceremonies, and knowledge and to remind young people to care for the knowledge of the elders and for the needs of the elders. They delivered a message of self-sufficiency and called upon Indian people to value the land and work the land as a project of culture-based community development (*Indian Country Today*, 2003).

At the forum, John Mohawk (Seneca) spoke about Wilma's leadership abilities in finding the right people to do the jobs, giving them the tools they need to complete the jobs, and encouraging them along the way. "You have to juggle ten balls at once and get everything to happen. The best way to do it is to get the people energized themselves so that they take over and do it themselves. This is the lesson in Wilma Mankiller 101. You discover that people have it within themselves to solve most of their problems when given the opportunity." Mohawk described how Wilma shared the leadership qualities of Crazy Horse (Oglala Lakota), Little Turtle (Mohican/Miami), and Tecumseh (Shawnee). As an honest person of integrity who could be trusted to do the right thing, Wilma also possessed a talent for recognizing the real potential in people (Mankiller, "American Indian Millennium: Renewing our Way of Life for Future Generations," 2001).

Wilma next traveled to Smith College in 2002 and joined Angela Davis, author Toni Morrison, East Indian scholar and environmental activist Vandana Shiva, Egyptian feminist, writer, physician, and activist Naawel el Saadawi, and Ghanaian author, poet, playwright and academic Ama Ata Aidoo as part of the national board to create *Meridians: Feminism, Race, and Transnationalism* as the first peer-reviewed journal addressing the expansion of the women's studies field into areas of ethnicity and identity. Smith College president Ruth Simmons proposed the idea to the college's Women's Studies department, and they collaborated with the African American Studies department to create a journal written by women of color, about women of color, and for women of color.

Wilma next traveled to Utah and delivered the Keynote Address at the University of Utah Women's Week as a part of Women's History Month. She spoke about women's activism, challenging stereotypes, having a brave spirit, international women's rights, and the role of women in the 21st century. The crowd was so large, the university president asked the audience to push the chairs closer together to make more room for people standing in the back of the room. He also announced it was okay to sit on the floor in front of the first row. Wilma's mother and two nieces traveled there with her.

Wilma discussed why tribal governments exist today and Why Indian communities rank lowest in terms of social indicators and how there were always government-to-government relations. She stressed how the Cherokee are a culturally distinct group of people, with tribal traditional knowledge and ways of life continuing to sustain the people. She spoke of how the Cherokee concept of being of good mind is the ability of finding something positive instead of negative.

> My identity, my sense of who I am, is derived from my family and my community. My family and community shaped my ideas and caused me to get involved in things around me. In our family, no one sat us down and said, "This is how you should live your life, and this is the way things should be." In our community we didn't have ceremonies where people told us how we should live. I learned about community, family, and how people should treat one another from watching people from my community. I saw that people survived by helping each other, by bartering, and by having a sense of community. The other thing I saw is that people, by and large, tried to look forward in a good way. Even when people were dealing with the worst circumstances, they would have something good to say. If there was a snowstorm, they would say, "Well, that's okay, we can do things in the house." They were grateful for what they had and did what they could with what they had. They tried to find a good way of thinking about things. The good way of thinking is symbolized on a wampum belt by a white arrow going toward the Creator; the white line with the arrow and the beads going towards the Creator represents the White Path, or the right way of living and being. That way of thinking in a good way probably also shaped my identity. (Mankiller, Keynote Address 2002 at the University of Utah Women's Week, 2002)

Closing the lecture, Wilma noted how people are redefining feminism. "As women in the larger society made gains, native women have as well. There is no area in the world not affected by the feminist movement, whether it's a small community in Oklahoma or in New York City" (Mankiller, Keynote Address 2002 at the University of Utah Women's Week, 2002). Yet, she also stated how women still have a major battle on their hands because even American society has a narrow view of what it means to be a woman.

The evolution of her leadership came about because Wilma cared about the issues. "I don't think a life is worth living if you are not engaged in the community and actively working to make things better. Don't be afraid to lead. It's very important to stay engaged" (Mankiller, Keynote Address 2002 at the University of Utah Women's Week, 2002). Wilma believed leaders needed to have a positive attitude as well as faith, hope, and optimism about the future. She also believed that leaders must show people respect, even those they totally disagree with politically. Talented leaders never give up and they see barriers as challenges. Wilma remarked on the negative stereotypes about Native American women and how they are seen as either an innocent child of nature or as a drudge. She advised the audience to live fully and love fully and to share their gifts with those around them. Wilma proclaimed, "To me, leadership is simply facilitation. If you listen to the people, talk to the people, it is clear that they know how to do things. They know what has to be done, and what they need to do to accomplish their goals. Most of the time all they need is some help with resources, and somebody to help them develop timeframes or kind of move things along. Besides facilitation, it is very important for people who are perceived as leaders to be positive" (Mankiller 2003, 56).

In an interview with *News from Indian Country* on May 15, 2002, Wilma further explained the importance of maintaining a good mind and balance. "In historical times, Cherokee people cared a great deal about balance. An important part of that balance was a measure of equity between men and women. They consulted women in matters of importance to the community, the clan, the family, and the nation. Tribal dignitaries, called War Women or Pretty Women, existed in addition to a women's council." She continued by offering her favorite prayer and a life goal. "First, let us remove all negative thoughts from our minds so we can come together as one." This quote represents how she tried to live her life. "I have always tried to find something positive about any situation I have found myself in, whether it is political or personal." Even during chemotherapy, when she was bald, thin, and sick, she never allowed herself to fall into despair. Instead, she played her guitar, planted flowers, and surrounded herself with positive things. Wilma closed the interview discussing the importance of the Cherokee language. She explained how the Cherokee language is very descriptive and, more often than not, loses meaning when translated to English. "The Cherokee language is key to the survival of Cherokee lifeways." Wilma believed education became one of the most critical aspects of Indian civilization to be continued and guarded (Rector 2002).

Two weeks later in an interview with *The Native Voice* in Rapid City, South Dakota, Wilma explained the importance of leadership in Native communities. "We need to look to ourselves for solutions to our problems, not to some mysterious 'they' out there who will come and solve our problems, or even a prophetic leader or a great Messiah or something like that." Always reinforcing her belief that the power to solve Indian issues comes from Indian people, Wilma remarked, "There's only us. We've got to figure out how to do things." She noted how more women are working in leadership positions at the local level and doing great work. On the theme of balance, she stated, "To me, things are out of balance as long as you don't have both men's voices and women's voices." She next spoke about being open and honest about domestic violence and how we cannot solve this vast problem without talking about it first. The interview closed on cultural survival and her continued optimism. "People are always asking me why I'm optimistic, because I'm always optimistic about Native people, and I always respond with the truth which is that if we've been through everything we've been through—wars and famine, massacres and mass removal, and having children taken away to boarding schools, losing our language in some cases and banning our ceremonies, if we've survived all that and we've still managed to stay together as a culturally distinct group of people, we can survive anything and we'll still be here a hundred years from now as a culturally distinct group of people—and five hundred years from now. I do believe that" (Kent 2002). Speaking about feminism and the changing role of women in Indian tribal life, Wilma stated, "It's important to take a woman's sensibility to leadership. Women should bring their own skills to leadership positions and not emulate men's." She also said, "I don't like the term 'leader' applied to me. It's a team effort" (O'Rourke 2005).

Wilma published her fourth book in 2004 entitled *Every Day Is a Good Day: Reflections by Contemporary Indigenous Women*. In the book, Wilma wrote, "Cherokee traditional identity is tied to both an individual and a collective determination to follow a good path, be responsible and loving, and help one another—or as some Cherokee traditionalists say, 'Not let go of one another'" (Mankiller, *Every Day Is a Good Day*, 2004, 50). "The whole self-help concept of community development and the founding of the Cherokee Nation Community Development Department was based on the simple premise that when given the resources and opportunity, tradition-oriented Cherokee people will help each other and take on projects for the larger community good. Gadugi, or working collectively for the common good, is an abiding attribute of Cherokee culture" (Mankiller, *Every Day Is a Good Day*, 2004, 51). In the book, 19 prominent Indigenous women share their insights into what their tribes have endured and what it means to be an Indigenous woman in the 21st century. As the editor, Wilma stressed one of her key issues. After all these years of interaction with Euro-Americans, Indigenous people still have no identity except that created by stereotypes (Mankiller, *Every Day Is a Good Day*, 2004, 42). She emphasized the importance of traditional tribal knowledge providing Native people with a sense of identity and of knowing their place in the world; it helped them to remain genuine in a world where material wealth is the goal. Traditional tribal knowledge is the unique knowledge and expertise that Natives have about their ancestral lands and customs. Indigenous knowledge, or local knowledge, refers to knowledge systems embedded in the cultural knowledge of regional, Indigenous, or local communities. Traditional knowledge includes types of knowledge about traditional medicine, craft skills, climate, farming, subsistence, botany, ecology, and celestial navigation. These kinds of knowledge are based on accumulations of empirical observation and interaction with the environment.

Wilma also published an essay in *Native Americas* magazine entitled "To Persevere as Tribal People." In the article, she argued it was up to the current generation of young people to continue traditional tribal knowledge. "If we have persevered, and if we are tenacious enough to have survived everything that has happened to us to date, surely 100 years or even 500 years from now, the future generations will persevere and will also have that same sort of tenacity, strong spirit, and commitment to retaining a strong sense of who they are as tribal people" (Mankiller, "To Persevere as Tribal People," 2002).

Continuing her advocacy for women's rights, Wilma delivered another keynote speech—at the Oklahoma Native American Domestic Violence Conference in 2002—and spoke of the great difficulty in communicating the undesirability of violence in the post-9/11 climate. "We need to teach our children there are other ways to settle disputes." She reminded the audience that besides the War Chief many tribes also had a Peace Chief. "Peace Chiefs always counseled us to think about peaceful ways to settle disputes." Mankiller urged tribes to find fresh ways of teaching old traditional ways. "We have to fight for the right to maintain our traditional values. Our old ceremonies reminded us of our responsibility to each other and our responsibility to the earth. We don't have those ceremonies anymore." She suggested creating communities in the absence of family values (Rector 2001).

Wilma was proud of who she was and her heritage because of its contributions to American culture and its respectful attitudes toward women. "I believe the single most important attribute of our culture, that we all have in common, is a sense of interdependence, and a sense of community, a responsibility to help one another. The fact that we still live within a value system and culture that enables us to care about one another and help one another is the most precious cultural attribute. We still feel very strongly tied to our extended families, our clans, our communities and our nations. Our sense of community is a very precious attribute of our culture" (Mankiller 2003).

Reflecting the tenacity and perseverance of the Cherokee people was a news story called *Inside Native America*, on KOTV in Oklahoma City on April 5, 2004. The episode featured George Tiger interviewing the new Cherokee principal chief, Chad Smith, on the importance of Cherokee history and what it can teach us. Chief Smith reflected on the advances made over the past two decades and gave much credit to Wilma for the work done during her tenure as chief. Tiger and Smith discussed issues such as the Cherokee language–revitalization program, the focus on *gadugi*, economic development and a de facto regional government, improved social services, housing for the elderly, and keeping the elderly engaged in the community. Tiger asked Chief Smith of the reason for learning the Cherokee language and about tribal heritage, and he replied, "Language holds the culture and children excel academically by being bilingual." Wilma agreed wholeheartedly.

Wilma continued with her writing and her speaking engagements across the country as she turned 60 years old in 2005. She punctuated consistent themes such as the effects of negative Indian stereotypes and the importance of Indian sovereignty and self-reliance with an increasing emphasis on the need for more Native journalists and the significance of traditional tribal knowledge.

In February, Wilma took part in an American Indian Journalism seminar at the University of South Dakota in Vermillion. The Diversity Institute of the Freedom Forum sponsored the event and also honored Wilma by electing her one of four new trustees of the Freedom Forum during that visit. The Freedom Forum is a nonpartisan, nonprofit, media-oriented

TRIBAL SOVEREIGNTY

Tribal sovereignty is the concept of the inherent authority of indigenous tribes to govern themselves within the borders of the United States. Originally, the U.S. federal government recognized American Indian tribes as independent nations and came to policy agreements with them via treaties. The sovereignty that American Indian tribes possess is inherent, which means that it comes from within the tribe itself and existed before the founding of the United States. The U.S. Constitution recognized tribal governments and, starting with Thomas Jefferson, America's founding fathers pledged that their sovereignty was to be protected. The U.S. Supreme Court has repeatedly recognized tribal sovereignty in court decisions for more than 150 years. In 1831, the Supreme Court agreed in *Cherokee Nation v. Georgia* that Indian nations had the full legal right to manage their own affairs, govern themselves internally, and engage in legal and political relationships with the federal government and its subdivisions. In 1942, Supreme Court Justice Felix Cohen wrote, "Indian sovereignty is the principle that those powers which are lawfully vested in an Indian tribe, are not delegated powers granted by express acts of Congress, but rather inherent powers of a limited sovereignty which can never be extinguished." Today, tribal governments remain for the same reasons they were founded—to provide for the welfare of the Indian people. Tribal governments build and maintain services like water, roads, waste disposal, emergency assistance, law enforcement, and transportation. Tribal governments are charged with protecting and developing an economic base, working to preserve and encourage culture, and supporting education.

foundation for media diversity (Lewin 2005). This was an important conference for illuminating the need for more Native journalists within the
profession. Continuing to educate non-Indians about the dangers of negative stereotypes and the role of the media, Wilma spoke at the Tulsa Press
Club in 2005 and focused on public perception and how it affects public
policy concerning American Indians. "I think the challenge now is to realize that public perception is just as important as a Supreme Court decision
where Indians are concerned" (Ruckman 2005). She described the importance of others knowing that tribes have businesses besides gaming, such
as schools, hospitals, and health-related services, emphasizing the need for
more Native journalists.

Vine Deloria Jr. passed away on November 13, 2005, and Wilma published an essay on his contributions to honor him and to assist the public
understanding of Native people. "I can testify as his contemporary that
reading his books encouraged me to be a more critical thinker and affirmed
my own beliefs about Native people. His provocative and revolutionary
ideas have also had a monumental impact on Indian policy and public perceptions toward Native people." Wilma wrote on how Deloria's influence
reached far and wide and he literally saved lives with his accurate words.
"His stature and moral integrity, knowledge of tribal law and history, and
ability to debate misinformed journalists, politicians and academics have
earned him our admiration and respect" (Mankiller, "An Original Thinker
with a Warrior's Spirit," 2005).

In fall 2005, Wilma became the University of Oregon's Morse Chair
professor, as a visiting lecturer in the Ethnic Studies Department, coteach-
ing a class with American Indian law professor Rennard Strickland on
tribal government, law, and life at the law school and delivering lectures.
Wilma shared the stage with old friend John Trudell at one of her lectures
for Indigenous Solidarity Day at the end of October 2005. Ron Marten, a
writer with the Confederated Tribes of Grande Ronde, attended and noted,
"she was incredibly knowledgeable and even a little bit feisty" (Radical Profeminist Blog, 2010).

Speaking of feminism in the modern age, Wilma said, "Every woman
figures out her own way to deal with sexism." She made her mark among
the men at the table by pulling her own seat up and getting down to business. "I never thought about being a woman. Nobody told me I couldn't do
anything. Girls and women have to have their own identity, not from their
boyfriends or husbands. Define it for yourself in your own way" (Radical
Profeminist Blog, 2010).

On November 9, 2005, Wilma delivered the Wayne Morse Center for
Law and Politics 25th Annual Morse Chair Address at the University of
Oregon. The topic was "Context is Everything: History and Culture in
Contemporary Tribal Life." A crowd of around 650 people gathered that

evening. Wilma began her lecture with the structure of tribal governments and how the manner in which we select leaders differs from nation to nation:

> The land base and population of tribal governments range from those with millions of acres to some with fewer than 25 acres of land. And the population ranges from the Navajo and Cherokee Nation, each with enrolled membership of over 225,000 members, to some governments with less than 100 members. It is important to note that the population or land base of a sovereign entity does not determine the degree to which it enjoys the rights to self-governance . . . Tribal governments exercise a range of sovereign rights. Some tribal governments, such as the Onondaga, continue their original form of government and even issue their own passports for international travel, while other tribal governments must fight for federal recognition after centuries of outrageous exploitation. (Mankiller 2005a)

Wilma said, "Though land was and remains critical to the cultural survival of tribal people and their governments, tribal governments now hold only a tiny fraction of their original land holdings. The dozens of anti-sovereignty groups who argue that tribal people should not have 'special rights' fail to understand that tribal people gave up millions of acres of land and sacrificed many lives to retain our right to self-governance" (Mankiller 2005a).

Wilma described the role of Native women:

> It is often said that the character of an individual or a people can best be determined in times of extreme crisis. By keeping their vision fixed firmly on the future, even during times of unspeakable hardship, Cherokee people have showed the depth and strength of their character time and time again. One underlying reason for the tenacity of Cherokee people is the key role women have played in tribal life. In the media, as in larger society, the power, strength, and complexity of Native women are rarely acknowledged or recognized. Prior to Cherokee removal, they consulted women in matters of importance to the community, the clan, the family, and the nation. A woman's power was considered so great that special women declared whether punishment was to inflict upon those who had committed offenses against the people, or whether we should instead pardon them. (O'Rourke 2005)

Many people who hear about present-day jurisdictional and taxation controversies between state and tribal governments are completely unaware of the long history of government-to-government relations between tribal governments and the U.S. government. In her Morse Chair Address, Wilma stated, "The lack of accurate information about Native people leaves a void that is often filled with stereotypes that either vilify or romanticize Native people." She also said that a great deal of media attention focuses on the wealthy tribes who distribute some of their casino revenue to tribal members through per capita payments. "While the casinos give tribal governments unprecedented economic and political power and generate much needed income for schools, scholarships, health care, housing, and other desperately needed services, the debate about the long-term impact of casinos on the social and cultural web of the community continues," Wilma noted. Economic growth is the most notable and positive aspect of gaming. Many opponents argue the negative aspects of gaming are the divisions within tribes created because of control and corruption of the gaming industry.

Many non-Indians often associate tribes with gaming just because they have casinos. Wilma said, "Oregon has a lottery, and the lottery doesn't define what it means to be a citizen of Oregon." Gaming is a tribal business like many businesses the Cherokee Nation operates. On sovereignty being able to address social problems such as poverty, poor health, and housing, Wilma described how outsiders usually focus on housing and economic issues when looking to successes with tribal sovereignty. "What we see in our communities that outsiders don't see is the strong sense of interdependence. We see a lot of self-help projects, projects where people will group together and help one another, whether it's to raise money for a scholarship or build their own waterline or build their own houses" (Cooper 2005).

Another critical point from the Oregon lecture was the importance of protecting Native culture, tribal sovereignty, and traditional knowledge. Wilma said, "Protecting tribal sovereignty is a universal priority for all tribal governments. Another common concern of great importance is the development of projects designed to maintain traditional knowledge systems, culture, and language. Tribal traditional knowledge and stories give Native people a sense of continuity and knowing their place in the world. The culture of Native people is not only important for tribal survival, it also holds potential gifts for the world. One of the most important challenges of our time is to develop practical models to capture, maintain, and pass on traditional knowledge to future generations" (Mankiller 2005c).

The Oregon lecture concluded with the importance of tribal values. Wilma said,

> Even with the rapidly changing racial composition of the population in the United States, a preoccupation with European culture remains. The larger society around us seems to promote the value that material wealth determines one's worth, that individual achievement is more important than the common good, and that kindness can be perceived as weakness. Those values do not hold much appeal to most tradition-oriented Native people. More and more, tribal people are trusting their own thinking again and looking within their own communities for solutions to entrenched problems. We have endured war, removal, loss of life, land, resources and rights; and wholesale attempts to assimilate us. But we are still standing, and we continue to have strong viable Native communities. After every major tribal

upheaval, we have almost had to reinvest ourselves as a people, but we have never given up our sense of family, of community, or clan, of nation. (Mankiller 2005a)

Wilma witnessed people helping one another and having a sense of responsibility for one another. She mentioned it is more important to focus on the things that are working rather than concentrating on all the social problems, which is what non-Indians or outsiders do. Wilma stated, "The thing that bothers me the most is people keep saying, 'You have to give up who you are, give up your identity and adopt the values of the larger society,' and yet they can't articulate what those values are." The reasons Natives are not interested in inclusion in the larger society is because they have their own governments, own lands, and have a culture that is thousands of years old. They are not seeking a new land, Wilma explained (Cooper 2005).

Wilma explained, "I grew up with the idea that whatever rights we have as Native people, that they are rights that we paid for dearly, paid for with many lost lives and many millions of acres of land, but that they are legal rights and that the United States government has a legal and moral responsibility to us as Native people" (Miller 2006). She returned to a favorite teaching topic by telling the audience that a fundamental challenge for those who care about tribal sovereignty and treaty rights is to educate the American public and the U.S. Congress about Native issues and history. She continued, "They don't know anything about us and that has got to change if we're going to survive." She said it is up to the tribal leaders to eliminate the stereotypes and negative publicity and give non-Indians accurate information (Miller 2006).

In 2005, Wilma's continuing influence in the Cherokee Nation became part of the Mission of the Cherokee Nation, as follows: "The mission of the Cherokee Nation is Gadugi—working together as individuals, families and communities for a better quality of life for this and future generations by promoting confidence, the tribal culture and an effective, sovereign government. We have developed a plan to help fulfill this mission and make our vision a reality. We must make sure that our daily work, our efforts in Washington, D.C. and every other part of our service to the Cherokee people is directed toward that goal" (Cherokee Nation website, n.d.). Principal Chief Chad Smith stated, "Under the great leadership of Chief Mankiller, we were able to fully realize our potential, not only as citizens of the Cherokee Nation, but also as human beings. It is of the utmost importance that we continue on as she would have wanted, to trust our own thinking, and to get the job done for our people" (Cherokee Nation website, n.d.).

Also in 2005, the Eastern Band of Cherokee Indians, the Cherokee Preservation Foundation, and Harrah's Cherokee Casino and Resort sponsored an annual event known as the Cherokee Day of Caring. Each community club within the Qualla Boundary, the Eastern Band lands, nominates 10 families in need of help with their homes, yards, gardens in order for an opportunity to practice *gadugi*.

From 2002 to 2006, Wilma saw a sea change in the way tribal governments and communities conducted their affairs.

> In the 1970s, the idea of exercising treaty rights seems a radical idea. But the federal Indian Self-Determination Act of 1975 set in motion changes that have allowed tribes to set their own courses based on their own tribal needs. We may always need outside experts, but we are experts on tribal government, tribal communities and the history of our people. I encourage our tribal people to think and look at their communities for solutions. Through self-reliance, tribes can build problem-solving capacity. Tribal governments are important because we are in charge of our future. We have been on this land for thousands of years. We're not from someplace else. This is our home, our land. (*Confederated Umatilla Journal*, 2006)

Wilma urged tribal leaders to control their own image to continue to educate the public about American Indians, stating that if they did not, then their opponents surely would (*Confederated Umatilla Journal*, 2006).

Wilma published an essay in 2006 on treaty and trust issues for modern Indian communities, which grew out of her Morse lecture at the University of Oregon. She emphasized:

> Some tribes make a conscious choice to establish relationships with states and execute cooperative agreements with state governments. Some other tribes choose to see the states as adversaries and choose not to enter into agreements with them at all. There are also different scales of tribal government. What I think is important for people to know is that the size of the land base of a tribal government, or the size of the population of a tribal government, has no bearing whatsoever on the degree to which it has the right to exercise sovereignty. The battle to protect sovereignty, I think, is the most important battle for all tribes—it's a universal concern. (Mankiller 2006, 43)

Wilma was one of the speakers, along with LaNada War Jack, at Idaho State University on January 17, 2007, during Human Rights Week. Dr. War Jack was the Shoshone-Bannock Tribes executive director. Wilma stated it is important that Indian people never give up fighting for the right to recognition of Indigenous rights. She emphasized the importance of traditions and women playing large roles in their communities. She said the negative stereotypes were being wiped away by women once again fulfilling leadership roles. She also stressed the role of mentors in the futures of Indian youth. Speaking of her own mentor Justine Buckskin, Wilma said, "Without her help, my life may have ended up very differently if she didn't extend her hand out to me." Buckskin had urged her to help Indian people. Wilma's advice to young people who were looking to build a career in tribal government was to get involved in their communities, be engaged in cultural activities, and get a wonderful education (Wahtomy 2007).

The state of Oklahoma celebrated its centennial anniversary in February 2007. Initially, Wilma declined to take part, given the history of the state and the Native people, then she reconsidered and thought of using the opportunity to educate others. "Reciprocity and interdependence are important to indigenous women, in particular. A lot of Americans think that because we dress like people around us, we drive similar cars, we live in similar houses, we think the same way. I would contend we not only think about different things, but we think about them in a different way" (Robinson 2007).

On May 22, 2007, Wilma joined Gloria and Alice Walker at the 92nd Street YMCA in New York City for a conversation about women and leadership. Wilma remarked that her role as chief did not define her because that was only for 10 years and represented only a small slice of her rich life. She said she was always happiest at home at Mankiller Flats and she certainly did not miss all the traveling back and forth to Washington. Wilma urged the audience members to get involved in leadership and said, "If you want to see a leader, look in the mirror." Wilma very much held community at the center of her servant leadership style. The well-being of the community was at the heart of her decision-making process. The three women—Wilma, Gloria, and Alice—each discussed the path they had taken to becoming feminist icons in America. Wilma then asked Gloria how she felt being listed on President Nixon's "enemies list." Gloria chuckled and remarked, "The less secure the man, the more he has to prove" (2007, 92nd Street Young Men's and Young Women's Hebrew Association, NYC).

Alice and Wilma had been friends for years when Alice remarked, "Seeing her (Wilma) stand so strong and tall, I have never seen so strong a spirit as Wilma. Anybody with spirit like that is supported by the Universe. She's incredibly beautiful and rare and wonderful. She's been a great teacher to me. She inspires energy" (Jones 1999). Wilma and Charlie spent a winter holiday with Gloria and Alice in Mexico. At the end of their stay, Wilma remarked, "This is the first time in my life that I've been with people who didn't need anything from me" (Steinem 2015, 230). This gave Gloria an important insight into the price Wilma had paid for leadership among people who had not been allowed to lead themselves for decades.

About her close friend, Gloria stated,

I think her greatness comes partly from the Cherokee tradition, because she's very much a part of that ancient wisdom. It comes partly from the activism of the '60s and the kind of populist belief that we can seize control of our own destinies. And it comes partly from some indescribable, unique place that is Wilma. She's like a large, wise tree. As a political force, she's a great leader because she understands how to empower people, how to help them make their own decisions, rather than making the decisions for them, which is the mark of a great leader. She creates strength, not weakness. As a friend, you can't be in Wilma's presence for very long without understanding how much compassion and intelligence there is in her. She makes each of us a little better than we would otherwise be. Her strength of spirit is evident. It is in her eyes, which stay fixed with a welcoming softness upon those with whom she speaks. (Jones 1999)

In June 2007, Supreme Court Justice Sandra Day O'Connor, the first woman to serve on the Supreme Court of the United States, visited the Cherokee Nation. In honor of her visit, the Cherokee Nation hosted a Youth Leadership Conference for which they invited several speakers, including Wilma. Impressed with her hosts, Justice O'Connor said, "I feel so privileged to be here and what touches me particularly is the extent to which traditionally the Cherokee people have placed a lot of reliance on the women" (*Native American Times*, 2007).

Wilma delivered a lecture at the Heard Museum in Phoenix, Arizona, on October 2, 2008, on the topic "Challenges facing 21st-Century Indigenous People." Poet Simon Ortiz (Acoma Pueblo) introduced Wilma, stating, "She has meant so much to us for what she has offered to us of her time and vision." Wilma stated she would live in Arizona if she did not live in the Cherokee Nation. Arizona is home to 20 tribal governments that are intertwined with local and state governments thereby having an economic impact. Wilma said,

> The Earth is our mother and we have a duty to preserve and protect the natural world. Remind people of their obligations to each other and to the land. The Hopi and Iroquois Prophesies state the world will end when people forget their responsibilities to protect the earth. Indigenous people have the benefit of being constantly reminded of their duty to the lands through their stories and ceremonies. There is an interdependence between humans and the land. Non-indigenous people are often distant from the land. How many urban dwellers go about their day never seeing the miracle of the natural world? (Mankiller 2008a)
>
> Public perception about native people must be framed by native people. We must frame our own issues to tell our own stories. What does the future hold? Look at the past. We survived massacres, wars, loss of land, life, and we must be hopeful. Efforts to eradicate our traditional knowledge and values failed. Ceremonial fires of many tribal people continues. Some have had to revitalize and reinvent themselves and adapt to change. There is still a strong sense of tribal identity remaining. We need to develop practical models to continue teaching traditional tribal knowledge. The entire system of knowledge must be maintained. Red Power is about tribal sovereignty and protecting indigenous human rights; political reform through intertribalism. (Mankiller 2008a)

During an interview with National Public Radio the following week, Wilma told host Michel Martin, "I think that in virtually every sector of society, Native people, whether they're in tribal government or whether they're in the private sector or an artist, they encounter people every day who have such enormously stupid, ridiculous stereotypes about Native people and have so little accurate information about either the history of Native people or their contemporary lives. We need more Native journalists and we need to produce more Native films" (National Public Radio Interview, 2008). Then she elaborated that it was in the late 1960s that she considered how "unfortunate it was that most Americans who have been living in our, you know, towns and villages for hundreds of years, know so little about us." Wilma described how the idea had changed a bit but whenever she gets together with other Natives who are active in the communities and around the nation they ask each other, "What kind of stupid questions were you asked recently?" Wilma was frustrated and exhausted having to constantly correct inaccurate information and negative stereotypes. Martin asked her what type of stupid question someone had asked lately. She related the story of an English guy with a thick British accent who once visited her office for an interview. He asked her if she rode a horse to work, and she had a bit of fun with him. "So I told him, yes, I did. I rode a horse to work. I described the horse. And I said, my husband and I live in a teepee along the edge of a river, and he fished and hunted every day, and this guy was writing the stuff down" (National Public Radio Interview, 2008).

Wilma delivered an address at Quinnipiac University in Hamden, Connecticut, on October 28, 2008, as part of the 60th anniversary of the Universal Declaration of Human Rights. Her speech closed out the day-long conference, "The Declaration of Human Rights 60 Years Later: A Look at Indigenous and Gender Issues." Wilma spoke of all the unique customs that bring each tribal group together. The main bond is a respect for the earth and the resources it brings forth. Mankiller said Indigenous people celebrate the earth in two ways: stories passed on through generations and tribal ceremonies. She further explained, "These ceremonies remind us of our responsibilities to each other and our land" (Taylor 2008). In addition, she pointed out how many environmentalists focus only on the land they are trying to save while overlooking the people who live there.

Wilma and Charlie visited an Indigenous community along the Rio Negro in the Brazilian rainforest and discovered that some leaders criticized many environmentalists for advocating to save the rainforest but saying very little about saving the inhabitants of the rainforest. Again, the familiar theme emerged from the dearth of information about Indigenous people throughout the world in educational institutions, literature, films, and popular culture. Wilma said, "This lack of accurate information leaves a void that is often filled with nonsensical stereotypes which either vilify indigenous peoples as troubled descendants of savage peoples, or romanticize them as innocent children of nature, spiritual but incapable of higher thought" (Mankiller 2009a). Indigenous people across the world share some common values derived from an understanding that their lives are inseparable from the natural world. It comes from living in one place for many generations and being familiar with the lands, rivers, and mountains.

While many ethnic groups care deeply about the environment, Wilma said, "The difference is that indigenous people have the benefit of being regularly reminded of their responsibilities to the land by stories and ceremonies. They remain close to the land, not only in the way they live, but in their hearts and in the way they view the world. Protecting the environment is not an intellectual exercise; it is a sacred duty" (Mankiller 2009a). Native environmental leaders speak of protecting the earth for future generations, but they not only speak of humans, they speak of future generations of plants, trees, water, and all living things. In conjunction with this is the continued value of cooperation in Native communities. Wilma described how the low-income Cherokee communities work together with Charlie to create walking trails, community centers, water lines, sports complexes, and houses.

Mankiller's tenure as principal chief helped alter many of the perceptions regarding the Cherokee Nation, particularly those regarding women. Prior to that, even some inside the tribe opposed being led by a woman. "Stereotypes about indigenous women are particularly appalling. In the media, the power, strength, and complexity is rarely recognized," Mankiller said. She continued that Indigenous people always have to reinvent themselves because of the changes constantly around them. According to her, the biggest task in the 21st century will be to create a practical model to communicate with newer generations of tribal people. "If we as a people have been able to lose such a staggering amount of land, resources, and we're still standing, how can I not be optimistic about the future? We're prepared for the future and [Indigenous people] have proved time and time again we can adapt to change" (Mankiller 2009a). In 2008, after a 30-year wait, the United Nations passed a Declaration on the Rights of Indigenous Peoples, outlawing discrimination against them while aiming to improve their development. Notably, the United States was one of four nations that voted against the declaration's passage.

In one of her last lectures, Wilma spoke at Kansas State University on April 2, 2009, during the conclusion of Diversity Summit Week. She spoke out against continuing stereotypes about Native people in America. She recalled that she had once been requested to wear a traditional dress for an interview with *Good Morning America* and she had replied, "Would they

ask the president to dress like a Pilgrim? I wear a traditional dress to ceremonies and I wear a business suit to work. I don't ride a horse. I drive a
station wagon."

She particularly focused on teaching about Cherokee history and the
establishment of their own government and how they established the first
public schools west of the Mississippi River. She further emphasized
that once Oklahoma became a state in 1907, all the progress and self-
governance actions made within the Cherokee Nation ended. The Cherokee people fell into tremendous decline with Adair County, Oklahoma,
becoming among the poorest in the United States. Yet, the tribe maintained their culture and language and traditional knowledge. Wilma
stated, "It's a miracle Cherokee culture has survived into the 21st century
and if you wonder why it's important, look at how we did when we governed ourselves and how we did when we did not control our destiny." She
added that it is possible to live in modern America and preserve ancient
ways (Strand 2009).

9

Enduring Legacy

In April 2009, Wilma revisited the site of Red Clay. She fought back tears as she recalled the first time she was there 25 years ago. "I came out just before dawn and there were people camped everywhere, and a few were already up drinking coffee at their camps—quietly, almost reverently." She had joined then–principal chief Ross Swimmer in a roped-off area close to where the Cherokee Joint Council meeting would begin. They stood in a place where their ancestors had gathered in the 19th century to discuss whether they should stay and fight to the death to keep their land or cooperate with the removal. "As I stood there, I tried to imagine again the anger, frustration and passion my ancestors must have felt," Wilma recalled. "And on that special morning, everyone seemed to feel connected to the Cherokee people who had met at Red Clay in the early 1800s." She recalled the crowd at that first Red Clay reunion in 1984 as she caught sight of the young Cherokee men running with the torch of the nation's eternal flame from North Carolina. "Many quietly cried. And I did. And I always cry again every time I say this. When I think about the Trail of Tears, I don't think about a big historical event. I think about the families . . . and how they must have felt as they were being told to leave everything they'd ever known," she said. "No matter how many generations pass, this is still home" (Sohn 2009).

She also recalled that while traveling to Red Clay in 1984, she and her family had discussed how a country that was "founded on democracy and equality for all could be so brutal to our ancestors." She felt anger over the past, she said, but learned to redirect her anger to something positive. "I learned at Red Clay how important it is to understand and acknowledge history and to understand past injustice. It's equally important to channel our past injustices into actions that will help us secure a future for our people," she said. "Our ancestors suffered greatly, but they kept their vision fixed firmly on the future. We today, as Cherokee people, can do no less." She said Cherokee people would acknowledge the hardships of the past and talk about them while they were at Red Clay but would not dwell on them. Mankiller closed with a Mohawk proverb, "It's hard to see the future with tears in your eyes" (Chavers 2009).

Wilma next traveled to Phoenix to the Heard Museum and delivered another lecture, but she had not been feeling well for several weeks. In March 2010, she received a diagnosis of Stage IV metastatic pancreatic cancer. The doctor at St. John's hospital in Tulsa gave her four weeks to live. Wilma declined chemotherapy treatments, telling the doctor they would only prolong her pain. She thought she had done what she was supposed to do while here on earth and it was time to go home. As she and Charlie drove back home to Mankiller Flats, neither said a word.

Arriving at the metallic cowboy boot hanging from the front gate, Charlie asked her what she wanted to do now, and Wilma said, "Let's drive." Returning home sometime later, Wilma and Charlie entered their one-story dark-red house. Lining the entrance were two picture frames. One held an invitation to Wilma and Charlie to a garden party with Queen Elizabeth II and Prince Philip of England in 1991, and the other frame held a certificate of the Presidential Medal of Freedom presented to her by President Clinton in 1998 (Whitehawk 2013). Wilma told her family and then called Gloria in New York with the news.

Wilma and Gloria were planning to coauthor a book on traditional tribal knowledge later that year. Wilma asked if Gloria could come now instead of waiting for May, which is when they had planned to work on the book. Gloria wanted to help. "I have been with her through dialysis because of kidney disease inherited from her father, a kidney transplant, cancer brought on by immune suppressants to maintain the transplant, chemotherapy and a second transplant, then a second bout with cancer" (Steinem 2015, 242). Gloria knew this would be by far the hardest and the last time she would be with her close friend.

Wilma's caregivers were Felicia, Gina, Charlie, Gloria, Dr. Gloria Grim from the Rural Health Clinic, and Kristina Kiehl and Bob Friedman, friends from San Francisco. Relatives, friends, and colleagues came to the house to pay their respects. They brought pies, cakes, casseroles, flowers, sweet tea, and cornbread. Mike Morris, Sherry's husband, was there for days and shared with Gloria that Wilma had helped him raise his daughter, Meghan, after the tragic car accident in 1979. Gloria learned about the value of community during her two weeks with Wilma that spring in 2010. Sharing with Wilma the many conversations taking place around her kitchen table, Gloria said, "I tell her that, thanks to her, I've come to understand the power of community." Wilma smiled and told Gloria, "You'll never be the same" (Steinem 2015, 246).

Wilma continued to be a warrior woman until the end. In her final public statement she said,

> I decided to issue this statement because I want my family and friends to know that I am mentally and spiritually prepared for this journey; a journey that all human beings will take at one time or another. I learned a long time ago that I can't control the challenges the Creator sends my way, but I can control the way I think about them and deal with them. On balance, I have been blessed with an extraordinarily rich and wonderful life, filled with incredible experiences. And I am grateful to have a support team composed of loving family and friends. I will be spending my time with family and close friends and engaging in activities I enjoy. It's been my privilege to meet and be touched by thousands of people in my life, and I regret not being able to deliver this message personally to so many of you. If anyone wants to send a message to me, it is best to email me at wilmapmankiller@yahoo.com. (Brakhage and Hood 2010)

Wilma asked that any gifts in her honor be made as donations to One Fire Development Corporation, a nonprofit dedicated to advancing Native American communities through economic development and to valuing the wisdom that exists within tribal communities.

In her last hours, Wilma asked Charlie if he could hear the horses running and their hooves pounding the earth. Charlie told her it was probably the warriors coming to escort her to the other side of the mountain. "Don't be sad. It's a happy day," she replied (Chavers 2010). Wilma died on Tuesday, April 6, 2010, at her home in Mankiller Flats, surrounded by her loved ones. During her last weeks of life, spring held off until she passed. The trees outside her house bloomed the next day. Following Wilma's cremation, the family spread her ashes around the spring behind her house at Mankiller Flats, her favorite place to pray.

Over 1,200 people attended Wilma's memorial service at the Cherokee National Cultural Grounds on April 10, 2010. They wore pink and black ribbons to honor Wilma's favorite color pink. Family, friends, and local and national dignitaries spoke about the impact Wilma had on their lives. She was one of the most highly regarded tribal leaders, and people came from across the country to honor her life. Wilma's greatest source of joy was her family. Usually, either Charlie or her daughters traveled with her and provided a significant source of strength in the face of her ongoing health challenges. Her friends, who she considered part of her extended family, had been another source of strength for Wilma. At the service,

Gina described Wilma as a gentle spirit who was funny, artistic, played the guitar, and sang. She spoke about what a great mom Wilma was. "Mom taught us to choose our battles carefully, but once we had chosen one, to never relent. Race, sexual orientation, or the economic status of people did not matter. Be accepting of all. Don't turn away from people because of how they look or what they have because you never know what they'll contribute to the world" (Snell 2010). Gina also read a statement Wilma wrote on April 2: "I know many people from around here believe in burial. But I would like them to bury something after today. I would like them to bury any unkindness or anger or hurtful things I may have done. Bury those with me" (*Native Times*, 2010).

Felicia read a statement that Wilma wrote four days before her death. "When I was seven or eight and living here, no one would have ever guessed what the future would bring. I hope people will learn from that—about themselves and about others" (*Tulsa World*, 2010). Wilma taught Felicia and Gina what a good mom looks like. She loved her two daughters and having them young allowed her to grow up with them. She carried them everywhere she went in California. She did not believe in killing bugs and found time to watch ESPN Sports Center to check on the Boston Red Sox and the LA Lakers. "Mom taught us to laugh, how to dance, to appreciate Motown music, to be a humble servant to our people, to love one another unequivocally and to cherish each and every moment we spent together as a family." Wilma taught them to gain knowledge through books. "When we were little kids, she told us reading books would afford us the opportunity to become more familiar to the world around us without leaving our home" (Olaya 2015).

As Charlie fought back tears at the memorial service, he related a story about a time when Wilma told him she wanted to plant a garden. He had no tiller, so he asked a neighbor to help, but the man never showed up. Charlie decided he would turn the soil with an old, two-horse-drawn plow that had belonged to his father. Not having the two requisite horses, Charlie hooked up the old plow to the back of his pickup truck, Montana. Gina drove the truck while he struggled with the plow. That worked until it was time for Gina to go to ball practice. Then, when Wilma came home from the office, he had her drive the truck. "She drove too fast," he recalled. They struggled with the plowing, sometimes with Charlie face down on the ground and sometimes with the plow underneath the truck, when Wilma backed up the truck too fast. "But that was the best garden we ever had," he said (*Native Times*, 2010). Prior to her passing, Wilma asked Charlie for one last favor. She wanted him to take the heavy steel leg brace she had to endure since 1980 and blow it to pieces with his shotgun. After her memorial service, Charlie returned home and fulfilled her last wish (Steinem 2015, 247).

Gloria, too, spoke at Wilma's service. She said, "Wilma always saw you a little better than you were, so you became better." She told the sizeable crowd how 23 countries with Indigenous people lit signal fires to brighten the way for Wilma's last journey. Gloria spoke of their long friendship and how she immediately knew Wilma was special. "Besides being unique in herself, she personified original values—community, balance between women and men, balance between humans and nature, peaceful ways of resolving differences, and being of good mind." Gloria reminded the mourners there was no difference in the private Wilma and the public Wilma; they were the same person. "Her gift for listening to the least powerful, so they knew their thoughts were worth listening to, was also her gift for talking to the most powerful so they learned to listen" (Adcock 2010).

Congressional representative Tom Cole spoke in Congress of Wilma as the first woman chief of the Cherokee Nation and called her the best leader the tribe has had since its removal from North Carolina to Oklahoma. "Frankly, she made the Cherokee Nation even more than it was—a force to be reckoned with, but a beneficent force, not only in northeast Oklahoma, not only within the lives of its citizens, but, quite frankly, in Indian Country and in American politics." Cole spoke of his close friendship with Wilma. "I knew Wilma Mankiller very well. She led a life based on principles. The first one was just absolute personal integrity. She was one of the most honest and honorable people I had ever met in my life. The second was humility. She was the most approachable person you would ever want to know. She had a total lack of pretension, and she believed very profoundly in service to others—in service, yes, to her tribe; in service, yes, to Native Americans; but in service beyond, as a creed and as a value, that she lived and acted on every single day of her life." He spoke of how every time he heard Wilma give a speech she introduced herself as either the former chief or the chief of the Cherokee Nation. Then she would talk about how if the U.S. government had its way, she would never have been chief and there would not even be a Cherokee Nation or any tribal nations. She always began her conversations that way.

Cole spoke about how Wilma was a role model not only to Native women but also to his mother, who was the first Native American elected to the State Senate in Oklahoma. "She was a close friend of Chief Mankiller's. Like me, my mother admired her quite profoundly. As a leader, she was always principled; she was determined; she was visionary, but she was supremely practical in her political pursuits. She was tough; she was shrewd; she was dedicated to the Cherokee people, and she was dedicated to Native Americans. She was an extraordinarily fierce defender of the concept of tribal sovereignty. She understood it in her bones; she advocated it and, frankly, enhanced it, not only for her own people but for Native Americans everywhere." One of Wilma's greatest qualities was her willingness to work with anyone, no matter their point of view or value system or political affiliation. As Cole explained, "She was a very devoted Democrat. My mother was a very fierce Republican. They found common ground again and again on issue after issue" (H.Res.1237—111th Congress (2009–2010) "Honoring the Life of Wilma Pearl Mankiller and Expressing Condolences of the House of Representatives on Her Passing").

Rebecca Tsosie, Indian law professor at Arizona State University, fondly recalled meeting Wilma.

> There are some people who have a rare quality. I guess "luminous" is the best word. That is how I will always remember her. She was powerful, but in a way that was so kind, so compassionate. As amazing as she was, however, she also had a way of just sitting down with you, like an old friend, chatting and laughing about some small thing that struck her as amusing. To me, she exemplified a Native woman's leadership, both in her manner and in her consistent and unfailing devotion to her family, her people on the land, and the ways in which we are connected to past and future generations. She knew these things. Practiced them, and had such a determination to make sure that this would be protected into the future. (Capriccioso 2010)

Chief Chad Smith wrote a commentary in the *Cherokee Phoenix* in May 2010 describing the qualities Wilma possessed. He wrote of her patriotism and her greatest strength being her absolute humility. "Some might think of humility as weakness, but Wilma showed that this Cherokee attribute was strength, rather than weakness. In her humility, she was decisive and determined. That humility gave her power to truly listen to people and to learn their perspective even when they were emotional, defensive, or antagonistic." He wrote of how her strength of humility allowed her to make well-reasoned decisions and gain the respect of those around her. "When you were around Wilma you could without a doubt sense her strength. That air of strength, of confidence in others, resulted in people wanting to follow her, listen to her and be inspired by her" (Adcock 2010).

On July 20, 2010, the Women Empowering Women for Indigenous Nations organization, which Wilma cofounded with Susan Masten (Yurok), honored Wilma. Her daughter Gina accepted the award on her mother's behalf. Gina said, "Mom's life and work wasn't about securing awards or someone patting her on the back for a job well done. Mom did what she did because she genuinely had a deep-seated passion and an over-whelming love for all Native people, especially women and children. She taught us so many things like to think outside of the box, to love all people unconditionally" (Good Voice 2010).

Among her many accomplishments during her tenure as chief, Wilma initiated a collaboration between the Cherokee Nation and the Cherokee National Historical Society, annually honoring people as Cherokee National Treasures. The honor goes to those who preserve and perpetuate

WOMEN EMPOWERING WOMEN FOR INDIGENOUS NATIONS

Women Empowering Women for Indigenous Nations (WEWIN) is a forum for women to come together and discuss the many issues of importance in their tribal communities. It is also a forum for community to draw upon the traditional and cultural values to create stronger networks, impact public policy, foster economic growth, and continue personal and professional development while offering encouragement and support to one another. The organization celebrates the strength, courage, and wisdom of the women who came before, uplifts and lessens the burden that the warrior women carry today, and prepares, supports, and inspires women leaders of tomorrow.

the lost arts of the Cherokee people—"Cherokee men and women with exceptional skill or historical knowledge of traditional Cherokee arts or crafts." The tribal council first recognized her for this honor through a resolution in May 2010 "for her cultural contribution, leadership and statesmanship to the Cherokee people." According to the resolution, "Wilma P. Mankiller was instrumental in strengthening the Cherokee Nation and was greatly responsible for making the Cherokee Nation government an example of excellence for all Native American tribes." The Cherokee National Historical Society posthumously honored Wilma in September 2010 for epitomizing the spirit of a Cherokee National Treasure (Adcock 2010).

She received another posthumous award on November 1, 2010. The Drum Award, sponsored by the Choctaw Nation of Oklahoma and the Cherokee, Chickasaw, and Muskogee Creek nations, recognizes individuals for their accomplishments and contributions to society. Wilma received the Lifetime Achievement Award, given "to honor an elder who exemplifies why we value our elders and their ongoing contributions to society" (Jackson 2010).

On October 6, 2011, Oklahoma City held a tree-planting ceremony for Wilma. Charlie spoke at the ceremony about how he learned so much from Wilma and the fact that she was a superb partner and an outstanding leader. Charlie said she had vision, and she had a strong will and the ability to get things done to serve the people. She represented survival, hope, and tenacity, to reinvent again and again, just like the Cherokee Nation. An inscription at the base of the planted tree reads, "Remember Wilma Mankiller." Gloria Steinem spoke at the ceremony about how Wilma and her family taught her about interconnectedness and how her friend never ignored injustice. Wilma taught Gloria that family is the paradigm of all human life, and we have to look after one another and to protect each other. Gloria wrote, in her book My Life on the Road, 2015, that Wilma was a quiet, warm, and listening woman and although she was 11 years Gloria's junior, she presented herself with such wisdom that she appeared to be much older. "Just being with her made it hard not to be as authentic and shit free as she was. Her humor did not come along often, but when it did, it was as natural as the weather" (Steinem 2015, 226).

Every so often, a leader emerges who changes things and leaves a lasting impression. Wilma was one of those leaders. Outsiders cannot understand the underlying values of the Cherokee community and their relationship to the land, as Gloria came to know in the last weeks of Wilma's life. Gloria learned that Cherokee women had power in the talking circles and a paradigm existed of linking instead of ranking. Wilma taught her that wealth is not what you accumulate, but it is what you give away.

In 2012, Charlie accepted the Brooklyn Museum Elizabeth A. Sackler Award at the Center for Feminist Art on Wilma's behalf. He spoke about her beginning the film, The Cherokee Word for Water, and how she made him promise to complete it. "She revived the gadugi concept and she always used to say we need a revolution in thinking before we put women in office" ("2012 Elizabeth A. Sackler Award," n.d.). A few months later, in January 2013, Northeastern State University (NSU) organized the Wilma Mankiller Day on campus as part of a weeklong series on service and volunteering. After a day of readings from Wilma's books and speeches by Felicia, Gina, and Charlie, there was a screening of the film The Cherokee Word for Water. As a teaching fellow at NSU, Wilma had planted the idea of an Indigenous Leadership Center and, through the work of the Indigenous Scholar Development Center, that plan was close to fruition. "This is a way for all to show that we appreciate and support the work Mankiller did throughout her lifetime," recalled Dr. Jennifer McCann, center director (Northeastern State University Newsletter, "Be the Change Week Includes Wilma Mankiller Day," 2013).

Wilma was always interested in filmmaking and had plans to pursue that interest in the future. She had served as a board member of a nonprofit film company in California and as a Cherokee consultant (Olaya 2015). She worked for 20 years on the 2013 story of the Bell project, entitled The Cherokee Word for Water. Eight days before her death, Wilma told Charlie she knew she would not live to see the completion of the film and made Charlie promise they would make it. "You have to help Kristina make the film," she told him. Charlie remarked to the audience at the film's screening in 2014 that he and Wilma used to talk about the need to educate non-Indians, and film was a dominant medium for that. Charlie directed the film along with Tim Kelly; and Charlie, Kristina Kiehl, Tim Kelly, Louise Rubacky, and Perry Pickert served as producers. Actress Kimberly Norris-Guerrero played Wilma and Moses Brings Plenty starred as Charlie. The focus of the film is the couple's efforts at bringing water to Bell in the early 1980s. It follows Wilma's life from the time she returned to Oklahoma until the successful completion of the water project. Charlie shared with the audience:

> I think the contemporary American Native has a lot to tell today. It was important to Wilma and me. We talked a lot about this together. There is a lot of need in the Native communities across the country in telling the history of the past. It's still important for everyone to know "gadugi" is very much alive—that kind of philosophy. That when we do community projects, that everyone is involved. To let all the people interested who are in the community to come and help. There was a lack of money for the Bell Water-line Project. We had to do something innovative, and Wilma and I got together and used this self-help method that would help the Bell community. We showed that if it could work in our community, it could work everywhere. It was to help get people in their communities to be self-sufficient. That was something in our early history that she and I believed in. It was one of the things we had talked—that "gadugi" would be very important. (Cardon 2014)

Wilma knew her people and the problems within Native communities. She was not afraid to tackle them, and she and Charlie worked together toward economic development and educational development. She believed in the people and in strengthening the nation's belief in *gadugi*.

Wilma was a people person working within the communities, working with *gadugi*. She had not wanted the film to be about her; she wanted it to be about community. Charlie stated, "She wanted to restore people's faith in their ability to do things on their own within the community rather than waiting for other people to come in from the outside, which is very important for a community that has been continually lied to and neglected like the Cherokee Nation. Wilma had wanted to show women and men working together under a woman's leadership, which is traditional for Cherokee communities. Most of all, she wanted people to see that if we can do it, they can do it" (Cardon 2014). Her memorial service program described Wilma as a rare person who was as comfortable in the White House as she was in a farmhouse. While Wilma's leadership took the Cherokee Nation and its people a long way in community building and having a richer life, there is still much work to be done.

Wilma had such vision and foresight that she built the new Cherokee Nation headquarters in such a way that they could add a second level on as needed, and it now has two stories. She bought the land next to the new Stilwell Medical Center so it could be expanded, and they expanded it in 2017–2018. Wilma started bingo halls in northeastern Oklahoma and eight casinos existed as of 2015. During her second term in 1990, she signed the Self-determination Act. She saw the need to build health care clinics, and future chiefs continued. Wilma laid the foundation to expand services to the tribe (Olaya 2015). People in the Cherokee Nation remember her for bringing the communities together. What would Wilma think of the state of politics today? She would not like the divisiveness of tribal and national politics, but she would have hoped for women to run for office. She was a staunch supporter of women candidates, be they Republicans or Democrats.

Director Valerie Red-Horse released a documentary entitled *Mankiller* in March 2017. The film explores Wilma's life from her childhood to the end of her life, with much focus on her time in California and in office as chief of the Cherokee Nation. Red-Horse interviewed many of the people included in this book. The documentary captures much insight into Wilma's early life in California. Throughout the film, it is clear how much the events of Alcatraz influenced Wilma and how much the Cherokee people energized and motivated her upon her return to Oklahoma after a 20-year absence.

On March 29, 2019, Wilma received another posthumous award—for being a champion for social justice. It was called the Courage Award and presented by the University of Oklahoma Women's and Gender Studies Board of Advocates. During her tenure as principal chief, Wilma tripled the tribe's enrollment, doubled employment, and built new housing, health centers, and children's programs. Infant mortality declined and educational achievement rose. After leaving office, she remained a vigorous champion for social justice, Native people, and women in the United States and abroad (*Tahlequah Daily Press*, 2019).

Wilma had worked hard trying to get the uranium contamination from the Gore plant cleaned up and removed. That did not occur until eight years after her death. It took from January 1986 to November 2018 to get the radioactive waste removed from the Gore uranium plant. Approximately 10,000 tons of nuclear waste, uranium-contaminated sludge, was taken to Blanding, Utah to the White Mesa Mill for re-milling (okenergy-today.com, 2018). The long-term environmental cost to the Cherokee people and to the lands they call home is yet to be determined.

Mainstream American society considered Wilma a feminist, but in Indian Country, she is a warrior spirit and beloved woman who did what she could for her people. Wilma embodied compassion and resilience. Wilma also had an immense love for the arts. She loved and collected American Indian art from all over the United States. She was part of the legislative team for the Indian Arts and Crafts Act of 1990. This law prohibits the marketing and misrepresentation of Native American arts and crafts products within the United States.

Wilma loved Aretha Franklin and Motown music, the Los Angeles Lakers, the Boston Red Sox, the color pink, spring flowers, literature, and art.

She loved to cook. She played the guitar, made ribbon shirts, and wrote poetry.

In summer 2021 Charlie was in the old barn on the Mankiller Flats property and found poems Wilma wrote from the 1960s until her death. They were published in a book entitled, *Mankiller Poems: The Lost Poetry of Wilma Mankiller, the Principal Chief of the Cherokee Nation.* Her friend of over three decades, Mark Trahant, wrote of the collection, "So many of us know Wilma Mankiller as a tribal leader, as a philanthropist, and as an American icon. These poems give us more because they transport us to another time when Wilma had yet to figure it all out" (Mankiller 2022, 7).

Wilma was funny, compassionate, nurturing, loving, and caring. She had a generous nature and was an advocate for women, Cherokees, and all Natives. She smiled a lot. She had an affinity for Toby Keith and Johnny Depp. She brought home stray animals; instead of killing bugs, she took them outside. Her nature was humble and tender. She had an affinity for opera. She could recite the statistics of any member of the Boston Red Sox.

Oaks and willows as well as hickory, dogwood, and redbud trees surrounded Wilma's home. She often commented on her connection to the people and land of eastern Oklahoma. "To think of myself outside the context of the tribe or my family or my community would be very difficult" (Koenenn 1993). A quote from Wilma hangs in the kitchen of the Mankiller home: "The meaning of life is to be in balance and harmony with every living thing in creation. We must also understand our own insignificance in the totality of things" (Plummer 2013).

Wilma stated,

> On balance, being here at home, among my own people, on my own ancestral land, is where I want to be, and where my spirit always was, even when I was in California, I never felt completely whole in California. When I came home, I felt whole again. If I am to be remembered, I want it to be because I am fortunate enough to have become my tribe's first female chief. But I also want to be remembered for emphasizing the fact that we have indigenous solutions to our problems. Cherokee values, especially those of helping one another and our interconnections with the land, can be used to address contemporary issues. (Mankiller 1993)

Wilma's story reminds us that each of us has a voice and we can use it to make a difference.

Timeline: Events in the Life of Wilma Mankiller

1945	Wilma Mankiller was born in Tahlequah, Oklahoma, on November 18.
1957	Her family moved to the Potrero District of San Francisco, California.
1958	She spent the year living with Grandma Sitton on a dairy farm in Escalon, California.
1960	Wilma's brother Robert died. Her family moved to the urban ghetto of Hunters Point in San Francisco.
1963	Wilma graduated high school. She married Hector Hugo deBardi Olaya in Reno, Nevada.
1964	Wilma's first daughter, Felicia, was born.
1966	Wilma's second daughter, Gina, was born. Black Panther Party was created.
1968	American Indian Movement (AIM) was created.
1969	Wilma became part of support group for Alcatraz occupation.
1970	Wilma began volunteering to help the Pit River tribes.
1971	Wilma's father, Charley, died of kidney disease. Wilma began courses at San Francisco State University.
1973	Grandma Sitton died. The Wounded Knee occupation took place.
1974	Wilma and Hugo got divorced. Wilma, Felicia, and Gina moved to Oakland. Wilma cofounded the American Indian Community School in Oakland, California. The International Indian Treaty Council was created on the Standing Rock reservation in South Dakota.

1975   Hugo took Gina and kept her for over a year.

1976   Wilma went to Oklahoma for a summer visit.

1977   Wilma attended Third International Indian Treaty Council Conference in South Dakota. She helped prepare tribal delegates for the United Nations Conference on Indigenous Rights in Geneva, Switzerland. She moved back home to Oklahoma with Felicia and Gina. She began working for the Cherokee Nation and completes degree. She met Charlie Soap.

1978   Wilma returned to school at the University of Arkansas-Fayetteville. Women of All Red Nations was created.

1979   Wilma created the Community Development Department with the Cherokee Nation tribal government. She Had a near-fatal car accident.

1980   Wilma was diagnosed with a form of muscular dystrophy called Myasthenia Gravis.

1981   Wilma returned to work at the Cherokee Nation.

1982   Wilma began work for the Bell and Kenwood waterline projects.

1983   Wilma won deputy chief election with Chief Ross Swimmer.

1984   Bell project was completed. Wilma participated in the first joint tribal council meeting of the Eastern Band of Cherokee Indians and the Cherokee Nation since the Removal period.

1985   Wilma replaced Chief Swimmer as principal chief when he resigned.

1986   Wilma married Charlie Soap. She was named American Indian Woman of the Year. She received the American Leadership Award from Harvard University for her notable contributions to American leadership and American culture.

1987   Wilma became the first woman to be elected as principal chief of the Cherokee Nation. She was inducted into the Oklahoma Women's Hall of Fame. She joined the board of the Ms. Foundation.

1988   Wilma was Alumna of the Year at San Francisco State University.

1990   Wilma underwent a kidney transplant due to polycystic kidney disease. She was awarded an honorary doctorate from Yale University.

1991	Wilma was reelected chief for another four-year term. She received honorary doctorate from Dartmouth College. She published an essay in 1991 entitled "Education and Native Americans."
1992	On October 16, Chief Wilma was honored at the Second Annual National Racial Justice Awards Dinner in Washington, D.C. She joined the Honorary Committee of the National Campaign of the National Museum of the American Indian in Washington, D.C.
1993	Wilma wrote an autobiography entitled *Mankiller: A Chief and Her People*. She was inducted into the Oklahoma Hall of Fame. She received an American Association of University Women's Achievement Award. She was inducted into the National Women's Hall of Fame. She was awarded the Elizabeth Blackwell Award and the John W. Gardner Leadership Award.
1995	Wilma's second term as principal chief ended.
1996	Wilma was awarded an honorary degree from Smith College. She received an award from Hobart and Smith College for exemplary service to humanity
1997	Wilma received Ms. Magazine Woman of the Year Award.
1998	Wilma was awarded the Presidential Medal of Freedom. She featured in a poster series on famous women. She underwent a second kidney transplant. *The Reader's Companion to U.S. Women's History*, coedited by Wilma, was published.
1999	Wilma was diagnosed with breast cancer.
2000	Wilma received the Hubert H. Humphrey Civil Rights Award from the Leadership Conference of Civil Rights.
2001	Wilma delivered speech at a conference on domestic violence.
2002	Wilma published an essay in a book entitled *Take That Ovaries!: Bold Females and Their Brazen Acts*.
2004	Wilma edited a collection of essays by Indigenous women entitled *Every Day Is a Good Day: Reflections by Contemporary Indigenous Women*.
2005	Wilma was named to Merrill Lynch's Diversity Board to identify issues and make recommendations about workplace diversity. She was appointed as representative of the National HIV/AIDS Awareness campaign.

2006   On March 11, Wilma received the "Circle of Honor" award from the Tulsa City-County Library American Indian Resource Center for opening doors for Indian women and all Cherokee people.

2010   Wilma was diagnosed with stage-4 pancreatic cancer. She passed away on April 6.

2013   The film *Cherokee Word for Water* was released.

2018   The documentary *Mankiller* was released.

Bibliography

BOOKS

Abbott, Carl. 1993. *The Metropolitan Frontier: Cities in the Modern American West*. Tucson: University of Arizona Press.

Ambler, Marjane. 1990. *Breaking the Iron Bonds: Indian Control of Energy Development*. Lawrence: University of Kansas Press.

Anderson, William L., ed. 1992. *Cherokee Removal: Before and After*. Athens: University of Georgia Press.

Awiakta, Marilou. 1993. *Selu: Seeking the Corn Mother's Wisdom*. Golden, CO: Fulcrum Publishing.

Barlow, William and Peter Shapiro. 1971. *An End to Silence: The San Francisco State Student Movement in the 1960s*. New York: Pegasus.

Blansett, Kent. 2018. *A Journey to Freedom: Richard Oakes, Alcatraz, and the Red Power Movement*. New Haven, CT: Yale University Press.

Bruchac, Joseph, ed. 1995. *Aniyunwia, Real Human Beings: Contemporary Cherokee Indian Fiction*. Greenfield Center, NY: Greenfield Review Literary Center.

Cahn, Edgar S. and David W. Hearns, eds. 1969. *Our Brother's Keeper: The Indian in White America*. New York: New American Library.

Conley, Robert. 2005. *The Cherokee Nation: A History*. Albuquerque: University of New Mexico Press.

Davis, Julie. 2013. *Survival Schools: The American Indian Movement and Community Education in the Twin Cities*. Minneapolis: University of Minnesota Press.

Deloria, Vine. 1969. *Custer Died for your Sins: An Indian Manifesto*. Norman: University of Oklahoma Press.

Deloria, Vine. 1974. *Behind the Trail of Broken Treaties: An Indian Declaration of Independence*. New York: Delacourte Press.

Edmunds, R. David, ed. 2001. *The New Warriors: Native American Leaders since 1900*. Lincoln: University of Nebraska Press.

Fortunate Eagle, Adam. 1992. *Alcatraz, Alcatraz: The Indian Occupation of 1969–1971*. Berkeley, CA: Heydey Books.

Fortunate Eagle, Adam. 2002. *The Heart of the Rock: The Indian Invasion of Alcatraz*. Norman: University of Oklahoma Press.

Gearing, Fred. 1962. *Priests and Warriors: Social Structures for Cherokee Politics in the 18th Century*. Millwood, NY: American Anthropological Association.

Gitlin, Todd. 1993. *The Sixties: Years of Hope, Days of Rage*. New York: Bantam Books.

Hippler, Arthur E. 1974. *Hunters Point: A Black Ghetto*. New York: Basic Books Inc.

Howell, D. Bruce. 2017. *Cherokee Echoes: Tales of Northeastern Oklahoma*. Scotts Valley, CA: CreateSpace Independent Publishing Platform.

Hurtado, Albert. 2008. *Reflections on American Indian History: Honoring the Past, Building a Future*. Norman: University of Oklahoma Press.

Janda, Sarah Eppler. 2007. *Beloved Women: The Political Lives of Ladonna Harris and Wilma Mankiller*. Dekalb: Northern Illinois University Press.

Johnson, Troy R. 1996. *The American Indian Occupation of Alcatraz Island: Red Power and Self-Determination*. Lincoln: University of Nebraska Press.

Johnson, Troy R., Duane Champagne and Joane Nagel. 1967. *American Indian Activism: Alcatraz to the Longest Walk*. Urbana: University of Illinois Press.

Johnson, Troy R., Alvin M. Josephy Jr. and Joane Nagel, eds. 1999. *Red Power: The American Indians Fight for Freedom*. Lincoln: University of Nebraska Press.

Lobo, Susan, ed. 2002. *Urban Voices: The Bay Area American Indian Community, Intertribal Friendship House, Oakland, California*. Tucson: The University of Arizona Press.

Lobo, Susan and Kurt Peters, eds. 2001. *American Indians and the Urban Experience*. Walnut Creek, CA: Altamira Press.

Longo, Peter J. 2018. *Great Plains Politics*. Lincoln: University of Nebraska Press.

Mails, Thomas E. 1996. *The Cherokee People: The Story of the Cherokees from Earliest Origins to Contemporary Times*. Chicago: Council Oak Books.

Mankiller, Wilma. 1988. *The Chief Cooks: Traditional Cherokee Recipes*. Muskogee, OK: Hoffman Printing Company.

Mankiller, Wilma. 2004. *Every Day Is a Good Day: Reflections by Contemporary Indigenous Women*. Golden, CO: Fulcrum Publishing.

Mankiller, Wilma. 2022. *Mankiller Poems: The Lost Poetry of Wilma Mankiller, the Principal Chief of the Cherokee Nation*. Clyde Hill, WA: Pulley Press.

Mankiller, Wilma and Michael Wallis. 1993. *Mankiller: A Chief and Her People: An Autobiography of the Principal Chief of the Cherokee Nation*. New York: St. Martin's Press.

Mankiller, Wilma, co-editor, Gwendolyn Mink, Marissa Navarro, Barbara Smith and Gloria Steinem. 1998. *The Reader's Companion to Women in American History*. New York: Houghton Mifflin Press.

Mankiller, Wilma, co-editor, Byllye Avery, Letty Cotin Pogrebin, 2000. *Woman: A Celebration to Benefit the Ms. Foundation for Women*. Philadelphia: Running Press.

McLoughlin, William. 1984. *Cherokees & Missionaries, 1789–1839*. Norman: University of Oklahoma Press.

McLoughlin, William. 1993. *After the Trail of Tears: The Cherokees' Struggle for Sovereignty, 1839–1880*. Chapel Hill: University of North Carolina Press.

Mooney, James. (1899) 1972. *Myths of the Cherokees and Sacred Formulas of the Cherokees*. Nashville, TN: Charles Elders.

Neely, Sharlotte. 1991. *Snowbird Cherokees: People of Persistence*. Athens: University of Georgia Press.

Shreve, Bradley G. 2011. *Red Power Rising: The National Indian Youth Council and the Origins of Native Activism*. Norman: University of Oklahoma Press.

Smith, Paul Chatt and Robert Warrior. 1996. *Like a Hurricane: The Indian Movement from Alcatraz to Wounded Knee*. New York: The New Press.

Smith, Sherry L. 2012. *Hippies, Indians, and the Fight for Red Power*. New York: Oxford University Press.

Solomon, Rivka, ed. 2002. *That Takes Ovaries: Bold Females and Their Brazen Acts*. New York: Crown Publishing Group.

Steinem, Gloria. 1992. *Revolution from Within: A Book of Self-Esteem*. Boston, MA: Little, Brown, and Company.

Steinem, Gloria. 2015. *My Life on the Road*. New York: Random House.

Steiner, Stan. 1968. *The New Indians*. New York: Delta Press.

Stremlau, Rose. 2011. *Sustaining the Cherokee Family: Kinship and the Allotment of an Indigenous Nation*. Chapel Hill: University of North Carolina Press.

Sturm, Circe. 2002. *Blood Politics: Race, Culture and Identity in the Cherokee Nation of Oklahoma*. Oakland: University of California Press.

Taylor, Carolyn, et al. 2007. *Voices from the Heartland*. Norman: University of Oklahoma Press.

Warrior, Robert Allen. 1995. *Tribal Secrets: Recovering American Indian Intellectual Traditions*. Minneapolis: University of Minnesota Press.

NEWSPAPERS, PERIODICALS, JOURNALS

Ablon, Joan. 1964. Relocated American Indians in the San Francisco Bay Area: Social Interaction and Indian Identity. *Human Organization* 23(4): 296–304.

Adams, Jim. 2001. American Indian Leaders Share Visions at New York Forum. *Indian Country Today.* December 7, 2001.

Adcock, Clifton. 2010. More Than 1,000 Attend Memorial Service for Former Cherokee Chief Wilma Mankiller. *Cherokee Phoenix.* April 10, 2010.

Akwesasne Notes. 1987. Thunderbird Free Press "Urgent Action Bulletin." September 30, 1987.

Allinder, Maridel. 1985. Cherokee: Achieving the Dream. *Tulsa World.* November 15, 1985.

Au-Authm Action News. 1994. White House Holds Historic Tribal Leaders Summit. May 1, 1994.

Barkdull, C. 2009. Exploring Intersections of Identity with Native American Women Leaders. *Journal of Women and Social Work* 24: 128–133.

Begay, Carol and Diane Tracy. 1986. *Boston Globe*, May 19, 1986.

Billy, Carrie. 2009. Dear Readers. *Tribal College: Journal of American Indian Higher Education* 20: 3.

Boston Globe. 1988. Reagan Says Indians Have 'Right to Choose' He Says He Does Not Remember Remark Made in Moscow on 'Primitive Lifestyle.' December 13, 1988.

Brakhage, Joshua and Terry Hood. 2010. Wilma Mankiller Dies. *News on 6.* April 6, 2010.

Britten, Thomas. 2017. Urban American Indian Centers in the Late 1960s–1970s: An Examination of Their Function and Purpose. *Indigenous Policy Journal* 27: 1–18.

Caldwell, Earl. 1970. Arrest Attempt by Indians Fails. *New York Times.* June 21, 1970.

Cardon, Dustin. 2014. Person of the Day: Wilma Mankiller. *Jackson Free Press.* March 18, 2014.

Chavers, Dean. 2010. Wilma Mankiller and Me. *Native Times.* April 14, 2010.

Chavers, Will. 2009. Cherokee People Honor Ancestors at Red Clay. *Cherokee Phoenix and Indian Advocate.* April 9, 2009.

Cherokee Advocate. 1978a. Cherry Tree Community Center Dedicated. November 30, 1978

Cherokee Advocate. 1978b. Center Open for Meetings at Bull Hollow. October 31, 1978.

Cherokee Advocate. 1978c. Construction Students Sought. September 30, 1978.

Cherokee Advocate. 1978d. Native Filmmakers Listed in New Directory. July 31, 1978.

Cherokee Advocate. 1978e. Program Offers Technical Training for Cherokees. May 31, 1978

Cherokee Advocate. 1979. TV Series to Address Ethnic Tensions. July 31, 1979.*Cherokee Advocate.* 1985. Mankiller Asked to Serve on State Boacrd. August 31, 1985.

Cherokee Advocate. 1987. Cherokees mourn former chief W.W. Keeler. September 30, 1987.

Cherokee Advocate. 1992a. Chief Delivers State of the Nation during Holiday. October 31, 1992.

Cherokee Advocate. 1992b. Eastern Band, Cherokee Nation Holds Joint Council in North Carolina. October 31, 1992.

Cherokee Advocate. 1992c. Judge rules in favor of Oklahoma Tax Commission on UKB lawsuit filed in 1990. May 31, 1992.

Cherokee Advocate. 1993a. Administrators Weary of Dealing with Current Leaders of UKB. January 31, 1993.

Cherokee Advocate. 1993b. State of the Nation Focuses on Housing. May 31, 1993.

Cherokee Advocate. 1994a. BIA Continues to Work Toward Consolidation. March 31, 1994.

Cherokee Advocate. 1994b. A Chief's Triumph over Adversity: This Cherokee Tale of Tears Is American Sage of Heroism. January 31, 1994.

Cherokee Advocate. 1994c. Mankiller Responds During State of the Nation. March 31, 1994.

Cherokee Advocate. 1994d. Relationship Between Cherokee Nation and UKB Clarified. September 30, 1994.

Cherokee Observer. 1994a. Arkansas Riverbed May Be Sold to Federal Government. January 31, 1994.

Cherokee Observer. 1994b. CNO Reaches Impasse with HIS. March 31, 1994.

Cherokee Observer. 1994c. CNO Take-Over Blocked by Commission. November 30, 1994.

Cherokee Observer. 1994d. Council Approves Grant Applications Totaling Nearly Three Million Dollars. May 31, 1994.

Cherokee Observer. 1994e. Indian Art Law Rules Written. December 31, 1994.

Cherokee Observer. 1994f. New Law Strips Cherokee Members of Rights. October 31, 1994.

Cherokee Observer. 1996a. TLJC Contract May Be in Jeopardy. *Cherokee Observer.* June, 30, 1996.

Cherokee Observer. 1996b. Trail of Tears Association Hold Historic Symposium. May 31, 1996.

Cherokee Phoenix and Indian Advocate. 1977. Tsa-la-Gi Funded for Rural Museum and Arboretum/Garden. September 30, 1977.

Cherokee Phoenix and Indian Advocate. 1978a. Center Open for Meetings at Bull Hollow. October. 31, 1978.

Cherokee Phoenix and Indian Advocate. 1978b. Cherry Tree Community Center Dedicated. November 30, 1978.

Cherokee Phoenix and Indian Advocate. 1978c. Economic Stimulus Seeks to Expand Indian Employment. January 3, 1978.

Cherokee Phoenix and Indian Advocate. 1979a. Cherokee Nation Hosts Indian Industrial Development Session. December 31, 1979.

Cherokee Phoenix and Indian Advocate. 1979b. Tribe Applies for $400,000 Block Grant. July 31, 1979.

Cherokee Phoenix and Indian Advocate. 1981a. Five Counties Withdraw EODD Membership. February 28, 1981.

Cherokee Phoenix and Indian Advocate. 1981b. Letter to the Cherokees. October 31, 1981.

Cherokee Phoenix and Indian Advocate. 1982. Cherokee Nation Industries: High Tech Jobs in Rural Adair County. August 31, 1982.

Cherokee Phoenix and Indian Advocate. 1984a. CNI Posts Record Year in Sales, Profits. October 31, 1984.

Cherokee Phoenix and Indian Advocate. 1984b. 1984: A Very Good Year for Tribe. January 31, 1984.

Cherokee Phoenix and Indian Advocate. 1984c. Red Clay 'Briefing' Delivered: Tribal Council Approves New Waterlines. March 31, 1984.

Cherokee Phoenix and Indian Advocate. 1984d. Study Targets Obstacles to Economic Development. October 31, 1984.

Cherokee Phoenix and Indian Advocate. 1984e. 32nd Annual Cherokee National Holiday Pays Tribute to Cherokee Communities. September 30, 1984.

Cherokee Phoenix and Indian Advocate. 1984f. Tribe Looks at Contracting BIA Area Office. May 31, 1984.

Cherokee Phoenix and Indian Advocate. 1985a. Block Grants Build Rural Communities. May 31, 1985.

Cherokee Phoenix and Indian Advocate. 1985b. East-West Cherokees Share Concerns, Culture. July 31, 1985.

Cherokee Phoenix and Indian Advocate. 1985c. Enterprises Report Record Sales. May 31, 1985.

Cherokee Phoenix and Indian Advocate. 1985d. New Waterline Biggest Self-Help Project. September 30, 1985.

Cherokee Phoenix and Indian Advocate. 1985e. Progress Pleases Kenwood Cherokees. January 31, 1985.

Cherokee Phoenix and Indian Advocate. 1985f. Today Show Airs Segment on Cherokees. April 30, 1985.

Cherokee Phoenix and Indian Advocate. 1986a. Community Development Efforts More Toward Economic Development in Indian Country. May 31, 1986.

Cherokee Phoenix and Indian Advocate. 1986b. Inaugural Address Charts Future Policy: Mankiller Stresses Economic Development. January 1, 1986.

Cherokee Phoenix and Indian Advocate. 1988a. Cherokees Working to Solve Area Solid Waste Problems. May 31, 1988.

Cherokee Phoenix and Indian Advocate. 1988b. Community Development Continues Winning Ways. January 31, 1988.

Clouston, David. 2009. Cultural Wisdom. *Salina Journal.* April 5, 2009.

Confederated Umatilla Journal. 2006. Mankiller: Tribal Leaders 'Up to Task.' September 1, 2006.

Cooper, Emily. 2005. Wilma Mankiller: Ex-Cherokee Chief, and Current UO Law Professor, Sounds Off about How U.S. Society Judges Tribes. *Willamette Week.* November 22, 2005.

Cornsilk, David. 1994a. Opinion: Arkansas Riverbed Sale or Sell-Out? *Cherokee Observer.* June 30, 1994.

Cornsilk, David. 1994b. Opinion: Mankiller Won't Run. *Cherokee Observer.* May 31, 1994.

Desert Sun. 1970. Indian Girl Dies from Alcatraz Fall. January 8, 1970.

Dowell, JoKAY. 2010. Donadagohvi, Wilma. *Native Times.* June 8, 2010.

Dullien, Thomas. 2016. Wilma Mankiller's Remarkable Leadership Journey. *Indian Gaming.* January 2016.

Dyer, Richard. 1993. A Full-Blooded Biography of the Cherokee Chief. *Boston Globe.* December 30, 1993.

Edmo-Suppah, Lori. 1994. Native American Journalists Association Dedicates Plaque at Site of First Native Newspaper: A Bittersweet Return Home for Mankiller. *Sho-Ban News.* August 11, 1994.

Fancher, John. 2006. Mankiller to Receive "Circle of Honor" Award; Former Cherokee Leader Recognized by Tulsa City-County Library. *Native American Times.* January 20, 2006.

Fogarty, Mark. 1995. Tribal Economic Self-Sufficiency a Gift from Eagle Staff Fund. *Indian Country Today.* January 19, 1995.

Fogelson, Raymond and Paul Kutsche. 1959. Cherokee Economic Cooperative: The Gadugi. Symposium on Cherokee and Iroquois Culture. *Bureau of American Ethnology Bulletin* 180: 83–123.

Gaines, Judith. 1988. 1st Female Chief Helps Cherokees Help Themselves. *Baltimore Sun.* February 9, 1988.

Gaines, Judith. 1991. Her Story Is History: Former Chief of Cherokee Nation Takes Mission to Dartmouth. *Boston Globe.* February 18, 1991.

Good Voice, Christina. 2010. Mankiller Also Left Behind Legacy as a Mother. *Cherokee Phoenix.* April 19, 2010.

Gulick, John. 1958. The Acculturation of Eastern Cherokee Community Organization. *Social Forces* 36(3): 246–250.

Hampton, Joy. 2008. Ga-du-gi: Working Together for the Benefit of Community. *Claremore Daily Progress.* February 19, 2008.

Hewes, Leslie. 1942a. Indian Land in the Cherokee Country of Oklahoma. *Economic Geography* 18: 401–412.

Hewes. Leslie. 1942b. The Oklahoma Ozarks as the Land of the Cherokees. *Geographical Review* 32: 269–281.

Hoxie, Frederick. 2014. Sovereignty's Challenge to Native American (and United States) History. *Journal of Nineteenth Century Americanists* 2: 137–142.

Indian Country Today. 1986. 7th Generation Meeting September 8. August 27, 1986.

Indian Country Today. 1998. Mankiller to Undergo 2nd Kidney Transplant. July 27, 1988.

Indian Country Today. 2000. Mankiller Honored for Civil Rights Achievements. May 17, 2000.

Indian Country Today. 2003. Dream of the Earth: Salute to the White Roots of Peace. January 20, 2003.

Jackson, Claude. 2003. Cherokee Leader Believes Protecting Family Enhances Economic Development. *Au-Authm Action News.* March 31, 2003.

Jackson, Tesina. 2010. Studi and Mankiller to Receive Drum Awards. *Cherokee Phoenix.* October 27, 2010.

Jenkins, Ron. 1992. Walters, Tribal Leaders Sign Compact. *Journal Record.* June 9, 1992.

Johnson, Dirk. 1994. Economic Pulse: Indian Country; Economies Come to Life on Indian Reservations. *New York Times.* July 3, 1994.

Jones, Charles T. 1999. An Honored Chief Wilma's Spirit Survives Adversity. *Oklahoman.* August 29, 1999.

Kent, Jim. 2002. Wilma Mankiller on the Importance of Native Leadership. *Native Voice.* May 23, 2002.

Koenenn, Connie. 1993. Heart of a Nation: As Chief of the Cherokees, Wilma Mankiller Meshes Traditional and Modern Indian Issues. The Tribe's Strength She Says, Lies in Self-Determination. *Los Angeles Times.* November 1, 1993.

Landry, Alissa. 2017. Today in Native History: Ronald Reagan Says, "We Should Not Have Humored (Natives)." *Indian Country Today.* May 31, 2017.

Langston, Donna Hightower. 2003. American Indian Women's Activism in the 1960s and 1970s. *Hypatia: Indigenous Women in the Americas* 18(2): 114–132.

Lewin, Sam. 2005. Mankiller Staying Super Busy. *Native American Times.* May 18, 2005.

Lobo, Susan. 1990. Intertribal Friendship House. *Ethnographic Exploratory Research Report*, No. 12. May 1990.

Los Angeles Sentinel. 2000. Southwest Museum Presents 'Native Women of Hope.' March 8, 2000.

Maltby, Jack. 1984. Thousands of Cherokee Indians Returned to Their Sacred Homeland. *UPI Archives*. April 6, 1984.

Mankiller, Wilma. 1991. Education and Native Americans. *National Forum* 71: 5.

Mankiller, Wilma. 1995. Guest Essay. *Native Peoples* . 8(Summer):4.

Mankiller, Wilma. 2001. And Finally... (Re)Constructing Community. *Continuum: The Magazine of the University of Utah* 10(Spring):4.

Mankiller, Wilma. 2002. To Persevere as Tribal People. *Native Americas: Akwe:kon's Journal of Indigenous Issues* 19(4): —60–70.

Mankiller, Wilma. 2004. My Home at Mankiller Flats. *Oklahoma Today* 54: 42–45.

Mankiller, Wilma. 2005. An Original Thinker with a Warrior's Spirit. *Indian Country Today*. January 12, 2005.

Mankiller, Wilma. 2006. Tribes, Treaties, and Trust: Modern Nation Relations. *Oregon's Future* (Fall): 42–44.

Mankiller, Wilma. 2009a. Being Indigenous in the 21st Century. *Cultural Survival Quarterly Magazine*. March 2009.

Mankiller, Wilma. 2009b. Indigenous People in the 21St Century the Unique Relationship Between Tribes and the U.S. *U.S. Department of State, eJournal* 14: 4–6.

Mason, Diane. 1992. How Wilma Explained Her Vision on March 23, 1992. *St. Petersburg Times*. March 23, 1992.

May, James. 2005. Tribe Member, Author Seen as a Moderate Radical. *Knight Ridder Tribune Business News*. January 12, 2005.

Miller, Robert. 2006. Wilma Mankiller: Tribes, Treaties, and Trust: Modern Nation Relations. *Oregon's Future* 107(3): 42–44.

Mohawk, John. 2002. Governance and Leadership: The Quality of Leadership, Honoring Tom Porter and Wilma Mankiller. *Native Americas* 19(4): 49–54.

Native American Times. 2002. Wilma Mankiller to Speak at USAO. March 15, 2002.

Native American Times. 2005. Celebs Turn Out for Indian Education. June 3, 2005.

Native American Times. 2007. Justice O'Connor Visits Cherokees, Praises Wise Use of Business Monies. June 8, 2007.

New York Times. 1994. Cherokee Losing Chief Who Revitalized Tribe. April 6, 1994.

Next Step Magazine. Native Americans—Walking in Two Worlds. Philadelphia. July 31, 1998: 5.

Northeastern State University Newsletter. 2013. Be the Change Week Includes Wilma Mankiller Day. January 24, 2013.

Ojibwe News. 1996a. Education a Must, Mankiller Says. November 22, 1996.

Ojibwe News. 1996b. Former Cherokee Chief Says She's Feeling Fine. September 27, 1996.

O'Rourke, Tim. 2005. The First Lady Chief. *Eugene Weekly.* October 27, 2005.

Phillips, Dan, 2013. Wilma Mankiller Day a Highlight of University's Service Week. *Northeastern State University Newsletter.* January 24, 2013.

Plummer, Sara. 2013. NSU Celebrates Wilma Mankiller Day. *Tulsa World.* January 25, 2013.

Rand, Ronald. 2013. "The Cherokee Word for Water"—A True Story of Wilma Mankiller. *Soul of the American Actor.*

Rector, Leta. 2001. Mankiller Pleas for Peace in Heightened World Violence. *Native American Times.* December 15, 2001.

Rector, Leta. 2002. The Measure of a Woman: Wilma Mankiller. *News from Indian Country.* May 15, 2002.

Red Sticks Press. 1994. Country Singer Up to Bootstraps in Controversy. June 30, 1994.

Reinhold, Robert. 1985. Cherokees Install First Woman as Chief of Major American Indian Tribe. *New York Times.* December 15, 1985.

Robbins, Catherine C. 1987. Expanding Power for Indian Women. *New York Times.* May 28, 1987.

Robertson, Dario F. 1998. Cherokee Government in Constitutional Crisis? *Cherokee Observer.* May 31, 1998.

Robinson, Judy Gibbs. 2006. Mankiller Foresees Indian Governor: Cherokee' Ex-Chief Is Not Planning to Move into State Government but to Stay with Tribe. *Daily Oklahoman.* December 16, 2006.

Robinson, Judy Gibbs. 2007. Mankiller Opens Up Dialogue: Centennial Offers a Chance to See New Perspectives, Former Cherokee Chief Says. *Daily Oklahoman.* February 23, 2007.

Ruckman, S. E. 2005. Perception Key for Indians. *Tulsa World.* March 15, 2005.

Savilla, Elmer M. 1992a. A Capital Outlook. *Char—Koosta News.* February 14, 1992.

Savilla, Elmer M. 1992b. Indian Tribes Should Realize Dangers of Monitored Retrieval Storage Sites. *Sho-Ban News.* May 14, 1992.

Schneider, Kevin. 1992. Troubled Nuclear Facility Is to Be Shut in Oklahoma. *New York Times.* November 25, 1992.

Sho-Ban News. 1991. Mankiller: A Code of Ethics Important for Tribal Members. December 12, 1991.

Sho-Ban News. 2007. Mankiller, War Jack Address Human Rights. January 25, 2007.

Smith, Paul Chaat. 2010. Wilma Mankiller's Trail of Triumph. *Special to CNN.* April 8, 2010.

Snell, Teddye. 2010. Leaders' Legacy. *Tahlequah Daily Press.* April 12, 2010.

Soap, Charlie. 2002. Life Chooses the Journey for You. *Native Americas* XIX: 63–65.

Sohn, Pam. 2009. Cherokees Mark Historic Gathering at Red Clay. *Times Free Press.* April 19, 2009.

Spaid, Elizabeth Levitan. 1992. Rebuilding a Nation Cherokees: Chief Wilma Mankiller Says Her Job Like 'Being President of a Tiny Country, a CEO, and a Social Worker.' *Los Angeles Times.* October 4, 1992.

Stephenson, Malvina. 1986. Wilma Mankiller Always Thrived on Challenge. *Tulsa World.* April 13, 1986.

Stogsdill, Sheila. 2010. Gloria Steinem Reflects on Friendship with Wilma Mankiller. *NewsOK.* April 8, 2010.

Strand, Michael. 2009. Proud Tradition. *Salina Journal.* April 3, 2009.

Sullivan, Patricia. 2010. First Female Chief of Modern Cherokees Excelled Over Hardship. *Washington Post.* April 7, 2010.

Swimmer, Ross. 1981. Letter to the Cherokees. *Cherokee Phoenix and Indian Advocate.* October 31, 1981.

Tahlequah Daily Press. 2019. Mankiller to Receive Posthumous Courage Award. March 9, 2019.

Taliman, Valerie. 1991. D.C. Environmental Leadership Summit. *Native Nevadan.* December 31, 1991.

Taylor, Glenn. 2008. Mankiller Speaks for Indigenous Cultures. *Quinnipiac Chronicle.* April 4, 2008.

Tickle, Phyllis. 1993. In Pursuit of the Intimate Native American Spirit. *Publishers Weekly.* December 13, 1993.

Tiernan, Becky. 2000. Cherokee Woman Enters Politics to Make a Difference: Teaches Leadership. *Tulsa World.* March 9, 2000.

Tomas, Lois. 1994. A Look at Wannabe-ism. *Red Sticks Press.* June 30, 1994.

Tribal College Journal. Heroes of Heroes: Everyone Has Someone to Look Up To. February 15, 2006, 17 (3).

Tulsa World. 2010. Former Cherokee Chief Wilma Mankiller Dies. April 6, 2010.

U.S. News & World Report. 1986. Chief Wilma Mankiller Helps Cherokees Build Pride: People Expect Me to Be More Warlike. February 17, 1986.

Vann, Marilyn. 2006. The Cherokee Freedman Story as of May 7, 2006. *Cherokee Observer.* May 1, 2006.

Verhovek, Sam Howe. 1993. At Work with: Chief Wilma Mankiller; The Name's the Most and Least of Her. *New York Times.* November 4, 1993.

Wahrhaftig, Albert L. 1968. The Tribal Cherokee Population of Eastern Oklahoma. *Current Anthropology* 9: 510–518.

Wahrhaftig, Albert L. 1969. Indian Communities of Eastern Oklahoma and the War on Poverty, in "Indian Education Hearings Before the Special Subcommittee on Indian Education of the Committee on Labor and Public Welfare US Senate, 90th Congress, 1st and 2nd Sessions on The Study of the Education of Indian Children, Part 2, February 19, 1968." US GPO, 1969.

Wahrhaftig, Albert L. 1970. *Social and Economic Characteristics of the Cherokee Population of Eastern Oklahoma, Report of a Survey of Four Cherokee Settlements in the Cherokee Nation.* Anthropological Studies No. 5. Washington DC: American Anthropological Association.

Wahrhaftig, Albert L. 1975. More Than Mere Work: The Subsistence System of Oklahoma's Cherokee Indians. *Appalachian Journal* 2: 327–331.

Wahrhaftig, Albert L. 1978. Making Do with the Dark Meat: A Report on the Cherokee Indians in Oklahoma. In *American Indian Economic Development,* edited by Sam Stanley. Berlin: De Gruyter Mouton, 2011, 409–510. https://doi.org/10.1515/9783110800029.409

Wahtomy, Roselynn. 2007. Mankiller, War Jack Address Human Rights. *Sho-Ban News.* January 25, 2007.

Weinraub, Judith, 1993. Mankiller: The Near Death and Life of the Cherokee Chief. *Washington Post.* December 10, 1993.

Whirlwind Soldier, Lydia. 1997. Women of Hope. *Tribal College Journal* 9(3).

Whitehawk, Rachel. 2013. Leader of a Nation. *Native Daughters.*

Willard, William. 1997. Outing, Relocation, and Employment Assistance: The Impact of Federal Indian Population Dispersal Programs in the Bay Area. *Wicazo Sa Review* 12(1): 29–46.

Willow, Alfred. 1993. National Health Conference Set. *Wind River News.* June 1, 1993.

Wilson, Linda D. 2010. Mankiller, Wilma Pearl (1945–2010). *Oklahoma Historical Society.*

Wind River News. 2004. Indian Spokeswoman Says Stereotypes Affect Health Policy. August 12, 2004.

Zizzo, David. 2005. Wilma Mankiller Reflects on Journey. *Oklahoman.* May 2, 2005.

DISSERTATIONS

Soza War Soldier, Rose. 2013. "To Take Positive and Effective Action": Rupert Costo and the California Based American Indian Historical Society. PhD Dissertation, Arizona State University.

Wahrhaftig, Albert L. 1975. In the Aftermath of Civilization: The Persistence of Cherokee Indians in Oklahoma. PhD Dissertation, University of Chicago. Appendix I.

FILMS

Cherokee Word for Water. 2014. Directors Tim Kelly and Charlie Soap. Producers Mankiller Project, Grey Hour Production Services, Toy Gun Films.

Mankiller Documentary. 2017. Director Valerie Red-Horse. Producers Red-Horse Native Productions and Valhalla Entertainment.

PRIMARY SOURCES

Cherokee Nation Tribal Council Minutes. Cherokee Executive Committee Meeting, April 1961. Western History Collection. University of Oklahoma, Norman.

Executive Committee Meeting, Cherokee Nation of Oklahoma, September 30, 1965, Tahlequah Oklahoma, Western History Collection, Tribal Council Meeting Minutes, 1961–1965, Hayden Library Microfilm Collection, Arizona State University, Tempe.

H.Res.1237—111th Congress (2009–2010): Honoring the Life of Wilma Pearl Mankiller and Expressing Condolences of the House of Representatives on Her Passing. Congress.gov, Library of Congress.

Intertribal Council Meeting, October 11, 1961, Tahlequah Oklahoma, Western History Collection, Tribal Council Meeting Minutes, 1961–1965, Hayden Library Microfilm Collection, Arizona State University, Tempe.

National Archives website. n.d. Dawes Records: Commission to the Five Civilized Tribes (The Dawes Commission), 1893–1914. National Archives.

Summary Report of the Meeting of the Executive Committee of the Cherokee Tribe of Oklahoma, May 24, 1963, Muskogee Area Office, Muskogee, Oklahoma Western Cherokee, Tribal Council Meeting Minutes, 1961–1965, Hayden Library Microfilm Collection, Arizona State University, Tempe.

United States v. Cherokee Nation, 480, U.S. 700 (1987). Justia US Supreme Court Center
Wilma Mankiller Collection, Business Structure Proposal, October 21, 1992, Box number 5, folder no. 7.
Wilma Mankiller Collection, Western History Collection, University of Oklahoma, Norman.

LECTURES AND SYMPOSIUMS

Mankiller, Wilma. 1992. Commencement Address, Northern Arizona University. December 18, 1992. Published in *Archives of Women's Political Communication*, Iowa State University.
Mankiller, Wilma. 1993. Commencement Address, Sweet Briar College. April 2, 1993.
Mankiller, Wilma. 1994a. Press Conference at Ball State University. https://www.youtube.com/watch?v=Vdye1Qjd0Kc
Mankiller, Wilma. 1994b. Wilma Mankiller | First Female Chief of the Cherokee Nation | #SeeHer Story | Katie Couric Media—YouTube.
Mankiller, Wilma. 2001. American Indian Millennium: Renewing Our Way of Life for Future Generations. University of Arizona Lecture. November 29–December, 2001.
Mankiller, Wilma. 2002. Keynote Address 2002 at the University of Utah Women's Week—YouTube video.
Mankiller, Wilma. 2005a. Culture Is Everything: History and Culture in Contemporary Tribal Life. The Wayne Morse Center for Law and Politics 25th Annual Morse Chair Address. University of Oregon. November 9, 2005.
Mankiller, Wilma. 2005b. The Fight for Treaty Rights. Native American History in the 20th Century Symposium, University of Oklahoma. April 2005.
Mankiller, Wilma. 2005c. The Wayne Morse Center for Law and Politics 25th Annual Morse Chair Address, "Context Is Everything: History and Culture in Contemporary Tribal Life." University of Oregon, Eugene. November 9, 2005.
Mankiller, Wilma. 2007. Wilma Mankiller: What It Means to Be an Indigenous Person in the 21st Century: A Cherokee Woman's Perspective. The University of Arizona Native Nations Institute.
Mankiller, Wilma. 2008a. Challenges Facing 21st Century Indigenous People. Heard Museum, Phoenix, Arizona. October 2, 2008.
Mankiller, Wilma. 2008b. What It Means to Be an Indigenous Person in the 21st Century: A Cherokee Woman's Perspective. Native Nations Institute. University of Arizona. September 2008.

INTERVIEWS

The Charlie Rose Show. 1993. Transcripts. Wilma Mankiller Interview.

Media Burn video. 1993. Wilma Mankiller, 1945–2010. YouTube.

Merina, Anita. 1994. National Education Association Today Staff Writer, Anita Merina—October 1994.

National Public Radio Interview. 2008. Wilma Mankiller Reflects on Columbus Day. October 13, 2008.

Olaya, Gina. 2015. Interview. Documentary Filmmaker Valerie Red Horse-Mohl and Gina Olaya Interview on Oklahoma PBS in 2015.

Voices of Oklahoma Interview. 2009. Wilma Mankiller: Principal Chief of the Cherokee Nation 1985–1995. August 13.

WEB RESOURCES

Capriccioso, Rob. 2010. Wilma Mankiller, Beloved Leader and Friend, Passes On. In A Radical Profeminist Blog. 2010.

Cherokee Nation Cultural Resource Center website. n.d. https://www .cherokee.org/cultural-resource-center/

Cherokee Nation website. n.d. Cherokee Nation Home. https://cherokee.org

Contaminated Sludge Sent from Sequoyah Fuels to Utah. December 2, 2018. okenergytoday.com.

Ishikawa, Tanya. 2006. Wilma Mankiller: Tireless Tribal Rights Advocate in the King Tradition. *Denver Urban Spectrum.*

Leaders as Guides of Return: Wilma Mankiller. Women's Media Center. April 7, 2010. www.womensmediacenter.com

Meili, Diane. 2017. Leader Challenged Convention to Get Things Done. January 28, 2017. Windspeaker.com

Nelson, Andrew. 2001. Wilma Mankiller: The First Female Chief of the Cherokee Nation, She Took Tragedy and Illness and Made Strength. And Don't Even Ask Where She Got Her Name. November 21, 2001. www.salon.com

A Radical Profeminist Blog. 2010. Honoring and Remembering the Life, Words, and Accomplishments of Wilma Mankiller (November 18, 1945–April 6, 2010 ECD), Former Two-Term Principal Chief of the Cherokee Nation, Community Activist, Author, and Tribal Legislator.

2012 Elizabeth A. Sackler Award. n.d. 2012 Sackler Center First Awards: Chief Wilma Mankiller—YouTube

Wilma Mankiller: An American Hero. National Women's History Museum. womenshistory.org

Winton, Ben. 2021. The Occupation of Alcatraz: Don't Give Us Apologies. Give Us What We Really Want. *Native Press.* October 20, 2021.

Index

About the Author

Tamrala Swafford Bliss, PhD, is adjunct professor at University of Maryland Global Campus, American Public University in Charlestown, WV, Grand Canyon University in Phoenix, AZ, and Bethel University in McKenzie, TN. She earned an MA in American History and Cherokee Studies from Western Carolina University, an MA in English from Jacksonville State University, and a PhD in American History from Arizona State University. She is a member of the Western History Association, the Organization of American Historians, and the international honor society Pi Gamma Mu.